THE BOOK OF
BANFF
Royal and Ancient Burgh

BANFF PRESERVATION & HERITAGE SOCIETY

HALSGROVE

First published in Great Britain in 2008
Reprinted 2009

British Library Cataloguing-in-Publication Data
A CIP record for this title is available from the British Library

ISBN 978 1 84114 790 1

HALSGROVE
Halsgrove House,
Ryelands Industrial Estate,
Bagley Road, Wellington, Somerset TA21 9PZ
Tel: 01823 653777   Fax: 01823 216796
email: sales@halsgrove.com

Part of the Halsgrove group of companies.
Information on all Halsgrove titles is available at: www.halsgrove.com

Printed and bound by CPI Antony Rowe, Wiltshire

Frontispiece photograph: *Mrs Smith, fishwife from Banff.* (© Dr David Findlay Clark ARPS)

Foreword

The history of the Royal and Ancient County Burgh of Banff was covered during the nineteenth and early-twentieth centuries by the authors Cramond, Imlach and Mahood.

This new history is quite different because it has been written by over 30 authors, each knowledgeable about different facets of the story, which collectively allows us to understand the placing of a coastal community in a specific spot, and how that community developed into the Burgh as we now know it. Over eight centuries have passed since its foundation, and many thousands of individuals have contributed to its heritage. Many of them lie in St Mary's Kirkyard, others were part of the Scottish diaspora and made the name of Banff synonymous with other parts of the world.

We hope you enjoy reading the stories and marvel at the visual images the book contains. The compilation has been a labour willingly undertaken by the editorial team of Julian Watson, Alistair Mason, David Findlay Clark and Christina Ord – all committee members of the Banff Preservation & Heritage Society, which was founded in 1965 to preserve the architectural heritage of the Burgh. Since then the society's remit has been extended to consider the social and cultural objects which make up the unique identity of Banff, and this volume continues the pioneering work of the 1965 founding members under the presidency of Sir John Betjeman, one of the followers of William Morris, and others, who were committed to the remembrance and preservation of our cultural inheritance.

When the reorganisation of local government in Scotland, involving the demise of the town councils, was carried through in 1975, there were many who feared that the loss of burgh status would mean loss of identity for towns like Banff and Macduff, and that, with the passage of time, civic pride and the spirit of independence would fade away. They were unduly pessimistic because they ignored an essential factor in the business of survival: that a town survives through the efforts of its people. As to the future, we can but hazard a guess, but with a conviction derived from the inspiration of its history we prophesy that Banff will survive and flourish. The Banff spirit is still there and we hope that in publishing this book we have produced a worthy souvenir.

It is our fervent wish that every reader will be inspired to find out more about Banff and its surrounding area, and come to appreciate why the Burgh holds a very special place in the heritage of our ancient realm of Scotland.

Charles J. Burnett, Ross Herald of Arms – Chairman
James A.S. McPherson CBE – Vice-Chairman
Banff Preservation and Heritage Society

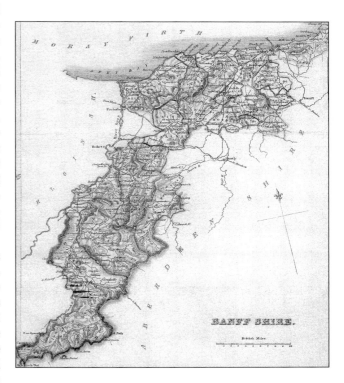

Map of Banffshire.

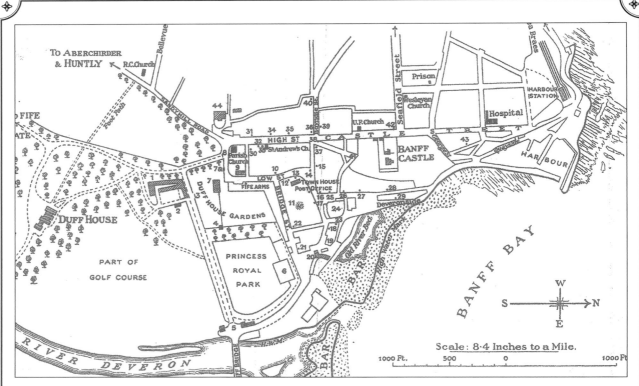

Banff in the 1920s.   Key: Duff House Grounds: 1. Nurses' Home and Barnyards; 2. Golf Pavilion; 3. Garden Entrance; 4. Part of Old Lodging of Airlie; 5. The Bridge Gate; 6. Blaes Tennis Court; 7. Vinery; 7a. Garden Door; 8. The Collie Gate in Collie Road. Low Street: 9. The County Buildings; 10. Union Bank (Carved Stones); 11. Carmelite Mound in part of the Great Garden; 12. Carved Stones by the Town Steeple; 13. The Market Cross; 14. Biggar Fountain. Strait Path: 15. Anderson Date Stone. Carmelite Street: 16. Old House; 17. Coat of Arms (J. Gordon); 18. Cottage with Leslie Buckles; 19. Old Salmon Close. Old Market Place: 20. Journal Office, formerly the Grammar School; 21. Castle Panton. Bridge Street: 22. Royal Oak Hotel. Church Street: 23. Old Boyne Dower-House. High Shore: 24. The Old Kirkyard; 25. Market Inn (1585 Date Stone); 26. The Old Manse; 27. Commercial Bank, Stewart Coat of Arms; 28. Shore House. Deveronside: 29. House of T. Edward, the Banff Naturalist. High Street: 30. Motto at the top of the Back Path; 31. Kyle's Close; 32. Museum and Library; 33. St Brandon's; 34. Murray's House, Date Stones; 35. Houses of Duff of Hatton; 36. Forbes's House; 37. T. Ogilvy's House, 1669; 38. The Grey Stone. Boyndie Street: 39. Provost Robinson's House, now the Town and County Club; 40. Formerly the Plough Inn. Old Castle Gate: 41. Former entrance to Castle Grounds, at the top of Water Path. Castle Street: 42. St Andrew's Hall. Braeheads: 43. St John's Lodge. Sandyhill Road: 44. Banff Academy.

The fine vernacular architecture of the building behind the lorry in the High Street (above) was demolished in the 1960s to make way for the 'modern' building (left).

CONTENTS

Aerial view of Banff in the late 1920s.

Acknowledgements

We should first acknowledge a grant from the Banff and Buchan Arts Forum, who do so much to encourage creativity in so many forms. We thank our authors, who are named at the head of each item. Some names are immediately recognisable as authorities in their field, others are new. We thank our artists, Roy Chillingworth and Derek Gray, and our photographers, David Findlay Clark and Julian Watson (Tommy Bod). As we mention Julian, we should say he made the original suggestion to bring out this book. David, for his part, spent many hours on the tricky work of computer manipulating and processing photographs. We thank everyone who hunted out old photographs and other memorabilia for us. We cannot name everyone, but must particularly name those who were so generous that we were unable to use all they provided – Helen Clark, Ronald Davidson, Harold Garner, James MacPherson and Anne Meldrum. Halsgrove have been very helpful, but their strict (and probably wise) rules about the technical standards of photographs have ruled out, for example, many interesting cuttings from newspapers.

Whenever we use the Bodie Collection we are grateful to Bill Bain. We also owe thanks to Neil Paterson's heirs for permission to use his evocative piece 'Home Town'. We are grateful to the Aberdeenshire Museum Service, and particularly the local staff in Banff, for all their help. We thank Jill Greig, who did a lot of typing for us at short notice.

If we have inadvertently published anything without acknowledging copyright, we apologise sincerely. If we have missed out something you know should have been in the book, we must say we were amazed how quickly we ran out of pages. It was first come, first served. There is so much more we could have written about. We must thank our subscribers, whose support has been a real encouragement, and the rest of the committee of the Banff Preservation & Heritage Society.

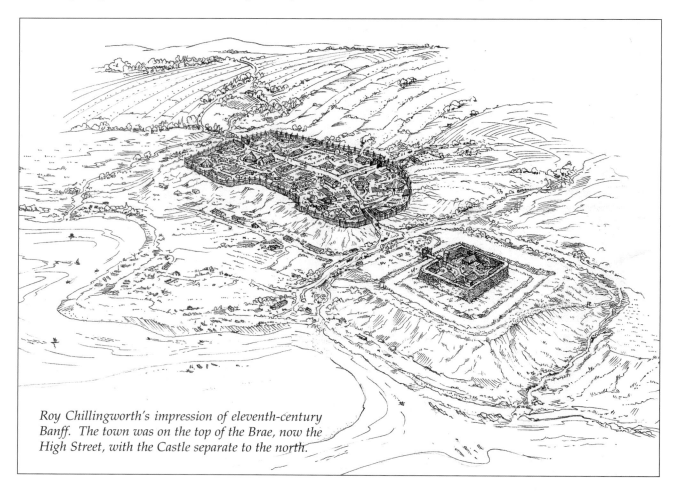

Roy Chillingworth's impression of eleventh-century Banff. The town was on the top of the Brae, now the High Street, with the Castle separate to the north.

HOME TOWN
Neil Paterson
The Scots Magazine, July 1949

The Fir Widdie (Wood), Banff. (© Dr David Findlay Clark ARPS)

Banff, county town. A miniature Edinburgh, douce, respectable, just a little standoffish. An old town with stately streets intersected by breakneck lanes; with spires and historical monuments and dignified public buildings; with a weekly newspaper of great repute and tradition; with venerated institutions including a Sheriff court, a fine neo-Grecian Academy, a museum, a Town and County Club. A proud town with a proud and imaginative war memorial: Banff castle and grounds, the town's in perpetuity.

Banff. Royal and Ancient Burgh. A gracious town with unexpected vistas framed between gables and chimney pots – a glimpse of the sea perhaps, and the sister town of Macduff across the Bay, with the links with their fringe of sleek, sophisticated sand, of the shifting shingle bar of the River Deveron, of Smeaton's noble seven-arched bridge straddling the estuary, of the Hill o' Doune with its temple of Venus (deserted by the goddess and currently a convenience for dogs), of the flat immaculate riverside golf course dotted with sheep, of the green Montcoffer woods of the upland, of the pilastered domes of Duff House, erstwhile gracious home, sanatorium, hotel, PoW. camp, and now decomposing white elephant.

Banff. An old name, half cousin to vulgarity, bastard through Bainiffe and Ooiniffe of Boyn. An ugly name for a bonny, bonny town.

Essentially a town is to be explained only in terms of geography and history, and, as this is even truer of Banff than of most towns, this exile claims the reader's indulgence for a little of both and in return, guarantees him no guide-book tarradiddle.

Banff is built on the upland of a peninsula bounded by the sea on the north and by the estuary of the Deveron on the east. It is sheltered to the landward by a yoke of rich, rising woodlands, and the setting – the co-ordination of land and sea and trees and river – is so felicitous that there could not but be a town here, and it could not but be beautiful.

The history of Banff goes back to the tenth century, and Banff is a town in which one can always hear the echoes of its history. But let us be frank. It is a history on a parochial scale. Nothing at all epoch-making ever happened in Banff. We have had illustrious visitors, from Malcolm Canmore through Burns and Byron to Dr Walford Bodie. But nobody ever murdered anybody worth speaking about in Banff, and we have had no great scenes of derring-do. In 1759 the appearance of a French privateer off the coast scared the living daylights out of us (an episode handled with great discretion in our official annals), and we sat very tight at the time of the Jacobite rebellions. The most warlike act we ever committed as a community was to hang MacPherson the freebooter, whom Burns has immortalised in 'Macpherson's Lament'. For this, because of the indulgence in certain irregularities – we are alleged to have put the town clock forward in order to forestall the reprieve, having observed its bearer riding hell-for-leather over Banff Bridge. He must indeed have been some bearer, as there was no bridge there at the time! For this innocent prank then, we, as a burgh, were deprived of the power of Pot and Gallows, and to this day are not entitled to hang or be hanged on our own home ground.

The sons of Banff have often been distinguished but seldom eminent. We claim as one of them Thomas Edward, the shoemaker-naturalist, who settled in Banff at the age of twenty, and who later said of himself in admirable understatement: 'I dinna think there'll be sic a feel as me for mony a lang year to come.' And, turning to the seventeenth century, we must confess to having given birth to Archbishop Sharp, that pious rascal who has been beatified in school histories, and who, not a day too soon, was most properly dispatched by bloody murder on Magus Moor.

The true history of Banff is not to be found in the lives of individuals or in national records, but rather in the annals of the noble families which have been connected with the town from time immemorial, and which in turn patronised and pillaged it. The Duffs, the Findlaters, the Ogilvies. These were and are great names, and in charity I think it should be said that the Earls of Fife and Findlater and the Lords of Banff have probably done Banff more good than harm. But I should not like to have to argue it. Banff has grown up through the centuries under their patronage and, for better or for worse, it is as it is today largely because of their influence. Their shadows still lie on the town, but they lie now lightly and graciously, and contribute in no small part to the pride and dignity which characterise the Royal and Ancient Burgh.

Until the advent of the railway, Banff was a port of consequence, serving a wide area of the countryside and exporting cattle, grain and salmon, but the town has now turned its back on the sea, and if you want to smell seaweed (or see the finest rock swimming pool in Scotland) you must cross the Deveron to Macduff. Banff has never been distinguished for its industries, and although it has had, and still has, flourishing trades, they exist not in justification of the town but in spite of it.

Banff has never been a town in which to work. It is a town in which to live, and I think it is possible that somewhere between these irreconcilables lie all its charms and limitations.

* ⚹ *

MEMORIES – THE FIR WIDDIE
David Findlay Clark
This explains the background of the preceding article by Neil Paterson

The contemporary Fir Widdie, behind Sandyhills farmhouse and the cemetery, is as much decid-uous as conifer in its content. In the 1930s and '40s, however, it contained some noble trees – Scots pines 40–50ft high and other strong conifers. They all contributed to the thick layer of brown pine needles which carpeted the space beneath them with a springy, if slightly slippery, surface on which we boys played football, enacted war games and became cowboys and Indians by turns. There was a natural largish area in the middle of the wood which became the pitch, and thickets on the periphery formed dens and hid a variety of secrets, such as caches of catapult stones, old tins of brambles in season and fading copies of small detective storybooks about Dixon Hawke and Tommy, his boy assistant.

Not many will know that the Fir Widdie has its place in literary history. I remember more senior boys telling of a tall boy who was a good footballer and would have been in the top class of the school when I was not yet at school at all. A year or two later, during the Second World War, I remember the same chap walking up Sandyhill Road and into his father's house a few yards up Bellevue Road. He was then in uniform as an officer in the Royal Navy, where he served, I think, in destroyers. His interest in writing, first as a hobby and then as a profession, was then just developing. He had graduated from Edinburgh University but went on to be a footballer of some quality, playing as an amateur for Scottish League teams such as Leith Athletic and Dundee United, of which he was captain in the 1936/37 season. He was briefly a sports writer with D.C. Thomson but after the war he went on to publish several well-known novels, such as *Man on a Tightrope*, *The China Run* and *Behold Thy Daughter*, the latter two of which drew on his knowledge of the sea, fishing and the life of North-East Scottish towns and way of life. It was in one of these books that the Fir Widdie is mentioned. Neil Paterson went on to write screenplays, one from his own story *The Kidnappers*

and, among several others, the screenplay for *Room at the Top*, a novel by John Braine. For this work Paterson was awarded a Bafta award and an Oscar. He won the Atlantic Award for Literature in 1946. Later he served as a governor for the British Film Institute, the National Film School and the Arts Council of Great Britain and was an executive for Grampian Television. He died in 1995 in Crieff, where he lived latterly.

Banff has been strangely reticent about this man's considerable achievements. Truly one is seldom a prophet in one's own country and the Nor'east put-down of 'Ah kent 'is faither' has perhaps played its part. The brief visits of the likes of Burns, Samuel Johnson, Boswell and Byron have featured more in the literary history of the town, but they never wrote about the Fir Widdie!

* ⚹ *

BEFORE BANFF EVER EXISTED
Alistair Mason

An historic town is not the place to look for pre-history. Generations of settlement have destroyed what was left thousands of years ago. But we can make guesses about what went before. There are flint-stones in the museum found locally, but they came from Buchan, so that is our earliest evidence of trade. Only with the Neolithic (New Stone) Age did men grow crops and breed cows and sheep. That means patterns of settlement, some of which are with us today. (Perhaps before that at the mouth of a river, hunter-gatherers might have come back generation after generation, and we would find their oyster shells in middens.) There is a large Neolithic burial mound at Longmanhill, behind Macduff. From their graves we can tell that these people were long-skulled and light-boned. Some time after 2000BC they were supplanted by invaders from across the North Sea, the 'Beaker folk'. These were bigger, round-skulled, and broad-faced, and you can see lots of their descendants walking round Banff today.

Prehistoric tumulus in the Fir Wood, Banff.

(© DR DAVID FINDLAY CLARK ARPS)

The remains of a stone circle, with Banff Bridge in the background. (© Tommy Bod)

Prehistoric beakers excavated locally. (© Tommy Bod)

Close-up of one of the standing stones.

(© Dr David Findlay Clark ARPS)

On the hills around, like the Durn behind Portsoy, you will find the traces of prehistoric hill forts. The most striking reminder of our prehistoric past, once in the Banff Museum, now in the National Museum in Edinburgh (we kept a replica), is the 'Boar's Head' carnyx. A carnyx was a war trumpet. To produce forts or war-trumpets, and indeed any metalwork, you need more than small handfuls of hunter-gatherers in clearings in the forest. They may not have left writings, but Bronze-Age and early-Iron-Age cultures were often complex and, when we can find them, they also left fascinating traces of a rich world of the imagination.

In Banff we are in Pictland, and the whole of the North East is full of their carved stones, and their

The carnyx (prehistoric war trumpet) in Banff Museum).

(© Tommy Bod)

11

place-names. Their language is a mystery to us, though probably it was nearer Welsh than Gaelic (these were P-Celts not Q-Celts). In no period should we underestimate the possibility of communication by water. There was coastal traffic; amber came from the Baltic across the North Sea, along the Moray Firth, down the Great Glen, along the West Coast of Britain to Cornwall, and then to the Mediterranean. So Banff was on a very early trade route.

The Roman fleet sailed up into the Moray Firth in AD84, and there is a Roman camp at Archaeolink, Oyne. Somewhere near Bennachie there was the battle of Mons Graupius. It is by no means unlikely that to get from the fleet to the camp Roman soldiers landed around Banff. The Roman geographer Ptolemy talks about the tribes of the Taexali and Vacomagi around here, but the names have not survived, even if we are descended from them. The Romans did not stay.

THE BEGINNINGS: IRISHMEN AND VIKINGS
Norman Allan, Julian Watson, Alistair Mason

There are many old spellings of the name of the town: Banb, Bainiffe, Boiniffe, Bainffe, Banef, Banf, and Bamf. The name is important as a clue to the history of the town. There seems little doubt that the word comes from Gaelic.

For the first mention of the word Banff we must go to an ancient Irish Gaelic manuscript called *Leabhar Gabhala* (*Book of Invasions*), a mythical account of the prehistoric settlers in Ireland, containing one highly imaginative explanation of how the island of Ireland acquired its name. The book says that when the Gaels arrived in Ireland they were met by the three territorial goddesses, called Eriu, Fodhla and Banbha, who were ruling the island. In a tale reminiscent of the Judgement of Paris on the three goddesses in classical literature, each goddess in turn requested the leader of the Gaels to name the island after herself. In the event Eriu won the contest, and hence the island came to be called after her – 'Erin' – which later was transformed into Ireland. Despite this we frequently find in older Irish literature the island being called Banbha, or Banbh. The Gaelic 'bh' is pronounced in English like the fricative 'f' or 'v'. The terminal element '-ff' is, in fact, a favoured way of portraying in English the Gaelic 'bh'; thus Duff (dubh – black), Crieff (craobh – a tree), River Tarff (tarbh – a bull), Corgarff (garbh – rough).

Ireland's most northerly point, Malin Head, used to be called Banbha's Point.

We know that the Scots came from Ireland to Scotland, and we know – who better than the Scots themselves? – that emigrants bestow upon places in their new country the names of their old country. Hence it is argued that it was settlers from Ireland who gave us the name of Banff, or Banbh. At one time there was also a Banff near Alyth in Perthshire and a Banff near Arbuthnott in Kincardine.

Professor Nicolaisen has pointed out that there is an obsolete Gaelic word 'banbh', meaning a pig. Could it be that the pig was the totem animal of the goddess Banbha and that is how she got her name? Some say that the town was named after the River Banb – river of the pigs – an older name of the Deveron. There was also a queen of the Siold Danum in Ireland called Banha.

There is, too, a suggestion that the Gaelic 'bunamph' could simply mean 'the town or village at the river mouth'. Others have pointed to another obsolete meaning of the word banbh, namely 'a piece of uncultivated land', though this seems an unlikely choice of name for a new settlement. We suggest, then, that the place-name 'Banff' simply means 'Ireland'. Professor Watson maintains that the name of the River Deveron itself is derived from the Gaelic 'dubh Eirinn', meaning 'black Ireland', and contrasts it with the River Findhorn, 'white Ireland' ('fionn' is white). However, Professor Nicolaisen disputes this translation and maintains that the element '-ern' represents an old Indo–European word simply meaning water.

Christianity came to this coast in the sixth century, probably from the Scots of Argyll (who had come over from Ireland), though there are dedications to the earlier St Ninian, the saint of Galloway, further north than you would expect (like Shetland). St Columba of Iona undoubtedly had dealings with the king of the Picts, but what is striking is how much of a cult of Columba there was along the Moray Firth coast, at places like Fordyce and Aberdour and St Combs. There may be truth in the story of how he and St Drostan together founded the abbey of Deer, so when we hear that the church at Alvah, just inland from Banff, was dedicated to St Columba, and there was a St Columba's well, perhaps he was here.

Our other neighbouring parish of Boyndie, at the other end of the bay, was traditionally an older Christian foundation than Banff. The dedication there is to St

An early 'pig' seal of the old town of Banff, 1408.

Brendan (or more often, locally, Brandon). St Brendan was abbot of Clonfert in Ireland, a contemporary of St Columba, and the story of his voyages was popular for centuries. He went to the 'northern and western islands', so why not to Banff Bay?

There was a medieval fair on his feast day in May in Brangan, where there is the Brangan Howe and the Brangan (standing) Stanes. It may be that the names of Boyne and Boyndie burn were called after the River Boyne in Ireland.

There is an ancient claim that Banff is linked with a woman saint, St Bey (or Baya, or Begha, or Vey), later than St Columba, who also has something to do with Little Cumbrae in the Firth of Clyde. There was another St Begha at Dunbar, and St Bee of St Bees in Cumbria, so women coastal saints are a possibility. However, by the time Banff was a burgh, our saint was the Virgin Mary. There was a Parish Church of Our Lady in Banff, certainly before 1199.

We should remember that this was a Gaelic-speaking culture. The oldest written Gaelic in Scotland is in the Book of Deer. In the margins of the pages, in the middle of the twelfth century, the monks wrote a description in Gaelic of the lands they had been given. Banff (Banb) is mentioned, though actually in a copy of a Latin charter of King David (1124–53). By the time there were burghs, even if the countryside spoke Gaelic, traders in the towns presumably spoke Scots.

The town's seals might hold a clue to the origins of Banff. The seal of Banff, the Virgin and Child, can be dated to at least 1472, and we do have one earlier seal of 1408. This is very different, and the inscription reads 'S. COMMVNE DE BANEF' and shows a pig – a boar. So possibly, when you look out over the Bay of Banff, you will be seeing the Bay of Pigs.

Traders and saints, on balance, were welcome; Vikings were not. Along the North East coast, from Cullen to Cruden Bay, there is a traditional memory of battles with the Danes. In 1004 there was a great battle at Gamrie, just along the coast, and for centuries men pointed out the skulls of the Danes in the walls of St John's Church there. During the same campaign there was a lesser battle on the Banff links, hence names likes Swordanes (the last five letters are the clue). They say that the fountain of Fountain Park was where the Vikings watered their horses – I wouldn't like to have been a horse in a Viking longboat! This is Scottish history, so we remember victories over the Vikings, but there must, more often than not, have been raids where no Scottish army was waiting, and settlements and monasteries were destroyed. What would become Banff was a dangerously exposed site. Even as late as 1151, Aberdeen was plundered by the Norsemen.

But the times were changing. The Norsemen were beaten off. The kings of Scotland, with their new Anglo-Norman ways, set up castles and burghs. Banff emerges into history.

THE ROYAL BURGH
Julian Watson

What was a burgh? To find the answer we have to reach back into history to the invading Normans in England. David I (1124–53) looked across the border of Scotland and was impressed by the Normans' organisation of the towns and country. The major benefits were greater control of the kingdom and an increase in revenue, two very good reasons for a monarch. Soon Normans were being invited to Scotland and given land and in return they gave allegiance to the king. With the Normans also came the burgh.

The status of royal burgh, granted by the king, came as a package. A group of traders known as burgesses were allowed to trade and in return paid a rent to the king. The greater the trade the higher the rent – effectively tax, or cess – to the monarch. It was therefore in all the parties' interests for the burgh to prosper and protect its trade.

The burgesses in a town had the right to protect the trading settlement with a wall or a palisade with a ditch. Gates to the town were not only for security but also to control the flow of trade. The burgh also elected its own council and magistrates. Its greatest privilege was the exclusive right to trade, including overseas, as a monopoly, thus operating a closed shop that was jealously guarded. All transactions had to pay a tax, similar to VAT today, at the stent stone in the market-place. There was also the right to hold annual fairs and markets to further increase trade. The surrounding countryside was defined as the burgh's 'liberty', which included all transactions. The burgh, besides the town, was also given lands and fishing rights to ensure it was self-sustainable.

The king, in return for all these privileges, received tax from the burgh. The charters for the burgh were renewed at times, so could, in theory, be withdrawn. The town's prosperity was dependent on its loyalty to the king. In addition, one-off taxes could be demanded, for example for wars, and men of arms could be called up.

In all this, Banff was a typical royal burgh, and its charters are evidence of this.

Part of the Royal Charter of Banff, 1372.

THE COUNTY OF BANFFSHIRE
Alistair Mason

From the reign of King David I (1124–53) to 1975, Banff was a county town. Counties with sheriffs were one of the many Anglo–Norman innovations introduced by King David I. They replaced rule by 'mormaers' (a Gaelic title meaning a high steward). The local mormaers were Moray and Buchan, so in 1975, when the old county was carved up, we were almost going back to what was before.

The county of Banffshire was a long thin one, getting narrower as it went up into the hills. On a map, it certainly looked squeezed between Moray and Aberdeenshire. Near Keith, it was only nine miles wide. The fact that the county town was on the coast might well say something about how effective the rule of law was in upper Banffshire. In the days when the Catholic Church was persecuted it survived, and trained its priests, in Glenlivet. Upper Banffshire, in early days largely illegally, specialised in producing whisky, and whenever anyone from Banffshire passes the sign on the county boundary of Moray saying 'Malt Whisky Country' they exclaim, 'But it's Banffshire's whisky!'

The Earls of Findlater and Seafield rebuilt Cullen, razing the old town to the ground because it was too near Cullen House. They then wanted their fine new town to be the county town. Banff had to fight hard to keep its status, and for a long time was suspicious of Cullen. The prosperous fishing port of Buckie was the biggest town in the county.

In 1975 (the Act was passed in 1973) the western part of Banffshire was put into Moray, and the eastern into Banff and Buchan. This was a two-tier system, so above Banff and Buchan was the Grampian regional authority. Banff was still the seat of the lower-level Banff and Buchan authority, even though Peterhead and Fraserburgh were bigger towns. When the two-tier system was abolished in 1994 (the Act took effect in 1996), Banff found itself part of the large Aberdeenshire authority. Quite understandably, many local people prefer 'Banffshire' to 'Aberdeenshire' as an address, and find local government from Woodhill House in Aberdeen remote. In the days of the Banff and Buchan authority, quite a number of attractive old buildings found a use as government offices. Banffshire seems to have done without purpose-built county offices. The little old counties of Scotland were a much smaller operation. Presumably many weighty decisions were made in the Town and County Club on Boyndie Street.

The county of Banffshire still has a lord lieutenant, and Banff still has something of the air of a county town.

THE ARMS OF BANFF
Charles Burnett

Banff received a charter as a royal burgh from Robert II, King of Scots, in 1372. Before then it was one of the Northern Hanse ports which traded with the Baltic in the twelfth century. The burgh required an official seal to conduct its business, and the first on record, c.1408, bears the image of a boar.

This animal occurs frequently in the heraldry of several Banffshire families, which indicates how common they must have been in Scotland during the medieval period. However, St Mary was the patron saint of Banff, and she appears for the first time in the burgh seal used from 1472 to 1764. The Virgin is crowned and holds the Child in her left arm. She stands within a Gothic canopy.

In 1672 the Scottish Parliament passed an Act creating the Public Register of All Arms and Bearings in Scotland. Every individual and every incorporated body who owned or used a coat of arms had to register the device in the Public Register. Banff Town Council was one of the first to register its arms. These bear the figure of the Virgin and Child and can be seen on the town signs at the three entrances to Banff from the west, south and east. In this version the Virgin holds the Child in her right arm.

Another seal matrix existed in 1893 which was crude in design and engraving skill; this set the Virgin beside a church building. She holds the Child in her left arm.

The final seal used by the burgh council of Banff was probably created some time after 1764. The Virgin and Child appear on a curvilinear shield and are thus represented as a coat of arms for the first time on the burgh seal. On either side of the shield are garlands in a classical style typical of late-Georgian craftsmanship. In 1897 a motto was added, 'OMNE BONUM DEI DONUM' – 'Every good is the gift of God'. This was recorded so as to be part of a new chain of office for the provost of Banff.

Epipactis atrorubens, *the flower of Banffshire.*

Above: *Seals of the town of Banff with* (far right) *its coat of arms.*

Right: *The coat of arms of Banff Town and County Club.*

Left: *The coat of arms of the Banff Preservation & Heritage Society.*

After the reorganisation of local government in 1975, Banff town council ceased to exist, and the burgh arms reverted to the Crown. If Banff and Macduff Community Council had the desire it could petition for a combined coat of arms incorporating the arms of both former town councils.

Two organisations within Banff have reflected the arms of the former town council in their own coats of arms. The first to do so was Banff Town and County Club, which recorded arms in 2000. The arms are impaled, i.e. divided in half, on the left the Virgin and Child, on the right a salmon symbolising the fishing tradition of Banff, along with a sheaf of corn to represent the agricultural heritage of Banffshire. The second organisation to record arms is the Banff Preservation & Heritage Society, which did so in 2007. Here the arms are made different from the old burgh arms with the addition of three shells. These are taken from the coat of arms of the Duff family, who played such a large part in the life of the burgh, and also represent the seaside location of Banff. These two local bodies therefore ensure the continuing visual identity of the Virgin and Child with the Royal Burgh of Banff.

⊷ ⊨✦⊨ ⊷

MEDIEVAL BANFF
Julian Watson

In the early Middle Ages Banff was located at the centre of one of many royal forests – land taken over by the crown as game preserves for hunting.

Pageant in 1972 to mark the 600th anniversary of Banff receiving its second charter from King Robert II.

Access was limited, as trees and animals were protected. Wild boar would appear to have been the favoured game. The Royal Forest of Boyn stretched from Portsoy to Gamrie along the coast and inland almost to Turriff. Over time the forests declined as pressure for land increased and the Crown gave land away to loyal subjects.

Banff, in its unique position at the head of the River Deveron, offered one of the very few safe harbours along the North Sea coastline. This was further enhanced by the shingle bar across the river mouth which formed a breakwater, thus creating a safe anchorage. Known as 'the lake', this ran inland as far as Duff House. A safe landing-point on the coast did, however, pose a threat from unwanted invading armies. The sea was the equivalent of our modern motorways for getting from A to B, and

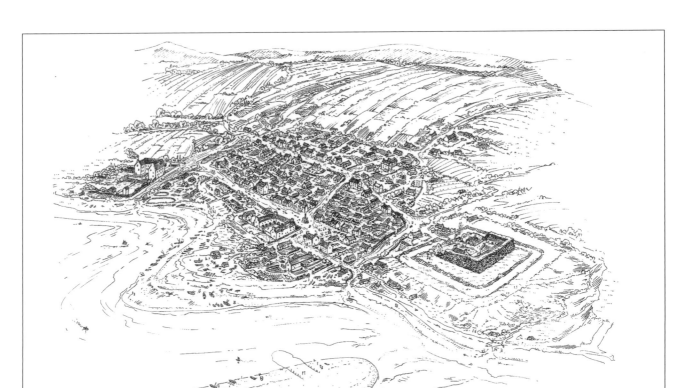

Roy Chillingworth's impression of Banff in the late 1500s, with the town expanding towards the sea.

although we do not know the age of the castle at Banff, with such a constant threat the area would have been fortified at an early date.

It was therefore a natural choice for the crown to create Banff a royal burgh. This occurred between 1189 and 1198, although the first surviving written charter is from 1372. Banff has remained a royal burgh ever since.

Burgh towns came in a set format as a blueprint plan. There was one main street, known as the king's highway, with a market-place. The two prominent buildings would have been the church and the Tolbooth (Townhouse). Burgesses' land strips, lined with wooden buildings, ran off the main street. In time, with further building back into the strips, these developed into pends, wynds, lanes and closes. The town in turn was surrounded by a ditch with a gated earth rampart. Scottish towns were very small.

Building a picture of Banff in these early periods is difficult in that we only have pieces of the jigsaw. There has been surprisingly little research on the town over the last century, and only a handful of archaeological digs. We have to refer back to Victorian research for the greater part of our information, especially as many of the burgh records were burnt by the Townhouse caretaker after the First World War. However, we do now have a far greater understanding of the workings of the old burghs. Morphology, the study of the position of buildings in the landscape, tells us what to look for and where we should expect to find it. Place names, frequently the oldest archaeology surviving, are often very descrip-

tive as to the use of the site. By combining all of the above we can today build a picture.

Banff lay on the principal medieval route from Aberdeen to Elgin and on to Inverness. It was the lowest crossing point of the River Deveron. The ford was located at Scurry Ford in Wrack Woods just beyond the mausoleum by Carmel Mount. This is just above the high-tide mark, and is where the Deveron emerges from Alvah gorge and spreads out on the river bend. Carmel Mount, identified as probably a motte and bailey by the Banff Townscape Heritage Initiative 2005 Archaeological Report, would have been a Norman-style timber castle protecting the ford. This land was also part of the burgh lands and was the location of the Mill of Banff, owned by the town.

The traveller, having crossed the ford, takes a refreshing drink at St Mary's Well and then gives thanks for his safe crossing at the chapel once located on the site of the mausoleum. Two tracks lead to the town; the lower route, known as the corn road, and the higher route, along the existing main road to Huntly. If we take the higher road towards the town on our left are the Carmelite lands and to our right are strips of land know as rigs, farmed by the burgesses, mostly put to corn. These lower slopes are named Cornhill. At the base of the hill is the marshy floodplain of the river, known as the Dawhaugh, now the golf course to the south of Duff House. The Dawhaugh is also owned by the industrious Carmelites who drained the meadowland.

Approaching the town from the south along Sandyhill Road, the town comes into view, positioned on the top of the braes with the castle behind overlooking the sea. Looking to our left up Gallow Hill the ground is open common land with some herds of pigs and cattle grazing. There are a few land strips reaching up the hill from the town. To our right are more land strips down to the water's edge. One of these strips of four acres is the toft of land granted to the church by King William the Lion in the 1190s. The 'lake' below the town stretches from what would become Duff House, over Princess Royal Park football grounds and the Temple View residential development, to the old market-place (Eastside shop) known as Shore Head and out to sea past the shingle bar. Boats are at anchor in the bay and pulled up on the shore in Gleddisgreen, now the Greenbanks. Along the shoreline near to the town are saltpans for the manufacture of salt to supply the fishing trade, as the Deveron was one of Scotland's main salmon rivers.

Continuing towards the town one passes over the boggy valley, used as the town's tip, called Fillicap, now St Mary's car park. One enters the town through the King's Gate, situated on the High Street at the top of Back Path. The main street stretches ahead, with buildings on either side within their burgess land strips. The writer would suggest that the church was on the right between the two existing churches. Banff was one of 24 parishes paying income for the upkeep of Arbroath Abbey, founded in 1178 by King William the Lion. At the head of the street was the market with the stent stone for paying taxes. Known locally as the Grey Stone, and now buried under the pavement by the pedestrian crossing, the Grey Stone continued to be a meeting-place well into the 1800s. Turning left into Boyndie Street and continuing to the corner of King's Well Lane by the old king's well, one leaves the town on the Elgin road via the West Gate.

At the Grey Stone the Tolbooth overlooks the square. The only alternative street is Castlegate, and on the right is an ancient chapel, probably St Ninian's or St Bey's, located on the highest brae within the town, called Droppane Craig. The castle gate is at the top of Water Path. The path then splits, one route leading to the castle while the other goes downhill, following Water Path to the seashore.

On the shoreline we do have one excavation which shows the remains of fish and shellfish processing from line baiting. On the peninsula of Gleddisgreen to Shore Head there would have been boats along the shore, while at night animals would be brought off the hills for safe grazing.

Expansion of the Town

Increasingly, stone would have been used for buildings, although roofs would be thatch. The town boundaries would be replaced by walls at the end of the burgesses' strips, the owners being responsible for each section.

As the town expanded there was increasing pressure for the development of land within the town, as it was considered too dangerous to build beyond the walls. With the increasing trade, the natural direction to expand was towards the sea. Buildings were built down the braes, Back Path marking the southern boundary of the town. Low Street, at the foot of the slope, was developed at first only on the west side, with some substantial merchant buildings acting as defences at the edge of the town. These looked out onto Gleddisgreen, the common town land, and to the 'lake'. The area along the shore, now Bridge Street, was known as the Butts, an open area put aside for the practice of archery, as decreed by the monarchy.

The most easterly buildings on the peninsula were the religious buildings, now St Mary's in the Old Kirkyard, which was the town church. Water Path marked the northern boundary of the town. The buildings along High Shore from Water Path to Carmelite Street became defensive merchant houses, with their main access from the rear. Number 1 High Shore, with its corner turret, would have been on an exposed corner overlooking open ground. Although the Market House Inn may have the oldest house date stone in the town, the oldest existing house within the burgh is undoubtedly Ingleneuk, with its massive medieval fireplace, at the bottom of Water Path.

With the town's main activities now down on the shoreline it was natural for the market to move to Low Street. The Tolbooth (Townhouse) was built on the corner of Strait Path and Low Street. Strait Path was cut down the hill connecting the old centre of the town to the new market-place and was the most direct route within the town walls. The market-place became the town centre with its Market Cross.

Further expansion led to the development of Gleddisgreen, with the town leasing out land for the

St Mary's Well in Duff House grounds.   (© TOMMY BOD)

construction of the Palace of Banff, built in 1538 on the site of what was later to be the Town House, with its gardens stretching approximately to Bridge Street and down to Reid Street. Collie Road, by St Mary's Church, continued from below the church, along the north wall of the Airlie Gardens, which became the southern boundary of the town, ending at the tower which would have stood on the lake's shoreline. Airlie House was built outside the town. Gleddisgreen was let out to a number of tenants, including the priest of the town and the town baker and blacksmith. The town's king's highway passed through Gleddisgreen, as stated, in the 1530s. This tells us that, although the ferry across the Deveron is not mentioned till 1622, it was in existence 100 years before. The King's Ford at Gellymill, opposite Duff House, had come into use with the drainage of the Dawhaugh, and could be crossed at low tide.

The second area of expansion was High Shore, below the castle. The decline of the castle meant the land on the shore was no longer important in its defences. This area was developed by the fishers and waulkers (cloth finishers) using the water from Water Path. Some think the Rood Chapel was built by the castle grounds overlooking the lake. The Order of the Templars was known to have land in and around Banff. Part of their property was a building located at the top of Water Path, an iron cross on the outside stating their ownership.

With the town full, Seytoune, or Seatown in the modern spelling, the area above the present harbour, became a satellite settlement to Banff, separated by the castle grounds. It was dominated by fishermen in their own community.

The medieval trade of Banff was chiefly with the Baltic city states. Wool, woolfells (fleeces), hides and salmon were the main exports. Salmon was the biggest export, accounting for an eighth of all Scotland's salmon exports. The Baltic cities formed a powerful trading monopoly, known as the Hanseatic League, that controlled the Baltic and the North Sea down to the Netherlands, reaching its peak of power during the mid-1300s. Banff's trade would have been dominated by the Hanseatic League. Banff would therefore have been hit hard by the league forbidding trade with Scotland due to the dire state of piracy by the Scots in 1416. This was to last 20 years, until 1436. The league slowly declined during the 1500s as new routes opened up for trade.

The medieval Mercat Cross of Banff. Unusually, on the reverse of the Crucifixion scene we see here it has the Virgin and Child.

(© Dr David Findlay Clark ARPS)

walk the boundaries, a ritual known as 'riding the marches', to ensure that neighbouring landowners had not encroached on town land. The town residents also needed to know the edges of the common land, where they had a right to graze their animals and cut turf for fuel. Many burghs ride the marches; the Burgh of Lanark can claim an unbroken history of riding the marches every year.

Banff's riding of the marches occurred in April or October. In 1676 this was accompanied by the drumming of the town drum. Freemen of the burgh were fined 4s. for failing to attend. In 1696 burgesses were expected to attend in full armour. In 1713 the walk commenced with the ringing of the Tolbooth bell. The last recorded riding of the marches was in October 1731, when, in celebration, 4s.8d. was spent on liquor.

The tradition was replaced with an annual town council inspection of the town's water supply. As the burgh increasingly let out the town lands the common land slowly disappeared, and thus many burghs only continued riding the marches as a local custom.

RIDING THE MARCHES
Julian Watson

Burgh boundaries were very important, encircling the common land of the town. Every year the provost, bailies, the town council and townsfolk would gather at the Market Cross. They would then

By referring to old maps and descriptions we have been able to locate the route of riding the marches of Banff. Today we can now relive history and again walk the marches, just as generations of Banffers did over the centuries. The walk along the boundaries takes us through the sheltered Deveron valley, up and over Gallow Hill, with its wonderful views to the open links by the sea. Take the walk as one or in sections, and remember all those feet that have gone before you.

Starting in Low Street at the Market Cross, proceed south and up Back Path. Turn left through what was once the King's Gate, leaving the old town and passing the present Parish Church. Cross the main road and continue onto Duff

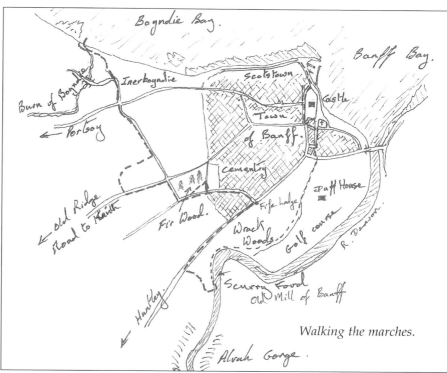

Walking the marches.

House grounds, past the rugby pitch and to Wrack Woods. Take the woodland path on your left, which brings you to the mausoleum. Below is St Mary's Well. Follow the main track at the bottom of the slope with, on your left, Carmel Mount, the old motte and bailey Scurry Castle guarding the ford. Moving out into the field by the river one is standing at Scurry Ford. The boundary included this field up to Wrack Mill. Returning to the bridge, the location of the old Mill of Banff, there is a track to the main road.

This brings one to Bauchlaw Bridge on the main Huntly road. Turn right along Sandyhill Road, following the pavement back towards the town.

On reaching the roundabout turn left up Colleonard Road through the new housing estates, with the cemetery on your right. Interestingly, the care home on the corner marks a kink in the boundary outside the burgh. However, follow the road along the base of the Fir Wood and turn right up the hill at the corner of the wood. At the crossroads

Banff town council waterworks inspection.

19

cross straight over the old Keith road. The boundary, in fact, turns left along the old Keith road for approximately 400m and crosses the field to the far field fence to double back to your lane. You rejoin the boundary of the town at the first field fence on your left descending the hill. To your right are the town's reservoirs at the top of Gallow Hill. Before you are fine views looking across Boyndie Bay. Continue down the lane and cross the main road to Portsoy from Banff.

Take the first right to the caravan site on the links. Walk through the site to where the Boyndie burn enters the sea, which was the most westerly point of the Burgh lands. Return along the seashore, across the links and past Scotstown to Banff harbour. At the harbour take the Sheriffs Brae up the hill into George Street. This brings us to Castle Street, where we turn left back towards the old town. This is in order to skirt the castle, which was not in the burgh lands. The castle's lands ran down to the sea. After the castle grounds turn left into Castle Lane, close to where Castle Gate once stood, back into the old town. Continue to your right up Old Castlegate to High Street and down Strait Path to the Market Cross.

Congratulations. You have just finished riding the marches, following what was an annual tradition for over 500 years, and have just covered over six miles. Best be in need of a dram, but I fear it will cost more than 4s.8d., which in today's money is 23p!

THE WHITEFRIARS – DRIVEN OUT BY FIRE AFTER 250 YEARS
Julian Watson

In the Middle Ages friars made an attempt to return to the austere lifestyle of the primitive church. The friars who came to Banff were the Carmelites, known as the White Friars (they wore white habits), dedicating their kirks to the Virgin Mary. They began as hermits on Mount Carmel in Palestine in the mid-twelfth century. As hermits they migrated from 1210 to Cyprus, Italy, Sicily, Spain and England. Sites were chosen in remote areas to reflect their hermit life.

They were, however, reformed by St Simon Stock (d.1265). This was to include working in towns, in the style of the other mendicant and preaching orders of friars, the Franciscans and Dominicans. Their later friaries are all to be found in or on the edge of towns. The Carmelites arrived in Scotland in 1262.

The first we know of the local Carmelites is a charter of 1324 granted by Robert the Bruce to set up a chapel and buildings 'juxta' (Latin for 'alongside') the town of Banff. Robert the Bruce had been excommunicated by the Pope in 1318 and it was not until 1324 that the Pope recognised Bruce as king.

It is clear from the charter that the Carmelites already held land in Banff. This is believed to have

been a large area of Sandyhills outside the burgh boundary, the Dawhaugh, part of the flood plain which had been drained, now the golf course south of Duff House. It is thought that this was a retreat established by Alexander III (1249–86). The chapel, it is claimed, was located on the site of the mausoleum in Wrack Woods, at that time overlooking the first ford, Scurry Ford, on the River Deveron by St Mary's Well. During the construction of the mausoleum, the remains of a chapel were demolished and many human remains were found on the site and placed in a large urn, since lost.

There are, however, many reports of the friary being in the area of Carmelite Street in lower Banff. This could well be the friary given a charter in 1324 by Robert the Bruce. On the south side of the street (Tesco) we do know that this was town land and let out, along with the right to build the 'Palace of Banff' with gardens (now the location of the Town House). Dr Cramond, in the *Annals of Banff*, clearly states that the friary could not have been in this area for the same reasons.

This leads us to a controversial observation that the old kirkyard could be the Friary. Historically, this does not appear to have been within the burgh in the 1300s. The Carmelite friary in Aberdeen was

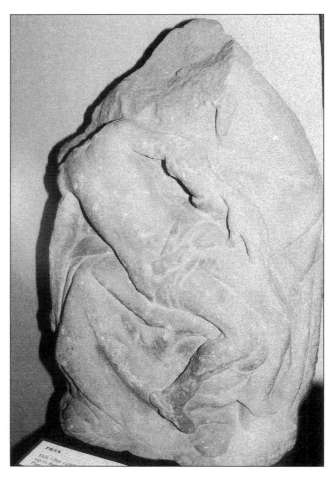

The only stone Pieta found in Scotland, discovered in St Mary's churchyard in the 1860s.

founded on reclaimed land beside the developing harbour in 1270. The friary churches have very similar dimensions, and it is highly unusual to find an ancient church in such a location. Friaries essentially required a good supply of water, which would have been obtained from the stream in Water Path. There are also reports of old friary cells along the south side of the kirkyard, and the Carmelite gardens extending to the old manse at the bottom of Water Path. Ingleneuk House has a very large and unusual medieval inglenook fireplace stretching the full width of the house, designed for cooking on a large scale. Could this be the friary kitchen? The Pieta Stone now held in the museum, a known symbol of the Carmelites, was dug up in the east side of the kirkyard. The jury is still out!

The Carmelite friary, a major part of Banff, was one of nine in Scotland. It would have looked after people's religious needs, but it also fed the poor, gave shelter to travellers, and tended the sick. Banff in the Middle Ages had a hospital, probably run by the friars. In Wrack Woods, away from the town on the River Deveron, is an island, Hospital Island, possibly run by the friars for lepers. Banff also had a school possibly connected with the friars. All of this was about to end with the Reformation.

In the 1500s, before there was any Protestant Reformation, there was already some pressure on the religious orders. The friary was wealthy, owning land and fishing rights. Noblemen and burghs schemed to appropriate church wealth. In response to local pressure the Carmelites leased out their land and fishing. In 1520 a plot of land was leased in the burgh overlooking the lake (the water behind the shingle bar). Then, in 1541, fishing on the Deveron was leased, followed in 1543 by lands in Dawhaugh and Sandyhill. The glebe went in 1549 and a net for salmon in the King's Water in the Deveron in 1555.

On 20 July 1559, under the cover of night, their kirk and some other buildings south of the town were set on fire by persons unknown. It was the final straw and the Carmelites concluded a deal with the Ogilvies, future Lords Banff, and departed.

Sir Walter Ogilvie of Dunlugas was the main beneficiary of these land deals, along with his son, George Ogilvie of Castletoun. Sir Walter was busy building up his estates in land and fishing from the church and town council. He was regarded in his time as a good friend of the church. Sir Walter also leased the lands left to endow the chantry altar of the Holy Rood, located to the north of the castle. Ministers of Banff also held the chaplaincy of the Rood Chapel. The church history of Banff for this period is not well known, and presbytery records only begin in 1622. It may be that the Ogilvies united the church of Banff with the Rood Chapel on the site of the friary. The earliest gravestone in the kirkyard is that of Sir Walter Ogilvie.

THE REFORMATION
Alistair Mason

The Scottish Reformation of 1560 came late, so the populations of trading ports such as Banff knew what had been going on in Germany and Holland for more than a generation. In a Banff document of the 1550s there is mention of 'heresy so long rampant', so there may have been Protestants already in Banff. The Stewart kings, largely for unworthy financial reasons, preferred the old church. There were structures in place to allow the king to milk a church which, in a very poor country, was relatively wealthy. In 1560 the Scots nobility, for very similar motives, deposed Mary Queen of Scots, put her baby son on the throne, and shared out much of the church's wealth. Banff was one of the burghs with a representative in the Reformation parliament. The church, thus reformed, was much poorer, and scarcely able to provide services. There was, however, no Catholic backlash, because the Catholic clergy were not driven out or martyred but were simply pensioned off. This meant that for a generation there was even less money to support a Protestant ministry.

So in Banff the last three Carmelites accepted a pension and disappeared. Their property in Banff, as we have seen, went to a lay owner, an Ogilvie of Dunlugas, part of the general transfer from the church to the gentry. On the other hand, the major part of the tithes paid to Banff Parish Church before the Reformation had gone to help run Arbroath Abbey. The abbey is now a ruin, and, after paying the pension to the last Catholic parish priest, the tithes could go towards the Protestant church in Banff. It is unlikely this happened across the board, because the gentry were very greedy and knew and administered the law.

Left: *A carved oak panel, probably sixteenth century, found in a house in Banff. It presents a number of interpretive mysteries.*

The first Protestant minister of Banff, William Lawtie, was also in charge of Cullen and Fordyce and Inverboyndie. He had 'readers' to help him. One of the readers had been the chaplain at the altar of the Holy Rood in the Parish Church, and a notary public. These readers, like other pre-Reformation clergy, are referred to as Sir George Scott or Sir William Martin. This did not mean they were county gentry. These are 'Pope's Knights'. If a man finished his course at King's College, Aberdeen, he would be a Master of Arts, and would be called Mr William Lawtie. If he didn't finish his course they called him 'Sir', which then was a less honourable title.

Left: *Banff aisle, old St Mary's Church.*

(© Dr David Findlay Clark ARPS)

One thing that did not change was that the only career open to a 'lad o' pairts' before and after the Reformation was the church. No wonder George Scott changed sides. The reformed church was very cautious about who would be allowed to preach, but reading from the bible was less risky. There was a shift from one sacred language to another. The old church used Latin, the new used English, both, doubtless, with a Scottish accent, but we should note that the new bible (not yet the Authorised Version) was not in Scots.

We know almost nothing about the details of the fittings of Banff Parish Church before and after the Reformation. All that is left of the old church today is the Banff aisle, a fine little annexe to the side of the nave, rather more to the glory of the Ogilvies than to the glory of God. It presumably had stained glass, which did not survive. We can naturally guess that Sir Walter's tastes in public worship were catered for before and after the Reformation. No one would be smashing his windows in his lifetime. We might wonder what the history was of the Banff Pieta (a carving of the Virgin and the dead Christ). That was put away, and not smashed. When?

A reformed church read the bible and sang psalms. The old Catholic church had had a great musical tradition, but it was for trained choirs. In Banff, money was left to have masses sung, not said. With the Reformation came congregational music; even women were allowed to sing. They didn't have books. The parish clerk, with his tuning fork, sang a line, and then they repeated it after him, which was slow work. Most congregations (or perhaps most clerks) had very few tunes in their repertoire.

Most religious change came from above, and we know almost nothing about what ordinary people thought. It might well take 50 years of strenuous preaching to make the people of Banff take their Protestantism for granted, and even develop a taste

for sermons. The ministers catechised, which means that children, and some older than children, stood in rows and recited prepared answers to prepared questions from memory. The Church of Scotland put no value on lay spontaneity, but its ministers were expected to preach and pray *ex tempore*. In practice they memorised, too. Their prayers were on well-tried themes, and a regular congregation could tell what was coming. The sermon was composed, very carefully structured and then memorised, a very challenging task.

Staying awake during sermons was a challenge too. The old Banff Parish Church was not a very tall building, and rather small for its purpose, so it presumably was normally full. In the centuries after the Reformation they kept adding galleries to get more people in. The service would last hours, people had had a heavy week of manual labour and there was no fresh air. Congregations slept.

The reformed church disliked the Christian calendar, saints' days and festivals. God had given us a weekly Sabbath, but nothing else. The evidence suggests that it was hard work and against the grain to suppress the Christian year. The Presbytery, coming to inspect Banff in 1625, blamed the parish for not stopping those who observed 'superstitious times' with special fires. These may indeed have been pre-Christian customs. The church banned Christmas in 1561, but even the Scottish Parliament dragged its feet for 30-odd years before enforcing it. Fasts, unlike festivals, were permitted, but fish on Fridays went.

There must have been many people who hankered after the old ways, but unless there was a local nobleman who could flout the law, there was no chance of Roman Catholic worship. Things were different, say, in Huntly, only some 20 miles away, and Banff was a port, so presumably anyone determined enough could find a priest. The Church of Scotland bullied its minorities, but disliked pursuing to the death. In the whole Reformation period there were only two Roman Catholic martyrs in Scotland. The North East of Scotland was theologically conservative, and tended to like bishops. In externals its churches and worship were like any other reformed church, but one might have found more traces of pre-Reformation Scotland still tolerated, like, perhaps, the Banff Pieta.

THE SLAUGHTER OF JAMES OGILVIE
Julian Watson

It was at the Michaelmas Sheriff Court in 1628, we hear, when the feud between two cousins came to a head in the streets of Banff. The story is told almost entirely in the words of the Court records.

The first attempt on James Ogilvie's life was at his home in Paddocklaw, just off the Huntly main road outside Banff. His cousin, Sir George Ogilvie of Banff, having a great hatred for James, came with William Ogilvie, George Braibner known as 'Joukie', and with several others armed with swords, dirks, steel bonnets, hackbuts, daggers, pistols and long guns. They arrived about midnight in silence under darkness of cloud. Margaret Ogilvie, pregnant with child, wife of the said James, was in bed when Sir George knocked on the main door. He claimed to be their friend John Gordon of Buckie, upon which Margaret rose from her bed and unlocked the door.

Thus in a great fury Sir George and his accomplices rushed in, drawing their swords and pistols. The servants were held with sword points to their naked breasts and threatened with death if they did not reveal the whereabouts of the said James. In a rage the beds were cut to pieces in the search. James was not at home.

Later, on 3 October, James had to go to the Head Court (a meeting of the burgh council) in Banff to remove some tenants for Lady Boyne. At the Head Court was Sir George Ogilvie of Banff, who, as a knight and the provost, was with the Laird of Carnowsie. There then developed a great argument with much malice and evil. Sir George hit James across the head with a baton, creating a great flow of blood. Swords were drawn in the court, James drew his sword and, although not in armour, was able to escape out of the Tolbooth and onto the King's Highway.

All was to no avail, as he was pursued by about 20 persons. Although many were in armour, they overtook him in 'the space of the two buttis and mair'. There they most barbarously, cruelly and inhumanly set upon him. James received many deadly wounds to both the head and body, and was thus shamefully and unmercifully murdered. Sir George, with his own hand, stuck James behind his back with a sword through the fifth rib and liver, being a deadly strike. The Laird of Carnowsie shot James with a pistol, with two bullets breaking the thigh bone.

The rest of the Sheriff Court records of the murder are lost, but we know that the original dispute was regarding land. From the church records it would appear that Sir George was not convicted and got away with the murder. The Presbytery Registers of 1630 and 1631 are not satisfied with Sir George over the scandal of the slaughter of James Ogilvie. Nor had his behaviour since been improving, with the further killing of the Laird of Rothiemay. However, Sir George appears to have made his peace with the Presbytery in the end with an apology!

COURT BOOK, 1624–50
Julian Watson

Burgh courts had great powers to enforce laws, especially on moral issues. They also covered building control, such as outside staircases. Punishments were handed out as fines, sitting in the stocks and banishment. Imprisonment for any period of time was too expensive. Hangings were surprisingly rare, which was just as well, as the trap door had not been invented and hangings were often agonisingly slow.

Price fixing was often required to control costs during times of shortages. The market was carefully controlled as tax was raised at the market cross.

Here is but a selection from the period:

Horse Bones
Alexander Jack, servant to James Tunour, ordered to sit upon his knees and crave the mercy of Patrick Cokburne for abusing his house door with horse bones. [1628]

Hanging
Francis Broune, son of John Broune, cloth maker, put in

The murder of James Ogilvie.   (© DEREK GRAY)

the stocks for a number of offences which were on the whole stealing around Banff. This included breaking into the James Kennedy building, and Patrick Schand's store which included silk buttons, silk, pairs of gloves and golf balls. Then going into the fields in the time of harvest and taking the corn. Found guilty on all accounts and sentenced to be taken to Gallowhill and hung upon the gallows. [1637. Rope for the gallows 3s.4d.]

Banishment

Thomas Wallace has an idle household of six or seven persons and furthermore did injury the bailies while they were collecting money for the harbour. Thomas is

Court adjourned.   (© Dr David Findlay Clark ARPS)

Instruments of punishment: jougs, stocks, branks and helmets.   (© Derek Gray)

to be discharged of his burghership and all his goods to be removed from his house. The keys are to be delivered up and he is never to have a house again in the burgh. He is to be placed in the stocks thereafter, then to be ejected from the burgh and not to be seen within 24 miles. [1626]

Isobel Mitchell is convicted for acts of theft and licentious life and being a whore. She is to be stripped naked (July) and banished from the burgh. If she should return she is to be burnt upon the cheek with a hot key and if she be found again in the Burgh is to be put to death as a notorious thief. [1629]

Isobel Watson having committed fornication is banished and if she should return she should be burnt upon the cheek. The hand bell man is sent through the town stating that no person should take her in under penalty of five pounds. [1642]

Beatrix Hendersone is banished for her scandalous life and if she returns to be drowned. [1643]

Katharen Robertsone vagabond banished and if she should be found within the Burgh she will taken to the Cross of Banff and burnt upon the face being stripped above the waist.

Marjorie Mylne and four other women are banished for their obscene and filthy crimes. [1644]

Pillar of Repentance

Returning from prayers two bailies did encounter a dispute. William Tailyeour with his wife Katherein Scherund and their daughter Janet were in dispute with Margaret Redheid, who was a bairn. Janet hit Margaret and when she was weeping on the road beside the Market Cross they did hit again. William Tailyeour is fined and loses his freedom of the burgh. Furthermore he with his wife and daughter must go to the pillar of repentance on Sunday during the service in public and repent. [1631]

Vagabonds and Idle Persons

Great harm and burden to Burgh to idle persons and strangers. They are to be removed from the Burgh. The houses are to be locked up or knocked down. [1629]

Janet Mylne with 24 other women as being idle living without any lawful living is referred to the Assize Court. [The judges went on tour round the country, so serious cases waited for the Assizes, when they were holding court locally]. [1633]

Beatrix Henrysone and John Browne and his bairns, with ten others who live 'idlie as codroches' [we think a 'codroche' is a layabout] *are ordered to find honest service within four days or be banished. Beatrix fails to find work and is transported by ferryboat over the*

Deveron by the Burgh officers, never to return. [1636]

Fines

William Ogilvy struck and bled William Fordyce in the shoulder with a 'durk' [presumably a dirk] while playing dice under cloud and silence of night. Fined £10 each and ordered to stand in the Tolbooth till eight in the morning. [1633]

William Wallace deprived of his burghership and fined £40 for insolence and abuse of the provost and bailies.

John Spence is fined 40s. to the town and 26s.8d. to William Stewart for striking him on the head with a hook and bleeding him, when he took grass from the kirkyard. [1628]

Barbara Scot fined 20 merks for hitting her servant and pulling out her hair. [1634]

Escaping

James Milne and Robert Alexander, sailors, imprisoned in the Tolbooth for certain wrongs done to the watch (guard) did 'out of a malicious and devilish intention' break out, but were recaptured. [1643]

Witches

John Philp suspected of witchcraft, charming and washing sick people at 'our Ladie Well' at Ordiquhill. The ministers brought him to court, where he was held within the wardhouse till a commission could be sent for and meanwhile placed in the stocks. Finally Philp was burnt at the stake at the Mercat Cross. [1630]

Margaret Nicol, suspected of witchcraft, handed over to the minister to be questioned and held to the next assizes. [Rope for binding the witches, 8s. 1636]

Orders

Beasts are not allowed to graze in the corn under penalty of a fine. [1628]

Nobody to trespass in the corn fields, and if so found to be placed in the stocks for eight hours. [1629]

Fixing of prices Ale 12d., Beer 14d. per pint. [1631]

All servants not to be out after six in the evening as abusing themselves. [1632]

Extra watch in the town from 10p.m. to 4a.m. as there are many vagabonds stealing. [1634]

For an imaginative reconstruction of life in Banff in the 1620s, the reader should refer to Shona MacLean's historical mystery *The Redemption of Alexander Seaton*.

THE CIVIL WAR AND COMMONWEALTH
Julian Watson

The Bishops' Wars

The Covenanting Revolution of the 1640s (named for the National Covenant of 1638, whereby the Scots bound themselves to uphold the king if he kept his country truly Protestant) was a power struggle between the Scottish Church and the king. In a series of wars intertwined with the English Civil War, King Charles was defeated and executed, against the wishes of his Scottish adversaries. Banff supported the Covenanters, the winning side, but at a great cost. Banff Castle played no part in the conflict, as it was already described as a ruin in 1642.

Palace of Banff

In April 1639, after a conference between the Marquis of Huntly and Montrose, many in Banff felt compelled to sign the Covenant. The Laird of Banff was not for signing and stood for King Charles. In July of 1640 the Earl of Findlater had orders to seize the Laird of Banff's rents. The following August Major Munro, with 800 men, marched on Forglen, one of the Laird's estates, and plundered most cruelly the country people. Then coming to Banff, he camped on the Dawhaugh (the present golf course) and set about the Palace of Banff, the Laird's house situated at the corner of Low Street, where now stands the Town House. The house and gardens were destroyed for firewood and shelter, with the assistance of the locals. The house had been one of the finest in the north of Scotland. Timber and iron-work were carried away, leaving nothing but the ruined walls. Inchdrewer Castle and Forglen were also rifled, being two other of his estates. King

An old mortar dating from 1641, in the period of the Civil War, now in Banff Museum, was probably used pharmaceutically.

(© TOMMY BOD)

A pillar, possibly from the Palace of Banff (early 1600s) found in Bridge Street. (© TOMMY BOD)

The murder of Alexander Douglas. (© DEREK GRAY)

Montrose, stripping Banff. (© DEREK GRAY)

Charles, for his allegiance, compensated him and created him a peer of the realm as Lord Banff.

In February 1643 all the burgesses and inhabitants were ordered to attend at Castle Hill in full armour, as there were sufficient grounds to call to arms.

In 1644 the Scots invaded England. Banff, in January, was put on alert as an easy landing place for Royalist forces from England. All men were called to arms with swords, pikes, or muskets within 24 hours, and failure to appear resulted in a fine of £10. Banff, under the provostship of Dr Alexander Douglas, was distinctly in favour of the Covenanters and the town needed to be on its guard.

Laird of Gight

The following April the town was caught off guard. The Lairds of Gight, Neutown and Ardlogie arrived with a force of 40 horse and musketeers and took the town. They were Royalists in favour of King Charles. They took free quarters and plundered all the arms they could get, buff coats, pikes, swords and carbines. Both town and merchants' money was taken. Dr Douglas, the provost, had fled and men

Provost Douglas's stolen tomb at the mausoleum in Duff House grounds.

had to swear allegiance to the king. The raiding party then left. The Laird of Gight was later prosecuted but claimed he had only borrowed the money. The spring of 1644 brought more trouble, with the King's Irish regiment plundering Banff due to lack of pay. The havoc also included what was left of the Palace of Banff, so it became the victim of both sides of the conflict.

Montrose

Banff survived the winter but worse was to come to its inhabitants. Montrose, one of Scotland's greatest generals, had at first supported the Covenanters, but felt they had gone too far and changed sides to support the king. Banff was on the wrong side. There was also the small matter of the destruction of the Palace of Banff by the Covenanters and locals. Montrose arrived in March 1645. He plundered the town pitilessly. No merchant's goods or gear were left. If a man was seen in the street he was stripped naked. But that was all: some two or three houses were burnt, but even so no blood was shed. There was no sign of the provost, Dr Douglas. On returning from victory at the battle of Auldearn in May of the same year, Montrose burned Cullen and also had troops quartered in Banff. The town at the time only escaped being burned as it had some strategic value.

In September 1645 the Presbytery Meeting was not held for fear of dangers from the north.

Petition to Parliament

The disastrous effects of the war are very clearly shown by a petition to Parliament in January 1647, a year and half later. The town was asking for relief on the burgh rent for the town, detailing its losses and praying for help. They had no animals or merchant goods. The kirk, Tolbooth, school and ferryboat were falling down or beyond repair, with no money for works, and the town was deeply in debt. Meanwhile troops were still quartered in the town demanding housing and food, while their horses roamed the fields and damaged the corn. The timber of the town had all been burnt by Montrose, and the inhabitants were living off the charity of their neighbours. Nothing seems to have come of it except for some relief on the Burgh rent.

Dr Douglas Assassinated

Dr Alexander Douglas was chief ringleader and agent of the Covenanters. The town elected him three times provost of the burgh. He was, however, liked by some and well hated by others. It is stated that he brought Munro to Banff in 1640 to sack the Palace of Banff. Cromwell, under the English occupation, had appointed him Sheriff of Banffshire. Furthermore, he was either a member of Parliament or sat on the Committee of State.

In 1658, returning home from the Court House in Low Street in the afternoon, Dr Douglas met his death by an assassin. He was stabbed from behind by a man who was selling peats on the street. The dirk passed through the Sheriff's body and came out at his breast. The murderer mounted the horse that had carried the peats and galloped up the Strait Path, making his escape, never to be heard of again.

A memorial to Dr Douglas may be seen over the gateway to the old kirkyard, and his monument, the figure of a knight, was later removed to the Mausoleum at Duff House, as a fake ancestor for the Fifes.

General Monk

All was to go full circle, as a letter from General Monk was read out in 1659 requesting attendance in Edinburgh to bring about the Restoration of the monarchy. Two years later came the 'Oath of Allegiance' to the Crown, with the proscription of the Covenanters and the National Covenant the following year.

THE LORDS BANFF
Jay Wilson

Three times 'Murder' –
George, 3rd Lord Banff

Standing isolated among unfurrowed fields, stripped of its orchards, its opulence and finally its occupants, Inchdrewer Castle merely gestures towards its past. Tumbledown walls and winds whispering through the medieval tower are the keepers of myth and legend. Truth, twisted in time and history, is unrecognisable. It is without doubt that George, 3rd Lord Banff, died violently when flames tore into the fabric of his bedchamber and dissolved the flesh on his back; but beyond that, rumour and speculation feed the myth.

Attracted by light from the inferno, neighbouring cottagers cut smooth paths through the wintered fields. Congregating, they helped Elizabeth Porter, the housekeeper, to safety. Whispers, threading their way through crowds, weaving rumours, competed with the roaring fire. 'She was beaten back by flames... smoke... too thick... couldn't get near his rooms.' With backs braced against the frost-filled night, faces glowed amber and feeling returned to frozen fingers. 'An' him just seen his boy married in Edinburgh too.' Smarting eyes blinked back ash-flecked tears; heads wavered, catching snippets of conversation dissolving in snowflakes drifting to the ground. 'No idea he was due back... should have stayed away.' Floor joists, wrapped in flame, cracked and bolted earthbound. 'Drunk, no doubt... never knew him sober.' Allegations attached themselves to servants, and neighbours filled with animosity

Inchdrewer Castle.   (© Dr David Findlay Clark ARPS)

Inchdrewer Castle in flames. (© TOMMY BOD)

instead of sympathy. 'Who could blame him... that George Mortimer of Auchinbady.' It wasn't a question, it was a dormant grudge reignited on a whisper. Women covering their mouths and nostrils, protecting their lungs from smoke, exhaled empathy. 'His poor wife, Margaret... savaged, she was... by Banff.' Men shielding their cheeks from heat corroborated that past. The blaze spread, intensifying rumour:

Saw them by his door... she did... Robert Stewart and James Miln... threatened her, Elizabeth... you know... to throw her on the pyre... paid her off... they say... to Ireland... three times... she said... three times Porter... three times Murder... from his blazing room... she heard.

Insolence, in place of remorse or denial, slipped off the boys' tongues as they witnessed the flames consume the castle and its contents. One was heard uttering, 'his Lordship deserved what has come to him.' Superstition and religion were in alliance on that Friday, 13 January 1713, when George's death was seen as apt, and mourned by few.

There was belligerent behaviour at the scene of the blaze, and rumour-fuelled relentless investigations by the new Lord Banff. Convinced that Robert Stewart and James Miln, along with William Brody, had not only robbed Inchdrewer on previous occasions but had indeed murdered his father, George set out to shape any proof of truth, picked out of the ashes, into his own form of justice. The 4th Lord Banff levelled charges of murder against the three.

As the only eye witness Elizabeth Porter's account of events was invaluable, and Lord George was confident that he had secured it in his favour. On the eve of the murder trial in Edinburgh, however, she fled for Ireland, leaving behind a note claiming that her flight was stoked by fear of the zealous Banff. Her withdrawal from the legal proceedings added further to myth and speculation. Was she. in fact. financially assisted by murderers? The defendants were not only released, having no case to prove, but were free to sue Banff for damages while incarcerated.

A Precarious Peerage
Lords Banff: 1642–1803

A peerage which lasts a mere 161 years could be deemed careless – careful marriages to women of good stock are tantamount to the survival of a line. But after only five generations the Banff line began to falter and break as lords repeatedly died prematurely and failed to produce heirs. The death of the unmarried eighth Lord of Banff in 1803 effected the demise of the title.

This ill-fated peerage was born in 1642 to an apparently self-serving and innately cruel laird, who was despised more for his personal proclivities than his political preferences. Having nurtured a quarrelsome and autocratic demeanour, George was quite literally let off with murder. See the 'slaughter of James Ogilvie'. The Sheriff accepted a plea, on Banff's behalf, of provocation.

Politically Sir George of Banff (1583–1663), the Catholic laird, could not and would not subscribe to the Presbyterian Covenant. His loyalty to King Charles I afforded him mixed fortunes, however, and he found himself frequently seeking sanctuary at court. Lands acquired by Banff, through not only inheritance and a good marriage but also those gifted for service to the crown, were indiscriminately attacked by marauding Covenanters. As we have seen, in 1640 General Munro's soldiers laid waste the grounds and buildings of Inchdrewer Castle and the Palace of Banff. This loyalty was rewarded, however, when Sir George was ennobled; giving birth to the Banff dynasty.

George, 2nd Lord Banff (1624–68) lived most of his life in the shadow of his father and only held the title for five years before he died; a relatively young man at 44. During one of his father's periods of exile (1640) the young, high-spirited George had an altercation with one of Munro's sergeants. The seriousness of the wounds exacted on this sergeant led to George's own exile for a time. He did return to Forglen, however, and fathered one son (George 3rd) and six daughters before his death; twins (one son and a daughter) were born posthumously. His eldest son's infamy had obviously taken root while he was still very young, as the 2nd Lord Banff gambled on his unborn child being a boy and made a deathbed change of will. Deemed an unworthy beneficiary of the Ogilvie estates by the time George the younger was 20, his father bestowed Forglen Estate upon the posthumous child.

George, 3rd Lord Banff, was born in 1649 and died, as we have seen, prematurely in mysterious circumstances in 1713. Before this incident, however, he had been declared a rebel by the Scots judiciary – due to the number of his violent assaults on neighbours and tenants. Unbelievably, the crown granted him a Remission of Crimes on the merit of his late grandfather. It appears that this did, however, result in a lull of activities against his neighbours while he continued to act with atrocious cruelty towards his wife, Lady Jean Keith.

George, 4th Lord Banff (1670–1718) was the protector of his mother and sisters during his father's years of violence and lawlessness, and seems to have lived a settled and domestic life at Inchdrewer following the death of his father and the restoration of the castle. While he took no official part in the Rising of 1715, he covertly supported the Jacobite cause through supplying arms, and his best horse, to George Gordon of Buckie.

Lord Banff and his wife, Helen Lauder, lost their first two sons (both called George) in infancy and, in an attempt to break the curse of the inherited family name, they called their subsequent son, and heir, John George. Lord George, the 4th Lord, died of a mysterious malady when John was not yet one year old and his brother Alexander was still in the womb.

The young Banff boys led sheltered lives at Inchdrewer until their guardian, Lord Findlater, decided it was time they should go out into the world. John went to London, and as 'a very fine [but naive] nobleman' befriended a Captain James Ogilvie and romantically married his daughter, Mary, after only a short acquaintance. John, however, returned to Scotland shortly after the wedding, while Mary mysteriously remained with her father. Despite not bearing the Christian name George, John's life was cut very short. After dining with friends at Cullen House he went swimming in the Moray Firth, near Black Rocks. Cramp appears to have wracked his limbs and rendered his friends useless as, despite being near the shore, he was neither able to swim back nor be rescued. He was a mere 21 years old when he drowned.

This event, in 1738, saw the peerage start its lateral slide, as John was survived only by his brother Alexander. When only 15 years old Alexander started a career in the Royal Navy, where he distinguished himself by reaching the rank of captain by the age of 23. Before his death in 1746 he had captured French and Spanish ships and had been given the freedom of the City of Glasgow. With his focus firmly on his career, family issues were not prioritised by the young Lord Banff. He never married. Illness and the curse of the Banffs prevented him from enjoying his glory for any length of time, and Alexander, 6th Lord Banff died, aged 28, passing the peerage sideways once more to his cousin, Sir Alexander Ogilvie of Forglen.

Alexander, 7th Lord Banff, was in fact the grandson of Alexander, the twin son born posthumously to George, the 2nd Lord. With his succession to the title, what remnants were left of the original seventeenth-century estates were reunited. Alexander, also the 2nd Baron of Forglen, held a commission in the Army. His marriage to Jean Nisbet of Dirleton, in Edinburgh on 2 April 1749, produced two surviving sons out of four, and five daughters.

Lord Banff died in 1771, leaving the title to William, his eldest surviving son.

William, 8th Lord Banff, followed a career in the Enniskilling (8th) Dragoons and remained unmarried. In 1803 his early death, at 49, brought to an end the Baronetcy of Forglen and the precarious peerage of Banff.

THE COUNTY FAMILIES
Charles Burnett

The story of Banffshire has evolved over the centuries through the efforts of individuals and family groups. Their concern has been to make a living from the land, the size of the holding dictating how large or small the income might be. Certain families have been consistent over the centuries in their connections with Banff, and many owned houses in the county town which were inhabited, particularly during the winter months, when social activity could be enjoyed at close quarters.

The Ogilvie family married into the Sinclair of Deskford family and established the foundation of a family eventually raised to the peerage as Earls of Seafield. Another branch of the Ogilvie family, descended from the Ogilvie/Sinclair marriage, became Lords Banff in 1642. They were the Ogilvies of Dunlugas, then 'of Banff'. Members had a close connection with the management of Banff and the first recorded provost of Banff was Sir Walter Ogilvie of Dunlugas in 1541. Thereafter, many of his descendants became provosts of the burgh. They held Inchdrewer Castle, south of Banff. The title became extinct in 1803 on the death of the 8th Lord Banff.

In the far south of Banffshire, within the Grampian foothills, is the estate of Ballindalloch, long held by the Macphersons. This family, like the Ogilvies, married into the Grant family and acquired a double surname, plus Grant heraldry in their arms. The family were not heavily involved in the administration of the county town, and did not possess a town house in Banff, but the head of the family at the time of writing, Mrs Clare Russell, is the Lord Lieutenant of Banffshire.

Auchmedden is in Aberdour parish, Aberdeenshire, not Banffshire, but the Baird family have always been closely involved with Banff. Two members of the family were provosts of Banff in the seventeenth century. Further west from Auchmedden, in the county, is the Troup estate, once held by the Garden family for many years. The family occupied Delgaty Castle, near Turriff, for a while and also inherited the Campbell barony of Glenlyon.

Like the Bairds, the Gardens used a boar on their arms. Two other Banffshire families also used boar heads on their arms, making the animal the most

Left: Arms of the Ogilvy Earls of Findlater and Seafield, who built Banff Castle. Centre: Arms of Sir Malcolm Innes of Edengight, Lord Lyon King of Arms, and local laird. Right: From St Mary's kirkyard, the sixteenth-century arms of Sir George Baird of Auchmedden.

popular heraldic subject in the area. These families were the Abercrombies of Birkenbog and Glassaugh, whose properties lay to the west of Banff, and the Gordons of Letterfourie, whose estate was at the western edge of Banffshire, just south of Buckie. They were descended from the fourth son of the 2nd Earl of Huntly.

The virtual kings of Banffshire were the Duff family, raised to the peerage as Earls Fife and later Dukes of Fife. They owned huge areas of Banffshire, Moray, Aberdeenshire, and Kincardineshire, and had residences at Duff House, Rothiemay Castle, Innes House, Fife House in Edinburgh, Fife House in London and Mar Lodge on Deeside. Eventually the family married into the royal family and received a dukedom. However, their vast inheritance passed away in Banffshire, though evidence of their once-greatness is still to be seen at Duff House, the mausoleum, and on a memorial in Banff Parish Church and in a stained-glass window at St Andrew's Episcopal Church, High Street, Banff.

The Innes family is another with a long county association. They are now linked to the properties of Edingight, Kinnairdy and Crombie. Shown above are the arms of Sir Malcolm Innes of Edingight as Lord Lyon King of Arms.

MACPHERSON'S RANT
Christina Ord

This is the story of James Macpherson, Highland freebooter and the Robin Hood of the North, c.1675–1700. His name lives on today through music and folklore.

James Macpherson was the illegitimate son of the Laird of Invereshie, near Kincraig in Inverness-shire. His mother, a beautiful gipsy, was cast out from her own people for forming a relationship with the laird. Growing up on his father's estate, and being the son of a Highland chief, James received a good education and, from an early age, travelled far and wide with his father to demonstrate his skills on the fiddle. It is said his performances were superb, and his folk music astonished all who heard him play.

While James was still a boy, his father was murdered by Donald Grant as he lay resting in a wood. On hearing the terrible news his mother took her son and fled the district, as she feared for both their lives. James, vowing to avenge his father's death, although he was still a youth, trained hard and became an excellent swordsman and athlete. He tracked down Donald Grant and took vengeance on his father's killer in a duel.

After settling this score, James and his mother lived peacefully in the neighbourhood of Strath Avon, where James had a long-lasting friendship with bonnie Annie Grant, the daughter of the laird of Aberlour. She was a beautiful and much sought-after girl. Annie enjoyed James's company, and the strange mixture of Scottish and gipsy fiddle music that James incorporated into a style of his own. After a long courtship, it is said, James married bonnie Annie. Everything went well until a jealous rival branded James's mother a witch, and the Macphersons' home was ransacked and burned to the ground.

After this atrocious act James Macpherson gathered a small army of friends, mainly gipsies and highlanders, and set out to discover who was responsible. During these searches he turned to the life of a freebooter. It is said he was following in the footsteps of Peter Roy Macgregor, who was caught near Keith in 1666. Unlike Peter Roy, however, Macpherson is said to have given most of his loot to the poor. Hence came the title of Robin Hood of the North.

Macpherson was a strong, handsome man, seven feet one inches high (they say) and very intelligent.

Celebrated throughout his lifetime for his skill on the violin, he was never charged with cruelty or atrocious acts. 'It is said his conduct often afforded evidence of his being imbued with feelings of generosity and pity.'

'James of the hills', as he became known, gathered tremendous support for his cause. He and his friends, Alistair Fraser and Peter and Donald Brown, and their band of freebooters led a daring and adventurous life. The Clan Macpherson, his father's clan, was always willing to help James either by feeding him, clothing him, or giving him money or shelter. They accepted James as one of their own clansmen, and even rescued him, with help from some locals, from prison when he was held at Aberdeen. James was a strong but fair leader. He pressed his opponents hard, but even his enemies conceded that he was an honourable and upright adversary, who never perpetrated acts of thievery or harm against the·poor or distressed.

Macpherson and his men made lightning swoops on market towns to drive off cattle and sheep to the hills. Keith, Elgin, Forres and Banff were plundered. All the time Macpherson was constantly looking for those responsible for the burning of his mother's home. They would make a spectacular entrance, sometimes using a piper, with their pistols, dirks and claymores much in evidence. Macpherson's two-handed sword, which survives, if it is indeed his, is 4ft 3in. in length and has a wavy-edged blade. It is described as a medieval weapon.

Macpherson's men had many narrow escapes from the authorities, which did not please his reputed arch-enemy, Lord Braco. At the Summer Eve's fair (St Rufus Fair) in Keith, Macpherson, accompanied by Peter and Donald Brown, mingled with the crowds, as they had done many times previously. But this time Lord Braco and his men spotted and closed in on the offenders. After a long chase through the town, and the exchange of steel, the men were cornered in the town's High Street, where the two Browns were captured. It is said a woman threw a blanket over the rebel leader, and Braco, aided by many townspeople, managed to apprehend Macpherson. The three were bound in chains and carried to the 'house of two storeys', which formed a section of the kirkyard's east dyke.

On hearing of the capture, the Laird of Grant and his clan, who were heavily armed, disturbed Duff (Lord Braco) and his friends celebrating their triumph, with banging and roaring at Braco's door: 'Nae Duff in Scotland'll stan atween me an ma freens.'

Left: *Doune Church with its blank clockface, Macduff.* (© TOMMY BOD)

The three offenders were set free, but Braco was determined to recapture them. He hastily gathered a force of 60 men and went after the freebooters. They engaged with the three highlanders again, and captured the Browns, but Macpherson fled, clearing a wall into the kirkyard, where a large contingent of men cornered him. With his back against the gable end of the church, Macpherson wielded his sword sufficiently to keep the pursuers at a safe distance. But when he tried again to run he tripped over a gravestone and, after a tremendous struggle, was recaptured. Fearing another visit by Macpherson's friends and clansmen, Braco had the three wild highlanders escorted to Banff under a heavy guard of mounted soldiers. On arrival at Banff, Macpherson and his friends were held at the Tolbooth in Low Street, and released from the chains that bound them.

James Macpherson awaited his trial within the cells of the Banff Tolbooth. It is said he played many a tune on his fiddle and crowds gathered daily to hear his music and lyrics. A young woman who claimed to have lived with Macpherson during his unsettled life, and to be of respectable parents (perhaps his wife Annie) was a constant visitor to Macpherson. It is said they were inseparable; in the dungeon she learned her lover's farewell lament.

On 7 November 1700 Macpherson, along with his associates, was brought to trial. The sheriff of Banff was Nicholas Dunbar of Castlefield, near Cullen.

The jury found them guilty, and the sheriff summed up the verdict by saying:

Forsameikle as you, Jas M'pherson and James Gordon, panels, are found guilty, by ane verdict of ane assyse, to be knoune, holden and repute, to be Egyptians and vagabonds and oppressors of his Matie's free lieges, in ane bangstrie manner, and going up and doune the country armed, and keeping the mercats in ane hostile manner, and that you are thieves, and receptors of thieves, and that you are of pessima fama..

According to folklore, Macpherson was marched to his place of hanging several hours earlier than had been specified at his trial, as the magistrates feared a reprieve. One came too late, and in consequence of

MacPherson being prepared for hanging.   (© DEREK GRAY)

visitor – perhaps his wife Annie – while he was held at the Banff Tolbooth. After witnessing his execution she is said to have wandered the land, singing the song he composed, the song she called 'The remains of her Jamie':

Then be content and not relent,
My silly soul until
The time may come wherein thou may'st
Perform thy latter will.
In hopes whereof I poured forth
This with a dying breath;
As joyfully as man could do
Who hath in sight his death.

Then wantonly and rantingly
I am resolved to die,
And with undaunted courage I
Shall mount the fatal tree.

I've spent my time in rioting,
Debauch'd my health and strength,
I squander'd fast as pillage came,
And fell to shame at length.
But dantonly and wantonly
And rantonly I'll gae,
I'll play a tune and dance it roun'
Below the gallow-tree.

So ends this account of James Macpherson (c.1675–1700), a great musician, freebooter, gipsy, vagabond and the son of a highland chief, who will be remembered by many as the Robin Hood of the North.

A Historical Comment
James A.S. McPherson

With such a long and memorable historic heritage it is difficult to understand why, in all the histories and commentaries about the royal burgh, the event which is mentioned and, in most instances, given greatest prominence, is the execution on 16 November 1700 of a man found guilty of offences which in modern parlance would be defined as theft and breach of the peace. After all, such executions were commonplace in the Scotland of that time. Perhaps the explanation is that, like Robin Hood or Rob Roy Macgregor, Macpherson touched the popular imagination. What is certain is that tradition and time have woven a marvellous web of fanciful myth and legend round his last hours.

His date of birth is not reliably recorded but it is believed that he was 30 when he was executed. He gave himself up to the life of a freebooter and eventually became the leader of a band of gypsies, or 'Egyptians', as they are styled in the records of the time. In the late-seventeenth century there were several bands of gypsies who went about the

this act of injustice it was alleged the town of Banff was deprived of the power of trying and executing malefactors. Legend also states that the town of Macduff, which faces Banff across Banff Bay, left a blank on the side of their clock tower facing Banff, as they were disgusted by the magistrates' decision to hang Macpherson, and that he was hanged because the Banff town clock was put forward when a reprieve was on its way to set him free.

More believable is the story that at the foot of the gallows Macpherson played a rant of his own composition, then offered his fiddle to any who would receive it, in remembrance of him. All who were present were afraid to accept the gift in case they were seen to be in league with the said thief and vagabond, so no one stepped forward. Macpherson took his fiddle across his knee and broke the instrument, throwing it to the ground. The Clan Macpherson claim that the fiddle was later picked up by a Donald Macpherson and taken to Cluny. It now has pride of place in the Clan Macpherson museum in Newtonmore.

The memory and story of James Macpherson, highland outlaw and renowned fiddle player, continue to live on through the many versions of 'Macpherson's Rant'.

There are, indeed, many variations of Macpherson's Lament, Rant, Pibroch or Dirge, the most famous by Robert Burns, but the one that I have chosen was said to be what he sang to his female northern counties of Scotland helping themselves freely to the property of the better-off farmers and country people. They attended markets, mingled with the crowds, inspected the livestock and produce and watched bargain-making in order to select suitable victims.

Macpherson's trial took place before Nicolas Dunbar of Castlefield, near Cullen, Sheriff of Banff. It lasted for three days. Part of the records of the trial still exist and are printed in the Miscellany of the Spalding Club. They disclose that on 7 November 1700 James Macpherson, James Gordon, Peter Brown and Donald Brown were brought to trial. The indictment has been lost, but the record shows clearly the nature of the charges. Preliminary objections were sustained in respect of all the charges, with the exception of that of robbery, and the charges eventually proceeded with were that the prisoners were known vagabonds and Egyptians and had committed the crimes of theft and oppression. Based on a study of the transcript of the evidence – some of it hearsay – given by witnesses, who numbered 21, it is generally accepted that if the current rules of evidence and criminal procedure had applied, a verdict of guilty could not have been sustained. However, the jury, through their foreman, or chancellor, James Gordon of Ardmeallie, found the accused guilty. Sheriff Dunbar pronounced sentence as follows:

Therefore I judge and decerne you, the sds James Macpherson and James Gordon, to be taken to the Cross of Banff, from the tolbooth yrof, where you now lye and yr upon ane gibbet to be erected to be hanged by the neck to the death by the hand of the comone executioner, upon Friday nixt being the 16 Nover instant, being a publick weeklie mercat-day betwixt the houres of 2 and 3 in the afternoon and... recommends the sentence to be seen put in executions by the magistrates of Banff.

However, there are few periods, if any, in the history of Scotland when the majesty of the law asserted itself so rigorously as at the close of the seventeenth century and, as the records disclose, the administrators of the law were not conspicuous for their fairness or clemency. Almost the only point in the proceedings after the trial upon which certainty exists is that Macpherson was hanged. Gordon is believed to have been pardoned and the Browns, who were subsequently sentenced, also escaped with their lives.

On 16 November 1700 Macpherson was led from the Tolbooth to the place of execution, which some allege was on the Gallow Hill and others beside the Mercat Cross in Low Street. If it was the latter it was on what is now the site of the Biggar fountain, where the Banff burgh cross stood until 1768, when it was moved to another site.

Macpherson was an accomplished musician and a poet of some repute. Local tradition, neither very abundant nor reliable, states that he played on his fiddle at the foot of the gallows and repeated the words of the ballad commonly attributed to him. The late Alexander Smith of Banff, author of the book *Philosophy and Morals*, wrote that a very old man informed him that he had been told by his grandfather, who was one of the guards at the execution, that the verses attributed to Macpherson were in fact those uttered by him. 'Macpherson's Rant' was printed on a broadsheet in the year 1701. Macpherson's sword, a heavy two-handed weapon, was preserved for many years in Duff House and thereafter in Banff Museum, but its present whereabouts are unknown.

A great many legends circulate regarding the part played by the magistrates of Banff in carrying out the sentence. There is no evidence that any are founded on fact. There would seem to be no substance to the story that a reprieve was on its way and that the magistrates, on learning that a messenger carrying a pardon was crossing Banff Bridge, put the clock forward so that the execution might be expedited. There was no bridge over the Deveron at Banff in 1700. The first bridge, completed in 1765, was replaced in 1780 by the present seven-arch bridge designed by Smeaton. There is also no substance in the fanciful claim that the citizens of Macduff, at that time still the village of Doune, were so outraged by this disregard of the law that the side of the clock tower of Doune Kirk facing Banff was kept blank so that Banffers would never know the time. The facts are that Doune Church, now Macduff Parish Church, was not built until 1805, and both the south and west faces of the clock tower were left blank because there were no houses on these sides. The mechanism of the Banff town clock, which eventually found its way to the clock tower in the square at Dufftown, is now also in the Clan Macpherson museum.

Macpherson's Rant or Farewell, both the original ballad attributed to the freebooter himself and the more popular version written by Robert Burns after his visit to Banff in 1787, has found its way into the repertoire of singers of Scottish folksongs. It brings together all the strands of fact and legend and has ensured that whoever he was and whatever he did Macpherson has left us a tune and a story.

THE GUILDRY AND INCORPORATION OF TRADES
Charles Burnett

From at least the middle of the sixteenth century Banff had three major public institutions deciding on the management of the burgh. The oldest was the town council, instituted by 1541, the second the guildry, composed of merchants and purveyors of foodstuffs, and the third the incorporation of trades of Banff. The last consisted of six individual incorporations; the hammermen, which included silversmiths, blacksmiths and those craftsmen whose principal tool was a hammer, the shoemakers, the wrights, consisting of carpenters and joiners, the weavers, the tailors, and the coopers. Each body had its own heraldic symbol based on a tool or basic commodity, such as a shuttle used by the weavers.

The guildry was headed by the Dean of Guild, the incorporation of trades had a convener, and the individual incorporations were each led by a deacon. Both guildry and incorporation licensed their members, who had to be burgesses of Banff. They ensured standards of business or craftsmanship, prevented non-members from trading in the burgh and supported members and their families if they fell on hard times.

In order to do this, members of the guildry paid annual sums to the Guild Box, instituted in 1676. This was built up for charitable purposes, but was also invested as loans – particularly to the town council, who had then to pay interest. Two of the loans were used to pay for kirk bells in 1718 (the loan was eventually paid back in 1734!) and for making improvements to Banff harbour in 1727. The incorporation had similar provisions, with a Convener's Fund used to invest in land and property.

The trades had their own meeting hall in Low Street, built in 1781, which was a very handsome building with three Palladian windows on the façade to light the second-storey meeting-room. Each incorporation had property. The wealthiest were the shoemakers, who owned land on the south side of the Gallow Hill Road and property on the west side of High Street and at the foot of Back Path, near Low

Above left: *The sign on the shoemakers' building, High Street.*

Below left: *The mark of the hammermen, High Street.*

Street. The hammermen held land on the east side of High Street, which was leased for the first Episcopal chapel in Banff; the wrights had a property on High Street adjacent to that of the shoemakers; the weavers owned a building in Old Castlegate (formerly Water Lane) and the coopers owned a piece of land on the west side of the Gallow Hill.

There are three carved stones which remind us of the incorporations. One is situated on the façade of the shoemakers' land in High Street and shows a crowned leather knife. Another stone, dated 1704 and in the possession of the Banff Preservation & Heritage Society, also bears the crowned leather knife. The third stone, with a crowned hammer, the mark of the hammermen, is built into a wall of the former Episcopal rectory in High Street.

Park House, No. 1 Gallowhill Street, in the early twentieth century, built on land owned by the Guild of Shoemakers.

High Street and the shoemakers' building before its restoration.

Fine Palladian windows in the Guildhall, Low Street.

In 1732 the incorporated trades complained to the council that people were selling things outwith the times set for the weekly market. The market opened by the ringing of a bell at 8.00a.m. between 1 May and 1 October, and at 9.00a.m. during the winter months. It is interesting to read in the Banff Town Council Minutes of the recurring complaints concerning underweight or poor-quality food and drink provided by those who were not members of the guildry or the incorporated trades.

THE JACOBITE RISING OF 1715
Alistair Mason

When the last Stuart king was deposed in 1688, Scotland was perceptibly less eager than England to see the back of him. The Stuarts were, after all, a Scottish dynasty. Seen from London, Scotland was very remote and mountainous, the natural setting for rebellions, and Scotland began to have reason to feel rebellious. First there were 'King William's lean years' (it wasn't his fault that the crops failed), then the Darien crash, when almost all the savings of Scotland were lost in one catastrophic scheme, and then the Union of the Parliaments, which didn't bring quick visible benefits to Scotland. So when Queen Anne died in 1714, Scotland was largely ready to give the Stuarts another chance. The alternative was the 'wee German lairdie', King George I.

Aberdeenshire and Banffshire were Jacobite heartlands. 'Jacobite' comes from the Latin form 'Jacobus' of the name James, and the Stuart claimant was King James VIII and III, whom some call 'the Old

The last surviving turret of the House of Airlie, Banff, in Airlie Gardens, as seen from the main road.

Pretender'. Several of the local gentry around Banff, the sort of people who had town houses in Banff, were actually 'out' in the Rising. Cramond lists Sir James Abercrombie of Birkenbog, Sir James Dunbar of Durn, George Gordon of Buckie, James Gordon of Letterfourie and the Laird of Farskane.

The Earl of Mar raised the Stuart standard at Braemar on 6 September 1715, marched to Perth and then stayed there. If he had been anything of a general, he could have taken all Scotland – his troops outnumbered the government forces there. Instead there was an indecisive battle at Sheriffmuir in November. King James, a decent man but an uninspiring leader, arrived at Peterhead on 22 December, and went in state to Aberdeen, Dundee and Perth, but by then it was clear the rising had failed, and, after six weeks in Scotland, he and Mar sailed from Montrose. It was a Banff boat that he sailed back on, and the shipmaster, Alexander Clark, made clever answers to the king in Latin (a credit to Banff schooling). With the money the chevalier gave him, he set up as a wood merchant in Banff, and more than 100 years later his granddaughter still had the royal snuffbox.

That's one Banff shipmaster. There is a story of another Jacobite who sailed from Banff, fled the country and was never heard of again. He was presumed lost at sea, but some said sailors were later seen wearing his clothes. He had been carrying a large sum of money. After the rising failed, quite a few Jacobites sailed from Banff, 14 sailing on one ship to Norway, carrying a cargo of meal.

For several months in 1715/16 the North East of Scotland was under Jacobite rule. John Donaldson, writer (the old Scots name for a lawyer) in Banff, was in charge of collecting taxes for the Jacobite government in Banffshire. The official collector was George Gordon of Carnowsie, but Mr Donaldson was the factor who actually handled the money. The cess (tax) was genuinely collected, and in 1718 the burgh was paying back the money borrowed from the Kirk Session to pay it. King James was solemnly proclaimed at the Market Cross of Banff. Poor Mr Hunter, the parish minister of Banff, was deposed, after the failure of the Rising, because he had attended the Proclamation at the Cross. His son, young and headstrong, had also read the Proclamation in the Parish Church and prayed for King James by name.

When Mr Hunter was hauled before the Presbytery after the failure of the Rising he wriggled. He told them he had shut himself into the manse with no intention of going outside, but that men in arms broke in and dragged him to the Mercat Cross. He wouldn't name who they were. 'His answers as to whether he prayed for the Pretender were not explicit.' He suggested that it was all very well for country ministers to say he should have testified against proclaiming King James, but they weren't in a county town with lots of men with guns around. He did not convince the Presbytery.

Almost certainly, Mr Hunter's sympathies were Jacobite. He had strong support in the town and, after the troubles had abated, they built him his own chapel.

Our wealthiest neighbours were careful. There is a famous saying from William Duff of Dipple, the father of the first Earl Fife: 'William Duff would have gone out, but Dipple would behold the event', that is, wait and see who won. The Duffs bought up estates forfeited by those who had gambled everything on a Jacobite victory, which perhaps could look as if they were exploiting an opportunity, but, like almost everybody else, they did their best to keep in with both sides. William Duff of Dipple had one son-in-law out in the '15, and two out in the '45.

A whole cluster of Jacobite heritors (landowners) of Banffshire surrendered to the government troops at Banff in 1716, and, after a time, the troops marched away and handed their prisoners over to the magistrates of Banff. The prisoners were gentry, kept under sentries, not in the Tolbooth, and the town council very discreetly took no further notice of them, so the prisoners sneaked away quietly. That would not have happened after the 1745 Rising. Perhaps the work that was done more efficiently was collecting arms surrendered after the Rising: '691 guns and gun barrels, 1,002 swords and sword blades, 360 pistols and pistol barrels, 48 axes, 20 targes, 120 durks' and so on were handed in at Banff.

John Urquhart of Craigston, in the 1715 Rising, fought at Sheriffmuir on the Jacobite side. In the 1745 Rising he secretly gave the Prince money, but stayed at home. He died in Banff in 1756, and left a paper of advice to his eldest son: '... on no account be concern'd in any Riseing against a Settled Government (however at first Established)'. With age comes caution, and the Urquharts have flourished since. In 2008 an Urquhart of Craigston is our Preservation Society's President.

<hr />

BETWEEN 1715 AND 1745
Alistair Mason

If you were transported back to Banff as it was in 1730, one thing you would notice was how the citizens were reminded of the time of day. Every morning at 4.00a.m. the drummer went round the town, at 5.00a.m. they rang the town bell and at 6.00a.m. the piper did his rounds. They had the same sequence in the evening, at 8.00p.m., 9.00p.m. and 10.00p.m. On wet days the drummer was allowed to perform inside the Tolbooth, but had to keep the windows open. The drum was a gift from Banffers in Danzig, and the bell came from Amsterdam.

The evening serenade on the bagpipes was to send you to bed. In 1733 Nicol Morison appeared before the magistrates for drinking and playing cards at unreasonable hours. He got permission to delay the trial until the afternoon, as it was a market day, and he had goods to sell. But other things happen on market days as well, and he and the witnesses turned up for trial drunk. They fined him, next day, £3 Scots (there were £12 Scots to £1 sterling; for most of the eighteenth century Banff was working with pounds Scots). He got off lightly; the fine for having a dunghill in the street was £4 Scots.

As is usual everywhere, people keep court papers, so a lot of our evidence is about law-breaking. (In fact the Court Book is missing between 1675 and 1736, so we have ten years' evidence of crime.) What is odd about Banff in this period is the number of people up before the magistrates for fornication. The probable reason is that the Kirk Session, which in most places handled these matters, did not dare throw its weight around in Banff because there were too many Episcopalians, and left it to the magistrates. If the man made an honest woman of her, the fine was much reduced. Imagine the scandal when Mr Shuniman, the organist of the Episcopal chapel, was one of those convicted of fornication.

Of course those who contravened social norms hadn't only the magistrates to fear. In 1740 poor Anne Milne was forced to 'ride the stang' (see below) by the young louts of the town. She was pregnant at the time, and the magistrates kept the perpetrators in jail until she was out of danger. Eighteenth-century Britain was prone to riot. Banff tended to riot at the thought of famine or dear food. If somebody was thought to be cornering meal or pork to force the price up, his windows would be broken. In 1741 the Banff magistrates were writing to the press anxious to make it clear they had not actually encouraged

Riding the Stang. (© DEREK GRAY)

such a riot. In 1743 a man was shot by the troops during such a riot, and the magistrates referred to it as murder, though no soldier was brought to trial.

There were soldiers in Banff. A regiment was quartered here in 1737, and the magistrates tried to arrange that widows be exempt from putting them up. The troops were there not to keep down the inhabitants, but to watch the coast. Again and again there was news of privateers, and presumably the people of Banff viewed sails on the horizon with mixed feelings. There was also a lot of smuggling. One of Cumberland's officers, in 1746, said: 'The town, I believe, lives chiefly by smuggling'. That is something you would not guess from the town council minutes. They hold up their hands in horror at the notion of contraband goods, condemn 'the immoderate use of Tea' – everyone drank smuggled tea – and their proclamation against smuggling was read 'with tuck of drum' in the town, and a copy sent to the Edinburgh newspapers. A few years earlier the unfortunate Banff exciseman David Couper, whose task was to prevent smuggling, was carried off bodily and put in the town prison by men pretending to be the town guard. The magistrates, after examining witnesses, '... find that the alleged imprisonment was groundless'. Well, yes. The poor exciseman did not get the support he might have expected.

The magistrates were tougher when they fined some poor fishermen for going on board a strange ship lying off shore 'in case of the plague'. But this was a trading port, and most ships were welcome. It was a thirsty age, and they did seem to import many hogsheads of wine from France. The town council met 44 times in 1727, a fairly ordinary year, and never without refreshments. They also had to entertain distinguished visitors. Almost anyone of any status would be offered the freedom of the burgh and put on the Burgess Roll, which meant another social event. Thus they treated 'the Linen Factors, the Officers of the Military, the London Factors'. One man was awarded it for providing them with a pair of thumbikins. 'Thumbikins' is a delightful name for a nasty thing, an instrument of torture used to extract evidence. If there was no one else to invite, the council turned to little boys, the sons of neighbouring gentry. The boys got raisins, but everyone else had wine.

These were welcome visitors. Unwelcome visitors got short shrift. Beggars were moved on. There is the pathetic tale of Christian Fraser, not a native of Banff, for whom the town council kindly made a wheelbarrow so that she could be wheeled into the next parish. Rather than being put in prison, people were banished – from Banff. They were likely to be whipped first. Travelling people often had problems. Benjamin Hay landed in court for beating Provost Shand's son. They only fined him £4 Scots, but they would not allow him to display 'the dwarf or miracle

of nature', so both his and the dwarf's livelihoods were gone.

For those leaving Banff, there was no bridge at that time. Alexander Steinson, the ferryman, was sent to jail, briefly, in January 1739, for: '... trusting the ferry boat to a boy, who, by his want of strength and skill, occasioned the loss of several people's lives.' Did the boy live on with that memory? Probably not.

+ ⊫◈⊨ +

THE 1745 JACOBITE RISING
Alistair Mason

The romantic story is well known; the young prince landed with a handful of companions in the Highlands, somehow outwitted and defeated the Hanoverian armies, held court in Edinburgh and marched south. The Jacobite army turned back at Derby and retreated to the Highlands, where they were defeated at Culloden. Afterwards there were massacres and cruel repression. No one betrayed the prince, and after many adventures in the heather he escaped to France. The general impression given is that the 1745 Rising was like a strange dream, and that Lowland Scotland, like England, watched the

A turret of the House of Airlie is on the extreme lower right. The house itself, where the Duke of Cumberland stayed, is on the left.

'The Turrets', on the site of the present museum, where meal was stored for troops.

Janet Duff (Mrs Gordon of Park), a Jacobite exile in France.

Highland army but did not stir a finger to help or hinder them. We should remember, however, that one-third of the prince's Army came from the counties of Aberdeenshire and Banffshire. The Banff Jacobites, quite understandably, to save their skins, and with the collusion of their neighbours, afterwards pretended the Rising had nothing to do with round here, but it did.

Consider the near relatives of Lord Braco. Braco (he would become Earl Fife) was an eagerly correct Hanoverian who joined the Duke of Cumberland at Aberdeen and accompanied him, through Banff, on his march to Culloden. But he had three brothers-in-law 'out' in the '45, and a son-in-law and a nephew. Baird of Auchmedden, who had a house in Banff and was one of these brothers-in-law, considered that Braco, by generous gifts, had bought off the Hanoverians to save his relatives' estates.

Lord Lewis Gordon proclaimed King James at Banff on 29 October 1745 and collected taxes for him there. According to a report to Lord Findlater in December 1745: 'David Tulloch is just now in Banff with about 60 to 80 men and as I am told demands no fewer Levies from that Town as 200 men.' During all the time that the prince was invading England, the north-east of Scotland was under Jacobite rule. They sacked Cullen House because the Earl of Findlater was on the other side. A very common defence later, when men had to explain why they joined the Jacobite army, was that they did it under duress, because look what the Jacobites were capable of doing, as at Cullen.

George Abernethy was a Bailie in Banff, an important man with a fine house. He joined the prince's army, and was a captain in the small Jacobite garrison in Carlisle, left behind to ward off Cumberland's troops. They delayed them a week and Mr Abernethy was taken to London for trial. Banff did everything possible to save him. The whole town council of Banff signed a petition in his favour, as did all the local ministers of the Church of Scotland, as did every voter in the county of Banffshire, beginning with Lord Braco. (We should remember that in those days there would be dozens rather than hundreds of voters.) Possibly in consequence, though condemned to death, he was reprieved at the last minute, but in fact died in prison. His widow later was unable to get possession of his house in Banff because it was requisitioned as lodgings for Hanoverian officers.

Another of the Carlisle garrison was William Clapperton, a ploughboy of 13, who was 'pardoned on account of his youth' but was transported to Antigua in any case. 'He gave his residence as Banff, and his height was 4 feet 11 inches.' Poor lad!

There is another sad story. Walter Ogilvie was a (scarcely qualified) writer in Banff, aged 19. He persuaded witnesses from Banff to swear that he was forced to join the Jacobite army, a not quite convincing story. The two witnesses, George Cay and Robert Gray, walked from Banff, as fast as they could make it, to London for the trial. They were a day late, and without his witnesses, he changed his plea to guilty, hoping for mercy. They hanged him. Think of walking for weeks in vain to perjure yourself to save a man's life.

Troops of both armies passed through Banff on the way to Culloden. The Duke of Cumberland gave his men a day's rest here. He stayed in the Old Lodging of the Earls of Airlie, now gone – it was on Low Street. The army, of about 7,500 men, encamped around the unfinished Duff House. Lord Braco, perhaps foolishly, gave them £250 of drink money, and they stole all his potatoes. Two poor men were hanged under suspicion of being Jacobite spies. We can no longer point out the very tree in the grounds of Duff House. The town was occupied by Hanoverian troops after the battle. The 37th (Hampshire) Regiment captured a man called Hugh MacKay and flogged him (the colonel called it 'a little encouragement') until 'he told me where some Rebels were lurking about this Town'. Banff was a frightening place to be.

The Hanoverian troops destroyed St Andrew's Chapel. First they took the roof off, and then made a bonfire of all the contents – seats, pulpit, altar, books, and the organ, probably the only organ north of Aberdeen. Every Episcopal church was destroyed, because the Episcopalians were nonjurors, that is, they refused on principle the oath of allegiance to King George. There is more to Episcopalianism than being Jacobite, but certainly the Episcopal chapels, week by week, were a focus of Jacobite feeling, and it is not totally surprising that they suffered under harsh penal laws from then on.

After a few years the chapel was rebuilt. Very carefully it was 'qualified' and they prayed for King George, but one might notice that Charles Cordiner, their minister, came from a family in Peterhead whose proudest moment was when his grandfather carried King James VIII (the Old Pretender) ashore in 1716. Like almost everyone else in the town, he had Jacobite roots. Cramond does not mention that Provost Alexander Dirom of Banff was 'out' in the '45. His daughter Sophia married Captain George Duff, killed at Trafalgar. Captain Duff's father, James Duff, was a very respectable sheriff-clerk in Banff from 1761 to 1801, and it was discreetly forgotten that he was 'out' in the '45 too. Provost Innes, who lived on the Market Place of Banff in a house called 'Castle Panton', which some may still remember, was another provost who had been 'out' in the '45. There is something of a trend here.

We have already mentioned Braco's Jacobite relatives. His daughter Janet, married to Sir William Gordon of Park (who comes up in the Chevalier de Johnstone's narrative), followed her husband into exile, but he died in France in 1751, and she came back to marry another Jacobite. Then there was the Dowager Countess of Findlater, who reigned over Banff society for many years in Banff Castle. She was a Murray of Atholl. Her own brother was Lord George Murray, Prince Charles Edward's best general. It would have been very tactless to speak ill of the white rose in polite circles in Banff in the eighteenth century.

The '45 brought sorrow and disaster to many people, and not only to men. In the government list of Jacobites is the entry: 'Elizabeth Clavering, Seamstress, Banff, transported'. What had she done?

The Chevalier de Johnstone in rags.   (© DEREK GRAY)

THE CHEVALIER DE JOHNSTONE
Christina Ord

James Johnstone (1719–c.1800), a Scottish soldier born in Edinburgh, was the son of a merchant. A Jacobite, he made his career abroad as the Chevalier de Johnstone, and accompanied Prince Charles Edward Stuart (Bonnie Prince Charlie) as his aide-de-camp in the 1745. After the defeat at Culloden, he escaped Scotland with difficulty and took service with the French. He was present at the capture of Louisbourg and the capitulation of Quebec in 1759. In later life he wrote his memoirs of the 1745 Rising.

As a fugitive from Culloden, Johnstone made his way to Banff, hoping to get safe passage by sea with the help of his brother-in-law, Mr Rollo (heir to the Jacobite Lord Rollo), who was established in Banff and was well acquainted with all the captains of the merchant vessels that sailed from Banff. He was, in

fact, the government inspector of merchant ships. Johnstone separated from his men, as the population of the seaward side of the county were seemingly loyal to the church of Scotland and violent against the house of Stuart. He spent a night, however, at a Church of Scotland manse (probably at Grange), where the minister, a Mr Stuart, had a secret fondness for the Jacobite side. The next morning he exchanged all his clothing, including stockings and shoes, with a servant. The highland garb was just rags and smelt offensive. 'It had the smell of dung to be felt at a distance.' Thus metamorphosed, he took his leave, passing many English soldiers as he entered Banff, his peasant disguise letting him pass unnoticed. 'My clothes were so bad the poorest beggar would have blushed to carry them on his back.'

Johnstone spent time in hiding at Shore House, his host being Mr Duff, provost of the town, as he waited anxiously for a meeting with his brother-in-law, Mr Rollo. There were around 400 English encamped in Banff at this time, but many residents, including the Duffs, were secretly partisans of Prince Charles Edward. Lives depended on people being prudent and discreet.

Johnstone had a full day on tenterhooks before his brother-in-law turned up. All this time he feared capture and certain death, not only for himself but for those who aided him. Just 15 minutes was all that Mr Rollo spent in Johnstone's company, and all the while he was very agitated. He made all the protestations possible of friendship, but at the same time excused himself for not being able in any way to arrange his brother-in-law's safe passage by sea to a foreign land. Rollo instead advised Johnstone to retire back to the mountains.

Johnstone was convinced that if Rollo had been willing to help, he could have got a ship's captain to take him, disguised as a sailor, on any number of vessels that sailed from Banff. This would have saved the Chevalier (he was only later given the French title) 'an infinitude of pains, and sufferings the most cruel' which he endured before he found a way to London, and then on to France.

There is the other side to this story, in that Johnstone was expecting people in official positions to risk their necks. None of them betrayed him.

THREATS FROM THE SEA
Julian Watson

Privateers

Between 1702 and 1815 Britain and France were engaged for a total of 64 years in six wars. Britain successfully boxed in the French fleets, in time forcing them into naval engagements leading to victory. However, the French diverted their sea war into filling the seas around the coast with privateers – vessels privately owned under commission to capture enemy ships and cargos as bounty. The effect during the wars was disastrous to trade in the Moray Firth. The French were using the Norwegian ports of Bergen, Stavanger and Egersund as bases to harry the Scottish coast. Banff once again stepped into the history books – or not.

François Thurot

François Thurot was a privateer, an agent extraordinary, a smuggler, an attempted saboteur and a French hero. In 1757 he was given command of a large 44-gun frigate, the *Mareschal de Belleisle*, with a supporting squadron of six frigates and sloops, to wreak havoc on the east coast of Scotland. On 5 October he appeared in Banff Bay in the *Mareschal de Belleisle* with a second frigate.

The provost called a Head Court meeting in view of the fearful emergency and there followed a rowdy debate. Could the French be paid off? The provost objected to paying a ransom as he would be held hostage until the monies were forthcoming, and he suggested running away! Thurot was manning his landing boats with troops at midnight when a hard gale blew up from the south-east and he was forced to cut his cables and leave the anchors. Banff was saved by a storm. It

later emerged that the ships had 1,100 men on board. Thurot was about to land 800 men to plunder and destroy the town that night.

In 1760 François Thurot captured and destroyed the town of Carrickfergus, in Ireland. Admiral Hawkes finally caught up with Thurot in the Irish Sea, and, after a terrible fight, captured his ship but was himself mortally wounded. The victorious sailors were so exhausted that the dead and dying were still on deck the next day when the reporter boarded the ship. Thurot is buried in Scotland. Such was the name of Thurot that in celebration church bells were rung across Britain.

The provost, in view of the possibility of such a strong force landing, probably had the most sensible suggestion! This lucky escape and thus non-event by the invading French was to have a profound impact on the town for the next 50 years. It was now regarded as prime coastline for an invading French raiding party or invasion. In 1757, due to a shortage of troops, there had been none based in Banff, but this was never to recur, with a garrison based in the town having the backup of up to 400 local volunteers. Military roads were built not for the fear of local rebellion following the 1745, but from the threat of invasion. The River Deveron became a major concern with the movement of troops in times of flood. The proposed military bridge at Fochabers over the River Spey was cancelled, and the money spent on building the military bridge in Banff in 1765.

Murder of William Robinson

There were many marriages between local girls and troops quartered in the town. However, on 10 April 1771 there was a dispute with the local guard, consisting of a captain and six troopers, who patrolled the town between the hours of 10p.m. and 6a.m.

William Robinson lived in Low Street in the house with the date stone of 1745 above the centre dormer window. Mr Robinson had been out for a merry supper at a friend's house and, returning late, found soldiers mucking around with his attractive nurserymaid. He took offence and a dispute developed, insults were hurled and a scuffle ensued. The redcoat

Left top: *The dormer window of William Robinson's house, overlooking the scene of his murder.*

Left bottom: *Thurot's anchor (1757), retrieved by fishermen and now on display in Macduff.*

soldiers had also been drinking. One of the officers ran across to the Black Bull Inn opposite and returned with his sword. 'Inflated with wine and frenzy, he ran William Robinson through the body'. Robinson was carried into his house to his sorrowing family, whereupon he died.

This murderous outrage caused a great sensation and was taken up by the town authorities. Although Lieutenants Gibbons and Thorn were arrested on a charge of murder, the case was dismissed without trial. The King's Advocate refused to prosecute, as the military authorities had little sympathy for such incidents.

American War of Independence

Banff in 1777 found that, although many miles from America, it was on the front line in the American War of Independence. The Americans had sent a number of privateers across the Atlantic Ocean. Captain John Grimes was sailing the *Tartar* of Boston from Massachusetts, a schooner of 50 tons, fully armed with 24 guns and 120 fighting men. The privateer was now off the east coast of Scotland and had taken seven vessels, including the *Royal Bounty* of Leith, the *Thomas and Elizabeth*, and the *Anne* of Banff. On 8 August the *Tartar* sailed right into the Bay of Banff and took the *Janet* of Irvine within view of the town. Just to add insult to injury, and creating more panic, later that day 36 crew were put ashore in the bay from the captured vessels.

The murder of William Robinson, 1771. (© Derek Gray)

The Battery

Invasions were feared in 1778, 1793, 1795 and 1803. Privateers were very active. The local firm of Robinson had two of its nine ships armed to the teeth with guns, but still lost the *Friendship* with Lord Fife's belongings on board.

The threat of invasion and privateers was so great that a battery was built above the harbour of Banff in 1781, now the Coastguard houses. Nine 18-pounder cannons were ordered, with a four-foot telescope, manned by local volunteers. The battery had to be ordered into alert four or five times a week in the 1790s, such was the threat. However, on 17 April 1799, at night, gunshots were heard in the bay. A French privateer had dared, under cover of darkness, to come within range of the battery and taken a Banff ship laden with barley. The battery did protect the town, but there was never a shot fired in anger. The battery was dismantled in 1815 at the end of the Napoleonic Wars.

A 'look-out' window at the corner of Water Path.

(© Tommy Bod)

Lookout at the Battery Green, Banff. We are told that the man in the uniform of the Merchant Marine was 'Packety' Watt.

41

THE STONES OF BANFF
Charles Burnett

Banff is unique amongst Scotland's county towns in having the largest collection of carved and dated stones. These were preserved when older properties were demolished to make way for new. Any carved or dated stones were then built into the replacement buildings. The tradition of dating the construction of a building has carried on to the present day.

The stones are either heraldic, dated or decorative, and provide visual interest for the visitor to Banff. Several have been painted or gilded by the Banff Preservation & Heritage Society to help preserve and enhance them. At least three stones have been found buried in private gardens, including one dated 1697 and another dated 1755. Many stones have been built into the rear of later properties, which means they are not frequently seen. One marriage lintel, with the names William Brown and Elizabeth Fyff, dated 1703, has been built into the high gable of a building on the High Street, which makes for difficult viewing. Several of the stones are skewputs, located at the bottom of an end-gable wall immediately on the wall head.

In Banff the skewput was a favourite location for a date of construction, or for the owner's initials. Six dated stones in Banff were carved by the same mason, as his numerals are unique, with curvilinear bottoms to the 1 and 7.

One of the treasures of Banff is Duff House, constructed between 1735 and 1740. It is covered on every elevation with carving of the highest quality, including 40 vases, two huge coats of arms, 38 Corinthian capitals and over 150 elaborate brackets.

Fine architectural details abound in Banff, many of them the result of the stone carver's skill. The former Trinity and Alvah Church in Castle Street is austere but has two Ionic columns on the entrance façade. The window frames of Banff Town Hall, on the corner of Seafield Street and Castle Street, are decorated with female heads, and there is an elaborate shell above a window on the north elevation. The Parish Church steeple is graced with elegant urns, and St Andrew's Episcopal Church bears Gothic crockets on the mini spires which flank the main entrance.

Banff also boasts an exotic carved stone from India with three human figures which is said to have been taken to the burgh by a sea captain and built into his house in Stuart Street. At the rear of another building on the corner of Boyndie Street and High Street there is a skewput with a human face like a gargoyle.

The twentieth century has also given Banff very good examples of the carver's art. The old Post Office in Carmelite Street was built during the reign of Edward VII and carries a crowned royal cypher as part of the decoration over an elaborate pillared window. There is a version of the Crown of Scotland on a Post Office telephone exchange built in 1958, and an inscribed oval stone with initials and the date 1968 within a rope pattern border on a building in North Castle Street.

Not all clients seek the most expensive examples of the stone carver's skill. Present-day techniques such as sand blasting can provide affordable decoration. This continues the well-established tradition in Banff of dating the construction of a building, thus adding to the interest of the townscape.

GEORGIAN ARCHITECTURE
Alistair Mason

This country had nothing but Georges on the throne from 1714 to 1830, and old Banff is basically a Georgian town. There are plain and fancy styles of Georgian. At the top end is Duff House, a masterpiece of baroque architecture. By contrast, some of the major Georgian buildings of the town rely on line and proportion and little else. Very little decoration was felt necessary for the façades of Banff Castle or the Town House, rectangular blocks with a regular pattern of windows. The Victorians, whose taste ran to fancy, called buildings like that mere barracks. Beyond plain was vernacular; the buildings didn't have an architect, but the masters-of-work followed rules of thumb, and the results are delightful.

Let us begin with a comparison with what went before. Look at two houses beside each other, Nos 1 and 3 High Shore. Number 1 is pre-Georgian, a tower house, irregular and turreted. Number 3 is early Georgian, with a regular grid of windows, with more window to wall than later Georgian styles. Up on the High Street Nos 31–39 are also early Georgian. These are vernacular, so they could never have afforded such large windows. The dormers, though they may well be a replacement, are authentic Georgian cat-slide. Most of the dormer windows in the old part of the town, like the good set on George Street, are late Georgian or even Victorian.

Two houses of the same vintage as No. 3 High Shore are Boyndie House and Forbes House, at the foot of Boyndie Street. Boyndie House has a slightly Dutch effect, and indeed all three might be taken in a metropolis for work of the reigns of William and Mary or Anne. Fashions moved slowly in Banff.

The castle, however, is a Georgian work by a Georgian architect, John Adam, from round about 1750, as is Carmelite House from 1753. There is a pleasant mixture of homeliness and gentility about Carmelite House which the castle misses. Around the end of the 1750s there was a fashion in Banff for dated skewputs, so several houses show us the vernacular varieties open precisely then. From 1756

Carved stone, probably Indian, now above a doorway in Stuart Street, Banff.

(© TOMMY BOD)

A beautifully preserved stone found in a garden in High Street.

A date stone from High Street. Note the curvilinear bottoms to the numbers.

To the rear of the Market Arms, the oldest surviving date stone in Banff.

Skewput stone with gargoyle face, mid-eighteenth century, foot of Boyndie Street.

(© TOMMY BOD)

Above: Coat of arms, Low Street.

Left: Marriage stone, Deveronside.

(© TOMMY BOD)

Numbers 1 and 2 High Shore and the Market Arms.

(© Dr David Findlay Clark ARPS)

Pre-Georgian architecture: the rear (once the front) of No. 1 High Shore.

(© Tommy Bod)

Late Georgian Bank on High Street on the site of what was once Forbes Watt's shop.

(© Bodie Collection)

Apart from Duff House and the fishing temple on the island in the Deveron, the most exciting piece of Georgian architecture in Banff is the town steeple from 1764. Architecturally speaking it is tragic that they put the big lump of the Town House immediately beside it. But disregard the Town House, and consider the abstract verve of the shapes that John Adam was using in that steeple.

In the 1770s the Robinsons were spending money, and we have both their mansions, which are now the County Hotel and the Town and County Club. The County Hotel, like the castle, owes much to the typical Georgian balanced pavilions (one missing) on either side. Look at the delicate detailing of the big curved fanlight above the door of the first, and the Venetian window at the back of the second. Later, humbler, versions of these recur in Banff's Georgian architecture. One of the marks of Georgian Banff is its taste for the three windows grouped together – look at St Catherine Street.

The older vernacular traditions continued. The Shoemakers' Land on High Street is dated 1787, but frankly it could have been built in the first half of the century. Architectural historians would be cautious in dating, say, George Street. It is definitely some time in the later eighteenth century.

From 1810 to 1820 the future King George IV was Regent, and the Georgian of his period is called Regency. The style is lighter and more graceful, and looks good with stucco rather than stone. Bellevue House of the 1820s is a good example of a Regency villa. The flattened arches to pends, like the one at

there is the wonderful four-storey gable looking down Water Path of Path House, with more routine proportions at No. 14 Old Castlegate and at the house on the corner of Low Street and Carmelite Street.

Back to a gentleman's house, the garden front of St Brandon's, with its spacious semi-circular bay, is from about 1760. (The delightful romantic tower on High Street is Victorian.) The whole block of Nos 1–5 High Street, three houses, each with its own character, is all from the early 1760s. Number 5, which was the town house of the Banffs, is another of these almost too regular façades. From much the same period, and here there is no skewput to help us, so it is anywhere between 1750 and 1770, are Nos 4–10 Castle Street, the sort of building where we must learn to look above the shop to see the centuries before.

George Street. A Georgian terrace, the dormer windows would have been later additions.

(© Dr David Findlay Clark ARPS)

Low Street in the early-twentieth century.

Ingleneuk, are characteristically Regency. In the north-east of Scotland, where we were building in granite, our late-Georgian buildings were sturdy rather than graceful, like No. 1 St Catherine Street, a fine but dour piece.

Those who know Banff will have noticed that we have not mentioned some of the most characteristic Georgian buildings in the town. Where are the Collie Lodge and the Old Academy? These fine pieces of Greek Revival date from 1836 and 1837. Victorian Banff was pleasantly behind the times, and carried on building in a Georgian style. The Parish Church

steeple of the late 1840s was the completion of a much earlier Georgian design. Trinity and Alvah (the Free) Church of 1844, like the Clydesdale Bank on Low Street, is a good classical building that looks earlier than Victorian. If you stand outside the bank and compare the Town House facing you with the old Fife Arms Hotel along to your right, you will see how Victorian fancy contrasts with Georgian plain.

There are good Georgian streets, like Back Path, we have not mentioned. Banff has more listed buildings than any town in the North of Scotland. Many of Banff's Georgian buildings have suffered because people no longer like wooden 12-pane sash windows, and the pvc replacements damage the surface pattern of the buildings. There was, when they were built, a canon of good taste; ordinary builders knew the proportions of wood to window to wall. This has gone in our day, and mass-produced replacement fittings ruin the appearance of Georgian buildings. In the Banff Renaissance scheme there is money available to put things right. We must hope more of the people of Banff develop an informed love of their own wonderful heritage.

THE ROBINSONS
Alistair Mason

The Robinsons dominated Banff for about half a century. They were the largest employers in the town, and father and son alternated as provost for many years. To this day their fine town houses are two of the best buildings in Banff.

William Robison or Robertson – the family settled on 'Robinson' rather later – was a linen weaver in Banff from the late 1740s. In 1753, jointly with a Mr Illingworth, he set up a thread manufacturers' business, partly in Banff, partly in Nottingham. In 1760 his younger brother George, only 17, joined the partnership. They may have had some Scottish roots – another Robinson, an uncle, was murdered in Banff in 1771 by a drunken soldier, who was never convicted – but their father was a linen manufacturer in Nottingham. By 1780 they had bought out Mr Illingworth. Young George was the dominant personality, and it was he who ran Banff. He married Miss Garden, a Banff girl, and settled here for life.

From Holland the firm imported raw flax which was milled and heckled in their works alongside the Robinson house (now the Town and County Club) on Boyndie Street. There were only about 60 men working there, but the firm had other employees beyond. Spinning was a cottage industry, and about 4,000 people earned their living spinning the yarn. It then had to be doubled and twisted, work for about 200 women and children, and then bleached, and there were bleachfields outside Banff, leased from Lord Findlater.

County Hotel, formerly Moray House and home of the Robinsons.　　(© Dr David Findlay Clark ARPS)

The other Robinson house, now the Banff Town and County Club.　　(© Tommy Bod)

In the late 1740s the total trade of the town of Banff was about £70,000 Scots. By the 1770s Mr Robinson's personal trade was as much as that, and the town as a whole was worth about £250,000 Scots. Finished articles probably make more of a profit than bleached yarn sent off to Nottingham, so quite soon the firm shifted to making stockings and patented their own design of stocking frame. By 1781 the stocking manufactory was earning twice as much as the thread business. The Robinsons had their own fleet of smacks sailing south, and travellers opted to sail in them rather than from Aberdeen. But then

there came war with France, and the Robinsons lost their export trade. The company went bankrupt in 1803, owing £100,000 in Britain alone, more overseas. The stocking works struggled on under different management until 1816. The Robinsons coped, and continued as leaders of Banff. George Garden Robinson, the son, was comfortably off. He could pretend to be landed gentry – Mr Garden Robinson, Esquire, of Towie Beg – and he was a bank agent in Banff and a perfectly acceptable provost, but he obviously didn't have the entrepreneurial drive of his father. None of the family carried on in the neighbourhood.

In 1784 George Robinson became provost of Banff. The term of office was three years, and then he would be off for three, and then back. From 1796 to 1828 he was alternating with his own son, George Garden Robinson. A large part of the business of a town council was entertaining visitors (it was a drunken age), and the endearing feature about Provost Robinson was that he picked up all the bills for entertainment. No wonder they re-elected him. He was, perhaps through calculation, generous, and Banff Parish Church grieved his passing. When they asked for money for good causes, they would say that the local earls had given something, but they would specify how much Mr Robinson gave, so he probably gave more.

In 1817 George Robinson stepped down as provost – they must have persuaded him later to change his mind – and he delivered a survey of what had been achieved under his watch. His first move had failed. It is a revealing story. In 1785 he had lobbied successfully for Banff to have its own Customs House. (Until then every boat leaving Banff had to have papers from Aberdeen, and there were only three posts in the week.) But this was the 'old corruption', there were jobs in the Customs, and the rival earls 'got so keenly interested for their protégées' that the government, rather than offend one or the other, stalled on the Customs House. It came later. But after that there was a great programme of building – a new pier in the harbour, a new Parish Church, new meal houses, a new Town House, a new road from the bridge to the town, at long last a new water supply, a new storey added to the Academy, and a new market built. They had also bribed fishermen to move to Banff with new boats and houses, because the town had no fishing fleet. They also coped with a flood. This is really quite an impressive programme, and, unlike bigger places whose ambitious building schemes had bankrupted the town, Banff's finances seemed in reasonable order.

There were those who did not love Provost Robinson. His portrait used to hang in the Town House he had built, and the historian Cramond, a tactful writer, speaks of his 'shrewd, if rather hard featured, countenance'. There were questions about the Town House itself, which is rather bigger than was needed. The reason is that Mr George Smith of Bombay, who built the Academy at Fordyce, also left £1,000 for a hospital in Banff. Provost Robinson decided, perhaps rightly, that £1,000 would not pay for a hospital, so instead the money was used to add another floor to the Town House. 'In years of scarcity, a great portion of the poorer classes was supplied from a soup kitchen established there.' That quotation is from a government commission, which did not say the money was misapplied. An occasional soup kitchen might be the next best thing to a hospital.

Provost Robinson had his finger in many pies. The Robinsons had branch concerns in Inverurie and Kintore and Elgin, and their representatives ran some of these town councils in the Fife interest too. For many years Provost Robinson rented the salmon fishing on the Deveron. In 1821 the Convener of the Incorporated Trades of Banff protested that the provost and town council had 'conducted the affairs of this burgh on a scale of wasteful extravagance, useless and unnecessary expenditure and often with negligence'. But the heart of the protest, where it went into long detail, was over the salmon fishing, a field that provosts entered at their peril. There was a long history of disagreement. When we look at what was thought extravagant in the early-nineteenth century, we may feel the provost was in the right. He had to fight hard to give any sort of salary to the teachers at the Academy.

On balance, the town is deeply indebted to the Robinsons.

Old Market Place, Banff.　　　(© BODIE COLLECTION)

Old Banff weights and measures.　　　(© TOMMY BOD)

MARKETS AND LOCAL HOLIDAYS
Julian Watson

The burgh had the right to hold markets. Banff had seven annual markets held on days of religious significance during the farming year. The markets were Candlemas (January), Lady Day (March), St Brandon's (May), St John the Baptist's (June), St Jerome's (October), St Dunstan's and St John's (both in December).

It may therefore be a surprise that by far the largest market was St Brandon's in May, and not one at harvest time. This was due to the custom of hiring and bidding for labour for the coming season. Large numbers of skilled, manual and casual workers would make their way to market for annual and seasonal work. It was a critical bargaining time for both employees and employers. This common method of hiring servants continued until after the rural depopulation in the later Victorian era. Regarding trade, by May overseas goods would also be appearing for sale, as ships would be coming into port having been laid up over the stormy winter.

Weekly markets were also held, with strict trading practices. All produce had to be sold at the market cross and trading could not begin before a certain time, say eight in the morning, with the ringing of the town bell. The selling of goods in private houses could lead to imprisonment and a fine. Standards of weights and measures were robustly enforced.

During the Middle Ages the market was in the High Street, but with the increase in trade at the port it later moved to Low Street by the market cross. The Georgians, requiring more space, then moved the market to the end of Bridge Street. Finally, after flooding, the 'old market place' returned in the 1830s to Low Street with the building of the Market Arch.

Banff's three main markets also became fairs: Brandon (May), St John the Baptist (June), and St John (December). Competitions held on such days included horse racing. Banff offered a silver cup for its horse race. Lord Huntly, having won the cup, generously returned it in 1684, thus saving the cost of another the following year.

Today we now have Local Bank Holidays reflecting those far-off once-hectic market days.

THE JAIL
Julian Watson

For centuries the town could not afford to keep prisoners for any period of time. They would be held until sentence was passed, paraded around town, then banished or hanged. The original prison, at the bottom of Strait Path on the corner of Low Street behind the Tolbooth, had an outside staircase that led up to the cells. Overlooking Strait Path, these had windows from which prisoners could let down bags on string for food. The building was rebuilt in 1712, though this did not stop a number of attempted and successful escapes, one of which involved setting fire to the timber doors.

A new prison was required and one for offenders and debtors was built in 1796 behind the new Town House in Low Street. However, this fared little better than its predecessor and was condemned in 1836 – more escapes had been made by deception and by tunnelling through the walls, whisky and improper food was being delivered via the windows in the courtyard, and the debtors' section was overcrowded.

In consequence, in 1844 a new prison was erected on Reidhaven Street in Seatown. This was a gaunt three-storey building with a curtain wall. In 1876 the annual cost of retaining a prisoner was £55. A sentence of hard labour meant the cranks and picking

The Tolbooth, site of the original prison.

(© Dr David Findlay Clark ARPS)

The remaining castellated corner tower of Banff jail, Reidhaven Street. (© Tommy Bod)

oakum. The crank was a revolving disk with a maximum resistance of 11 pounds. Each day males had to do 14,400 revolutions and females 12,000 revolutions! Having finished this task, and no doubt feeling a bit cranky, you moved on to the painstaking task of picking oakum, the picking apart of old rope to be used for caulking in boat building. Males had to produce up to five pounds in weight of rope and females up to three pounds. In 1877 there were 105 prisoners in total held throughout the year. It is interesting to note that of that figure 55 were local and 50 strangers, 81 male and 24 female. Of these, 94 were under the influence of drink and only 11 sober at the time of the offence.

The prison ceased to be a main prison in 1878, from which date prisoners were sent to Elgin. It was thereafter used as a local holding jail. The Chief warder, Coutts, who is still remembered, was also responsible for having to take the birch to children caught scrumping, a task he thoroughly disliked.

During the 1939-45 war, the roof of the jail was the site of the air-raid siren.

The jail shut in the 1950s and was later demolished. A housing development is now on the site, but the stone corner buildings of the old curtain wall can still be seen today on Reidhaven Street.

⊶ ⋙⊹⋙ ⊷

DR JOHNSON'S VISIT
Christina Ord

Dr Samuel Johnson (1709–84) the English writer, critic, conversationalist, lexicographer and compiler of the greatest of English dictionaries, visited Banff with his faithful biographer, James Boswell, while on their tour to the Hebrides in 1773.

Dr Johnson, born in Lichfield in Staffordshire in 1709, was the son of a bookseller. He read voraciously in his father's shop and was educated at Lichfield Grammar School and then at Pembroke College, Oxford, which he left in 1731 without taking a degree. In 1735 Samuel Johnson married Elizabeth (Tetty) Porter, a widow 20 years his senior. They opened a school in Edial, near Lichfield, which failed in 1737, and that same year they moved to London, where he struggled to earn a living by the pen. In 1747 he issued the prospectus of a dictionary of the English language which took him eight years to complete and which appeared in print in 1755. Although, when his wife died in 1752 he was plunged into a lasting depression, by 1760 he was financially secure, with a state pension for life of £300. In 1763 he met James Boswell, a Scot who became a good friend and his faithful biographer. In 1764 Johnson founded the Literary Club.

Johnson often teased Boswell about Scotland, but was persuaded to visit in 1773. They arrived in Banff at night, crossing the River Deveron by ferry, there

Above left: *Dr Samuel Johnson in Banff in 1773.*
Above right: *The Fife Arms Hotel, Low Street, site of the Black Bull Inn.*

(© BODIE COLLECTION)

being no bridge at that time. They stayed at the Black Bull Inn on Wednesday, 25 August 1773. Sadly, the inn was thus immortalised as the 'indifferent inn'. The site is now occupied by Fife House on Low Street.

Expecting an elegant reception from the Earl Fife at Duff House, Johnson and Boswell were displeased to find him absent from his residence, and would probably not have stayed in Banff if they had known the earl would be away.

Dr Johnson, while in his room at the Black Bull, wrote a long letter to his great friend Mrs, Thrale. He also wrote up his journey in his journal, mentioning that he craved fresh air and had tried with great difficulty to open the windows, which had no pulleys so he had had a struggle to hold one open.

In his journal, describing Banff, he at first wrote that 'arriving at night nothing particularly claimed his attention', but then proceeded to generalise:

The ancient towns of Scotland have generally an appearance unusual to Englishmen; the houses great or small are for the most part built of stone. Their entrance is very often up a flight of stairs, which reaches up to the second floor. The ground floor is reached by going downstairs inside the house. Window frames are of wood; the windows move up and down in grooves not hinges.

He also wrote of ventilation in Scottish homes that:

It has not been found a necessity by our northern neighbours. Also the art of joining squares of glass with lead is little used in Scotland; the Scots are more frugal with their glass.

The forestair of Bede house, Carmelite Street, demolished in 1903.

(© BODIE COLLECTION)

Dr Johnson and Boswell passed a night of discomfort at the Black Bull Inn, according to Boswell's account in the *Tour of the Hebrides*. They left Banff early next day, hiring a very good chaise and horse to carry them to Cullen for breakfast.

Mrs Hester Thrale, the woman Johnson had written to while sitting in the Black Bull Inn in Banff, cared for Johnson for many years after the death of her husband, also one of Johnson's friends. The doctor, who clearly had feelings for her, was devastated when she married an Italian musician in 1784, and it is even said he died in dejection. He is buried in Westminster Abbey.

SILVERSMITHS AND GOLDSMITHS
Grace Law and David Findlay Clark

In his *History of the Scottish People*, T.C. Smout remarked that the Scots had contributed little of the highest quality to the furnishings of their buildings, but went on to say how striking it was that they should have excelled 'to a remarkable degree' in the single art of making fine silver. In its earliest days the silver trade was centred largely in Edinburgh – and almost wholly in the High Street. Teapots and milk jugs were the main items produced by the silversmiths of Scotland, and probably one of the oldest surviving teasets in silver is at the Aberdeen Museum and Art Gallery. It was made by George Cooper some time after 1730. Scottish tea wares were more stoutly

Banff silver teapot, one of the oldest teapots in Scotland.

(© Tommy Bod)

Banff silver salt cellars by William Byres 1775-92.

(©Tommy Bod)

made, and generally larger, than the English equivalents. They were the work of skilled and confident craftsmen, many of whom worked in a row of shops known as luckenbooths in the centre of Edinburgh opposite Parliament Square. The work produced there set a pattern for silversmiths in provincial centres such as Aberdeen and Banff, Elgin, Dundee, Inverness, Glasgow, Dumfries and elsewhere. The designs were similar but the only assay office was in Edinburgh, so silversmiths elsewhere marked their wares with their own town mark, for example ABD for Aberdeen and a pot of lilies for Dundee.

The silversmiths and goldsmiths of Banff, like their fellow craftsmen of Aberdeen, were incorporated with other hammer-wielding trades under the general title of 'hammermen'.

From 1670 to 1885, William Scott the elder, William Scott the younger, Patrick Scott, John Reid, Patrick Gordon, Thomas Forbes, Ernest Mearns, Alexander Shirras, John Argo, Alexander Mackay, William Byres, David Izat, John Keith, George Elder, John McQueen and William Simpson all crafted communion cups, toddy ladles, ewers, spoons and forks, watch cases, buckles and so on. From such a source also came a beautifully made teapot brought back to Banff Museum some years ago and paid for by public subscription.

There are variations in the town mark of Banff. The earliest known was that of William Scott the elder (1670–99), consisting of his monogram followed by ABC, and later he added BANF (sic) as a town mark. This was subsequently used by Patrick Scott, John Argo, William Byres and John Keith.

William Scott the younger used a fish c.1720, as did John Keith. Another worker, using SA, has not been identified. The mark BAF was sometimes used, or the initial B, or an ornamental ribbon-type B. On a Banff communion cup, the letter D appears, and a small Old English d appears in William Scott the younger's marks.

Patrick Scott (1710–29) used a crowned heart, his initials, with a mullet below them, within a heart-shaped shield. Similar devices were used by some English and Irish goldsmiths in the seventeenth and eighteenth centuries but are rare in Scotland. John Keith (1794–1894) used a stamp resembling a man's head, the meaning of which is obscure. Another mark is the letter H in a square stamp, and this is occasionally found with the marks of John Keith and William Simpson (1840–55).

George Elder (1819–1843), in addition to his initials, plus B, used the figure of mother and child on a communion cup in Rhynie.

There is a round silver teapot which bears the town mark BANF, silversmith unknown, dated 1715–20 and engraved with a crest, Pennycuik. At the time of writing it is on loan to a major exhibition in the National Museum in Edinburgh, but is due back in Banff Museum.

John Hyman writes, 'The heyday of specifically Scottish silver tea wares ended about 1770.' He attributed that to the building of the New Town in Edinburgh. New interior styles followed and old designs were lost in the rush to 'modernise'. Even the familiar spherical teapot underwent a series of adjustments, emerging with an oversized oval body and a flattened cover, reflecting Neoclassical influences overlaid with Scottish ideas.

FOOD SHORTAGES AND FAMINE
Jay Wilson

In the early-twenty-first century the slogan bandied around has been 'Make Poverty History', but poverty has always been history. In medieval Scotland prospects were good. A favourable climate, forests teeming with game and a wealth of fish-filled waterways should have seen the population want for nothing while enjoying a relatively healthy diet. However, due to adverse weather conditions, diseased crops and animals, war and fire, the supply and availability of fish, meat and grain (mainly oats), as well as of fruit, vegetable and dairy products was frequently disrupted, during which times the poor suffered most. The whole of Europe was struck between 1315 and 1318 by famine initiated by bad harvests and poor climate and compounded by war.

As temperatures started to fall and rainfall rose in fifteenth-century Scotland, the growing season shortened, with detrimental results for wheat production. The aristocracy of the time favoured wheat over oats and subsequently forced farmers to set aside land for its cultivation.

Reeling from the effects of the previous century's intermittent outbreaks of the Black Death, the depleted seventeenth-century Scottish population became vulnerable once more. Destruction, as a result of the wars of the 1640s, laid waste east coast towns, including Banff, and trade languished. In 1690 the onset of famine, born of bad highland harvests, which spread south, reduced an already depressed population by a further 13 per cent. Death, emigration and a falling birth rate dominated a dark period between 1693 and 1700 known as King William's 'seven ill years'. These years were mythologised in Jacobite interpretations as God's curse on Scotland!

Migrants swarmed the country, searching for food, swelling town populations. By this time the Fiscal's office was well established and its officers in Banff organised night watches in order to apprehend all vagrants and thieves. Outwith times of emergency, the burgh was happy to appoint a handful of officers with responsibility for specific areas of town. Under the special circumstances of famine, however, townsmen were co-opted, and in the 1690s 44 men were deployed to secure the boundaries of Banff.

Food, and its shortages, have occasionally been the cause of uprising in Banff, and Mr Thomas Murray should have known better when he took it upon himself to cause a 'dearth [of pork at] the flesh mercat'. He had bought up great quantities of the meat and refused to disperse it in accordance with the bailies' orders. An incensed Elizabeth Smith, of the burgh, with her cohorts, gathered on a moonless March night. The sky hung low with cloud that night, 5 March 1741, and the constancy of a restless sea silenced their footsteps and masked their shadows sidling through streets. Murray's home came under sustained and relentless attack from an angry crowd, which was finally dispersed at about 4a.m.

Elizabeth Smith received a fine for her part in inciting this riot, which was in protest against one man stockpiling supplies of pork for profit. It appears, however, that no arrests were made during a subsequent riot in the Victorian era (1874), when Banff's harbour was blockaded by civilians. Men and boys laid a boom across the harbour entrance in order to keep at bay the vessel *Boyne*, whose cargo of meal was earmarked for export.

It is often felt that in hard times communities pull together. With our cynical perception of public office and commercial banks, it may be surprising to know that these very institutions kept the welfare of the public to the fore in time of famine. During the latter half of the eighteenth century Banff town council came to the aid of famine-afflicted residents. On average, during this period, one year in every five saw the council supply meal, and soup kitchens were organised to feed the poor. Conditions were so 'calamitous' by 1783 that even the banks were moved to charity. On 17 January of that year the directors of the Bank of Scotland and the directors of the Bank of Aberdeen offered an interest-free loan over the period of a year to towns where they had branches, in order to buy corn for the 'relief of their poor'. Not only was grain scarce but what was available had reached exorbitant prices. The £500 from each of these banks was accepted by Banff.

Another important benefactor of Banff was Lord Fife. His efforts to secure grain at an affordable price

The old meal house, Bridge Street (1796).

for the hundreds of families living on his estate led him to declare that, 'This state of the country has made me a notable corn merchant. I am quite fit to enter into business.' On 30 December 1782 he wrote to the Convener of Trades in Elgin highlighting the extent of his efforts:

Sir, In the present distress of the County I consider the towns and the Highlands as the places that require most attention. I have several hundred familys on my estate that are in the greatest distress for meal and seed, and several villages in the same situation that I have under-taken to provide for. I wish as far as in my power to extend this to Elgin, and I have directed my Factor the first of my Farms that are pay'd in to send in a weekly supply for the Trades and Labourers and to be sold at one shilling a peck. I hope you will be so good as to take the trouble to see that it is sold only to those.

With an eye on the future it was decided to expand Banff's meal house (1796) and create a stockpile which would prevent famine on the scale it had reached in the 1780s. This meal house now stands empty and semi-derelict in Banff's old market-place, perhaps foreshadowing the severity of the food shortages ahead.

PUBLIC HEALTH AT RISK
Jay Wilson

Alex Hay must have felt that the gods had deserted him as he put ashore in Banff in 1709. Suffering symptoms similar to those of the plague, he was immediately seized and quarantined. There had been no reported cases for more than 60 years in Banff, so his condition must have been quite alarmingly alien to the town. The location of the town's houses, built on hard, dry ground a few feet above sea level, meant that residents benefited from living conditions which were freely ventilated and resistant to damp. Even the proximity of the River Deveron posed no immediate threat to health, as there were

Chalmers Hospital with all its turrets.

neither swamps nor stagnant waters harbouring disease. Orchards were abundant and fish were plentiful. However, the apparent paradise was marred by prevailing winds blowing through the town from the Moray Firth. Residents, therefore, were more liable to rheumatism and inflammatory complaints than they were to coughs and colds.

With the threat of plague replaced by the fear of its return, it was not surprising that the local council acted in accordance with strict quarantine measures put in place in the seventeenth century, and segregated Hay. While the advance of the plague from Sicily across Western Europe in the late 1340s could not have been within living memory, its incidence would have been engrained in the history of all European ports. The Genoese ship docking in Messina, Sicily, would have been no different from other merchant ships arriving that October in 1347. Without warning, however, thousands of people were soon dead and most of Sicily's residents had been infected.

There are three varieties of the Black Death, but it was poor comfort to know that one was less virulent than the others when death was delayed merely by a matter of hours. The pneumonic variety was passed from human to human through coughing, sneezing and spitting. Despite the salutary 'Bless you' after sneezing, the infected droplets ensured that 'we all fall down' within three days. The septicaemic variety, which involved an intense infestation of the bloodstream, delivered the quickest death, only hours from the time of contracting it. The bubonic, and most common, plague caused death within five days. It was this type which reached Scotland in 1349 and which had wiped out a quarter of her population within a year.

Scotland, however, was not a good host to the disease, as a warmer climate than she could offer was needed for its survival. As a consequence the death toll here was generally lower than in the rest of Europe, where up to a third of the population perished. As the plague feathered its way along the Sicilian trade routes, news of its advance must have been met with total incomprehension and impotence. It took less than two years for it to reach Scottish shores and wipe out a quarter of the population. Following this initial and devastating outbreak the plague became a regular visitor. Localised incidents terrorised each decade at least once at the end of the fourteenth century, and its recurrence was recorded at this rate throughout the fifteenth and sixteenth centuries. For over 200 years the recovery of a depleted population was postponed.

Although by the seventeenth century the plague was fast becoming a thing of the past, the fear of it began to fester. Banff Town Council convened on 13 December 1624 (the day before market day) and posted a guard of 19 people on all routes into the burgh, for fear of the plague entering with strangers.

No outbreak was reported. It was believed that the last instance of the plague in Scotland was 1645, though in 1648, towards the end of the Covenanter and Royalist manoeuvres, 'Banff was exempted from supplying its full portion of men to a levy on account of the pestilence.' Alex Hay was found to be clear of the plague by the end of his stint in quarantine.

Out of the plague rose a growing awareness of the link between ill health and poor hygiene. Seventeenth-century living quarters were no better than squalid hovels overrun by vermin and ringed by outside privies and dung heaps. Despite the potential for good public health among the lower classes, it was their own practices which put them at risk, that is overcrowding and poor personal hygiene. Beds and bedding in particular were washed seldom and ventilated rarely. The water supply was brackish, the effort to extract domestic water from local springs being considered unnecessary by the general population, as was cleaning the streets of 'putrid substances'.

With sanitation less of a priority than it is today, hands were never washed when preparing food, meat was butchered in public, flour was mixed with dust, oats and barley bore remnants of the millstone that ground them and dunghills were the 'muck' that was the 'money'. A by-law passed in 1676 forbade the storage of dung in heaps on public streets. Despite the threat of a £4 Scots fine for non-compliance, it does not seem to have been enforced effectively, as almost 100 years later, in 1762, dung was once again banned from the streets and anyone leaving their heap in public for more than 12 hours was fined £6 sterling. Dunghills and muck middens were a constant source of nuisance.

Time and again Banff town council tried to clean up the streets. In 1714 they ordained the services of Common Officers, employed to keep the town free of dung and vagabonds. The punishment for not keeping the streets clear was levied at 12s. Scots or imprisonment in the 'pit'. Recognisable by their distinctive coats, the officers could be seen scouring the streets for perpetrators on market days, public days and, more regularly, on Sundays. Included in their remit was the eradication of dogs which roamed into the kirk while a service was in progress. They would stand guard at the kirk door each Sabbath in order to prevent the stray dogs entering. The incentive to carry out this duty conscientiously came in the form of 40 pennies per pelt.

Dung heaps were not the only by-product from animals which threatened public health. In 1766 complaints were made against butchers, whose practices proved a perceived threat. Where Eastside now stands these butchers plied their trade at the Shambles. Unlike today, butchers not only sold the meat but actually killed the beasts before selling them. You would be forgiven for thinking that the only threat to public health would be from cleavers and knives or even from contaminated meat. No.

Discarded entrails were the culprits. Unsuspecting horses were startled as butchers threw yards of bloody intestines into the road and riders feared death as a result of being thrown. Under threat of a 5s. sterling fine, butchers were made to carry their waste products 'north west of the bulwark within flood mark' and allow the tide to carry it out. In 1778, however, the Shambles was moved to a more convenient area of town, west of the kirkyard, where the tide was within easy reach.

BURNS IN BANFF
Christina Ord

Robert Burns (1759–96) is Scotland's national poet. Born in Alloway near Ayr (though his father's family came from the North East of Scotland), he was the son of a small farmer. Among his early influences were the popular tales, ballads and songs of Betty Davidson, an old woman who lived with the poet's family, while being in the company of sailors and smugglers broadened his outlook and his interest in the fairer sex, and he became something of a rural Casanova.

On his northern tour Burns visited Banff in 1787. The account of his visit appears in *Chambers' Journal* for 1840, written by George Imlach (1775–1863), who was a native of Banff.

Robert Burns and his friend William Nicol, while on tour, stopped for a night in Banff on 8 September 1787. Nicol looked up an old acquaintance, Dr Chapman, the rector of Banff Academy. The friends were invited for breakfast, and George Imlach, aged 12 years, who was the dux of his class and, it is said, a 'pet scholar' of the rector's, was also present. After breakfast George was asked to give Nicol and Burns a quick tour of Banff and then of Duff House. George recalled Burns paying particular attention to the paintings of the Stuarts while visiting Duff House.

Formerly Banff Grammar School, where the headmaster, Dr Chapman, entertained Robert Burns, and now Banff County Garage.   (© DR DAVID FINDLAY CLARK ARPS)

Burns wrote his song 'Macpherson's farewell' as a consequence of what he heard from the Banff locals of this celebrated freebooter. In doing so he gave the lament renewed life with his catching refrain:

Sae rantingly, sae wantonly, sae dauntingly gaed he;
He played a spring and danced it round below the gallows tree.

He also wrote 'My bonnie Mary':

Go fetch to me a pint o' wine,
An' fill it in a silver tassie,
That I may drink before I go
A service to my bonnie lassie."

It is suggested that the original of this song was composed by Alexander Lesly of Eden, near Banff, in about 1636.

While visiting Duff House, Nicol asked the boy George Imlach which of Burns's poems he liked best. The reply was: 'I liked by far the Cotter's Saturday Night, although it made me greet when my father read it to my mother.' Burns, looking at George, said: 'Well, my callant, I don't wonder at your greeting at reading the poem. It made me greet more than once when I was writing it, at my father's fireside.' George also told them what other poems he liked of Burns: they were 'Twa Dogs', and 'Death and Dr Hornbook'. Within two years of their first publication, Banff was reading Burns's poems - that is impressive.

While Burns was still working on his father's farm as a young man he wrote some of his best poetry, which included George's favourite, The Cotter's Saturday Night. Burns wrote songs, ballads and poems, gathering his material from his own and other people's life experiences. From his humble origins and his identification with Scottish folk traditions, which he rescued, refurbished and in part embellished, he gained the title of the national poet of Scotland. He was never without money worries, and his health was damaged by hard outdoor work. He died, relatively young, in 1796, and is buried in Dumfries.

⤙ ❈ ⤚

SUSANNAH EMMETT, 1765–98
Christina Ord

Susannah Emmett, an English girl, died a short time after giving birth to her daughter, also called Susannah, on 2 April 1798 in Banff. She had come to Banff by boat, the *Friendship*, chaperoned by her brother, who returned to England. Susannah was married to John Duncan, a native of Oyne, the gardener to Earl Fife, and they lived at the Lodge at Banff Bridge. She is buried in St Mary's kirkyard.

Susannah Emmett lived in the gatehouse on the left.

All that remains of her house, by Banff Bridge

(© TOMMY BOD)

Through her letters to her family back in England we get an interesting insight into life in Banff 210 years ago.

Walking through the kirkyard, your eyes may be drawn to the unusual pillar-like tombstone erected to her memory. For many years her husband put flowers on it, a custom which was seldom heard of then. Later, when the stone fell, a Mrs Coutts, a resident who remembered the tale told to her as a girl, had it reset.

Susannah was born in Watton in Hertfordshire. Her father was a bailiff on the Watton Estate and she had three brothers who adored her. Over 100 years later one of their descendants was searching for information on his family's history. Mr John T. Emmett, following the letters written by Susannah, came to Banff, where he found Mrs Coutts, who had a rich store of antiquarian knowledge. She showed him the house where Susannah had lived, had written her letters home, and had died, and the tombstone raised in her memory. They soon realised that Mr Milne, the captain of the *Friendship* which brought Susannah to Banff, was, in fact, Mrs Coutts's grandfather. He had also carried the letters between Susannah and her family.

'Banff May 2nd 1797' is the date of the first letter written home to her mother and father. Susannah wrote of her journey to Banff 'being six days upon the water', for three of which she was sea-sick. There were three gentlemen, herself and her brother as passengers all going to Banff. Two of the men were Indian chiefs who came for an education; they both spoke good English, and the other gentleman was their guardian. Susannah wrote:

When we arrived at Banff we went to an inn and dined. I'll tell you our bill of fare – roast beef, a broiled chicken, beef steaks, potatoes, an apple pie with cream, a rice pudding, cheese and butter, three bottles of red port, two bottles of London porter. All this amongst six people.

The captain joined them for their feast. Susannah was not allowed to pay anything for her meal, and she wrote: 'This was my first dinner I partook of in Scotland, and an excellent one indeed, after eating but little for several days.'

She wrote of her meeting with her husband, and of their neat little house which stood in the park very near to his Lordship's house (Duff House). She told her parents of the milk and cream they got from the dairy close by, also about the sheep and deer which grazed close to their door. She described her house, one side facing into the garden, the other onto the park, two bedrooms with closets each side of the chimney, the walls painted white and the doors of mahogany. She writes of there being grates in the kitchen and parlour, and of a nice pantry and wash house with shelves and dressers all around. They got as much coal and firewood as they needed.

Her clothing and furniture, which were shipped from home, arrived safely, and the expense of carriage was charged to his lordship. The same ship also carried his lordship's servants, and took ten days longer than Susannah's ship to arrive at Banff. She thanked God Almighty and her family and friends for their blessings for her safe carriage, and for her new husband and home. She told her parents that his lordship had not yet arrived in Banff, but when he did she would try and get some franks so she could write again.

Susannah's second letter was written on 1 June 1797 to her brother. John Emmett, at Grosvenor Square in London. She wrote again of her safe passage, thanking God for no rough seas and for not being taken by the French. She tells him of her beautiful little house and of the large garden with an abundance of fruit trees, of the grandeur of Duff House and the cattle and the walks in the park:

The Town of Banff joins the garden wall, tis a large place. There is a great number of ships come into this port. Banff is reckoned a dear place for provisions, as there are so many people of small fortune comes to reside here. You will see hundreds of people walking of a Sunday, and all well dressed.

Left: *Susannah Emmett's grave with flowers.*
(© Tommy Bod)

She found it hard to comprehend that there were so many smartly dressed people in Banff, after all the stories she had heard about Scotland.

Susannah wrote about the weekly market on a Friday where she purchased her provisions, buying a fine piece of cod for sixpence, 'weighing upwards of ten pounds'. She took her maid with her to the markets as she understood the local dialect better, and the prices. The maid also showed Susannah how to spin cloth. She and her husband attended chapel (St Andrew's) on a Sunday; there was, she said, an excellent preacher and a fine organ, with most of the congregation singing along with it.

Susannah asked her brother to write back via Captain Milne, who would be back in Banff within five weeks. He was to:

... direct his letter to her husband Mr Duncan. It will be more proper than to me, and he was to put the letter under cover and direct it to the Right Hon. Earl of Fife, Duff House, near Banff.

By doing this they received their mail free of charge. She asked her brother to let her family and friends know they were both well and happy, and requested that her mother send her 'a bladder of Hog's lard, as she can get none here under a shilling a pound'.

On 4 December 1798 Susannah wrote again to her mother and father. She thanked her mother for the present of lard – 'very acceptable to fry our fish'. She wrote:

'Tis not because there are no hogs, the reason is the people in general are not fond of pork. There are numbers fatted, killed, pickled up and sent to London for sale. We have the best of beef, mutton and veal for 5 or 6d the pound.

She mentioned the weight differences, saying butter was 24oz to the pound; meat was 17oz to the pound. She would have liked her parents to visit after Christmas and told them she had made elderberry wine, but she suspected the journey would be too difficult for them. His lordship was going to London for the winter. Most of his servants were English, with a lot of English families settled in Banff. 'Tis a great place for visiting each other and having balls in the winter season', although she and her husband enjoyed their fireside. The parties would have been for the upper classes. She finished her letter asking affectionately after all who knew her and sending prayers to keep all in good health. She also commented on the weather, saying it was not so much colder there and that the snow did not lie for long.

A few months later Susannah was dead, aged 33, leaving a baby girl and a distraught husband.

The old manse at the foot of the Water Path, with a famous pear tree in the garden.

BYRON
John Mackie

The word 'Byronic' has come to describe an idealised but flawed character whose attributes include: having great talent, exhibiting great passion, having a distaste for society and social institutions, expressing a lack of respect for rank and privilege, being thwarted in love by social constraint or death, rebelling, suffering exile, hiding an unsavoury past,

The home of Lady Gight, grandmother of Lord Byron, on the site of the present Court House.

The house of Mary Duff (Byron's first sweetheart) on the site of the present Co-operative shop.

Lord Byron, from a painting housed in a private collection in Banff.

Shore House (right) *was left to Byron by his great-aunt, Elizabeth Gordon. The building on the left was once a bank and is the present Police Station.* (© TOMMY BOD)

being arrogant, overconfident or lacking of foresight and ultimately, acting in a self-destructive manner.

George Gordon Byron, 6th Baron Byron (22 January 1788 – 19 April 1824), commonly known as Lord Byron, was a poet and a leading figure in Romanticism. Among his best-known works are the narrative poems 'Childe Harold's Pilgrimage' and

St Brandon's, High Street. Note the balcony above the bay windows.
(© Tommy Bod)

'Don Juan'. He is regarded as one of the great European poets and remains widely read and influential, in the English speaking world and beyond.

He was the sole child of the marriage of John 'Mad Jack' Byron and Katherine Gordon, heiress of Gight. Poems and songs surfaced in Aberdeenshire at their union – mostly warning or reminding Katherine of her folly in marrying a rake:

Your Johnnie's a man frae England just come,
The Scots dinna like his extraction ava
But tak ye gude tent, for he'll spen' a' your rent
And fast draw the lands of Gight awa'.

How prophetic this doggerel proved to be is demonstrated by the fact that within two years of their marriage most of Katherine's property, including her castle and estate, to the value of about £21,000 (a lot of money in 1786) was sold to pay off Mad Jack's debts. The *Annals of Banff* state: 'Mrs Byron... thus in two years found herself reduced from competence to a pittance of £150 per annum.'

The poet Byron was born of this gambler's union in London in January 1788. His mother brought him home to Scotland shortly thereafter and took up residence with him, and without his father, in Aberdeen in 1790. From then until about 1798 he was a frequent visitor to Banff, where both his grandmother and his maternal uncle lived. Additionally, by his own account, he and his mother lived in Banff for a while (this seems to have been in 1795) when he was seven or eight years old. Byron's enduring fame rests not only on his writing but also on his life, which featured extravagant living, numerous love affairs, debts, separation, allegations of incest and marital exploits. He was famously described by Lady Caroline Lamb as 'mad, bad, and dangerous to know'. He served as a regional leader of Italy's revo-lutionary organisation the Carbonari in its struggle against Austria, and later travelled to fight against the Ottoman Empire in the Greek War of Independence, for which Greeks revere him as a national hero. When he died from a fever in Missolonghi, crowds lined the streets at his funeral.

If it is true that 'the child is father of the man', then we may catch glimpses of the future in Banffers' contemporaneous description of him as 'that little deevil Geordie Byron', and in the account in the *Annals of Banff*:

> *Memories still linger in Banff of Byron's violent and improper conduct in his youthful days. On Miss Abercromby of Birkenbog remonstrating with his mother thereupon he butted her like a ram, and threatened to throw her over the balcony. Byron had then arrived at the mature age of seven or eight years.*

The *Annals* snootily note: 'It is very evident that Byron did not attain to the high standard of moral excellence then prevalent in Banff.' It may have been good for poetry that he never did. In many ways the adult Byron embodied the Romantic Spirit – espousing the value of the irrational, embracing intellectual and sexual freedom for himself and his women, living out his emotions, animating the virtues of the warrior poet, revering wild places and distant cultures, able to both philosophise and fight, his life was as vivid as the wind and has added an adjective to the language.

There are five locations in Banff with which 'that little deevil Geordie' is most closely associated:
- 'Little Fillacap' at No. 15 Low Street (where the courthouse now stands) was his grandmother, Lady Gight, and her sister's house. Byron and his mother stayed there for a time when the poet was about seven years old. Byron is reputed to have planted a thorn tree in its garden, which was later moved, felled and used to make 'a fancy work table'.
- The Old Manse (Abercromby Gordon, a relative, was the minister), which stood at the corner of Water Path and High Shore and boasted a massive pear tree, which the boy Byron scrumped in and fell from. In what he later described as an over-estimation of his hurt from a fall, 'the old red-nosed doctor was called for'. Faced with the prospect of being bled better (using lancets) the not-so-injured child threatened the doctor with a pulled nose. The doctor 'gave the bleeding up'. The child recovered quickly, with a permanent aversion to bleeding as a cure.
- Number 25 High Street, where a cousin, Mary Duff, whom he later described fulsomely as his 'first love', lived. The Co-op now stands in its place.
- Shore House, next to the Police House on High Shore, a property inherited and quickly passed on to a cousin.
- St Brandon's, in the High Street, which is widely cited as the location of a morbid practical joke. As

1748 AND 1798 COMPARED
Alistair Mason

Anyone wanting to see what Scotland was like in the late-eighteenth century will turn to the *Statistical Account* (later known as the *Old Statistical Account*, because the idea was too good not to repeat). A questionnaire was sent to every parish in Scotland, and normally filled in by the parish minister. The parish minister of Banff in 1798, the Revd Abercromby Gordon, a lively and interesting man, went beyond the call of duty, and not only described his own day, but drew up a table of comparisons with 50 years before. This is well worth re-reading, and we can mentally make comparisons with today. Scotland, and Banff, was becoming wealthier, even though there was inflation.

1748

A gown of linsey-woolsey was the usual dress of a laird's daughter. Her mother appeared on great occasions in a silk gown and fine laces, which were considered as part of the paraphernalia destined to the succeeding generation. Ladies seldom wore any other than coloured stockings. The town could only boast of one silken pair, and these were black. The occupation of milliner was totally unknown.

A four wheeled carriage was a luxury seldom enjoyed, unless by the nobility.

A gentleman and his wife generally rode together on the same horse.

Drawing-rooms and dining parlours were no less rare than carriages.

Mahogany was seldom seen save in the tea-tray, the round folding table, and the corner cupboard.

Most of the useful articles of merchandise might be procured in the same shop. Almost every trader was denominated 'merchant'.

A joyous company, after dinner, have been seen quaffing the wine of a dozen bottles from a single glass.

Agreeable to Queen Mary's Act of Parliament, AD1563, all butcher meat was carried to market 'skin and birn', and, agreeable to custom, was sold amidst abounding filth.

The annual wages of a great man's butler was about £8; his valet £5; and his other servants £3.

The farmer had his ploughman for 13s.4d. in the half year, with the allowance of a pair shoes. The wages of a maidservant 6s.8d.

Dr Johnson complained (1773) of our windows.

A draught ox cost £1.13s.4d.
20 sheep, small size, £4.
Beef and mutton 1d. and 1½d a pound.
A hen, together with a dozen eggs, 4d.
Dozen eggs 1d.
Goose, 2s. a pair.
Turkey, 3s. a pair.
Pigeons, 1½d a pair.
14 haddocks, 1½d.
Claret, 1s. a bottle.

1798

The decoration of our persons is now become a more general study among both sexes, and all ranks. The art millinery affords employment and profit to many; and every trading vessel from London brings a fresh assortment of dresses, adjusted to the prevailing mode.

Post-chaises are now in general use. Several private gentlemen keep their carriages.

The pad is become the exclusive property of the country goodwife.

The minister of the parish must have his drawing-room.

Mahogany is a species of timber in general use for articles of furniture, and the corner press is superseded by the splendid sideboard.

The several distinctions of tradesmen are better understood.

A sober party sometimes meet, whose libation consists of a solitary bottle with a dozen glasses.

There are convenient slaughterhouses apart, and meat is brought to market seemly, and in good order.

The nobleman pays at least in a quadruple ratio for his servants.

The wages of a ploughman vary from £10 to £12, and of a maidservant from £3 to £3.10s. per annum.

Many of our windows are furnished with weights and pullies.

£15, £20, and £25.
£12.
5½d and 6d a pound.
Hen, without eggs, a shilling and 1s 3d.
4d and 6d.
5s 6d.
7s.
6d.
1s.6d.
6s.

some ladies sat taking tea with Byron's mother, the boy, bored with the occasion, made his way to an upper room with a balcony, where he dressed a pillow in his jacket and tossed it into the garden, alarming the tea drinkers below. In one version of the story the eight-year-old Byron's response to being told off was to retort: 'Miss Abercromby, my only regret is that it was a pillow and not you that I threw from the balcony.'

Claims have been made that he began a life-long love of the sea at Tarlair and found inspiration for his work in local landscapes, but to no great effect. As soon as George Gordon inherited his title from an uncle at the age of ten, his mother took him off to England to claim his house, estates and whatever money there might be. There is no record of his ever having returned to Banff.

When Byron died his agent burned most of the memoirs he had written. We can only guess that there were too many scandals to risk his reputation by, for at the end of his life he was a huge success – a literary colossus with enormous sales, even though for some, who had good cause to dislike him personally, he was merely 'a poet for parlour maids'.

CAPTAIN GEORGE DUFF RN
BANFF'S TRAFALGAR HERO
James A.S. McPherson

George Duff was born in High Shore, Banff, in 1764. His father, James Duff, was Sheriff Clerk of Banffshire and his grandmother was a daughter of the 1st Earl Fife. He had an instinctive genius for the sea and as a boy spent much of his time in boats at the harbour. His father arranged for George, at the early age of 13, to join the Royal Navy as a midshipman, and he was sent to join his grand-uncle Commodore (afterwards Admiral) Robert Duff at Gibraltar.

Over the next 12 years he saw active service in the Mediterranean and the West Indies, gaining early promotion to lieutenant. He proved to be an audacious, able and conscientious officer, and in 1790, at the age of 26, he was promoted to Commander. Shortly after this promotion, while on leave in 1791, he married Sophia Dirom, daughter of Provost Alexander Dirom of Banff. Held in high esteem by his superiors and much loved and respected by the officers and men of every ship on which he served, he was promoted to captain in 1793 and in April 1804 was given command of the *Mars*, a 74-gun ship, part of Vice-Admiral Collingwood's squadron, which joined the British fleet

The unveiling of a stone to commemorate Captain George Duff, Banff Castle, 2005.

under Vice-Admiral Lord Nelson off Cadiz in September 1805.

On 21 October 1805, off Cape Trafalgar, the British fleet joined battle with the much larger combined Franco–Spanish fleet in what has been described as the first Battle of Britain. The annihilation of the enemy fleet, thanks to Nelson's strategic brilliance and the skill and determination of the British captains and crews, dealt a fatal blow to Napoleon's plans to invade England and ensured Britain's world-wide naval supremacy for more than a century.

Sadly, both Nelson and Duff, one of his most experienced and trusted captains, were killed by enemy fire during the battle. Captain Duff was buried at sea, while Nelson's body, preserved in a large cask of brandy, was returned to England to a state funeral in St Paul's Cathedral.

Although in the crypt of St Paul's Cathedral there is an impressive monument to the memory of Captain George Duff, there was no local memorial in Banff until this was remedied on the bicentenary of the battle.

Captain Duff's son, Norwich, who sailed with his father as a midshipman on the *Mars*, was, at the age of 13, present at Trafalgar. He survived the battle and had a distinguished career in the Royal Navy, reaching the rank of Vice-Admiral.

Banff Rotary Club, celebrating the centenary of Rotary International, together with Banff Preservation & Heritage Society and Friends of Duff House, funded the provision of a memorial. This comprised an inscribed plaque mounted on a locally quarried sandstone pillar erected in the grounds of Banff Castle overlooking the sea and Captain Duff's birthplace in High Shore.

Left: *Captain George Duff RN.*

The unveiling ceremony was performed by Commodore Charles Stevenson, CBE RN, Scotland's most senior naval officer, on 21 October 2005, the bicentenary of the battle.

⊷ ⊟ ⊶

MEMORABLE ASSOCIATIONS
John Mackie

Throughout history, sections of the populace of Banff have come together to form groups with a common purpose or aim: to repel a perceived danger, perhaps, or to confront an unwelcome social development; to evangelise a shared vision or to ensure the town's economic survival.

Here is a small selection from the many such groupings and associations that have sprung up over the years.

The Banff Volunteers, 1794–1802

In a world awash with notions of equality, fraternity and liberty (ideas that had animated two revolutions), the British crown and the aristocracy that governed locally on its behalf felt threatened on three fronts simultaneously. Firstly, there were the expected predations of privateers sanctioned by France, secondly the prospect of an invasion by revolutionary France and thirdly, the expectation of internal insurrection: riot and revolution by a discontented local population. The Earl Fife, Lord Lieutenant of Banffshire, like most of the governing class, took all three threats very seriously. In fact it might be argued that the threat of insurrection and seizing of private property was the most pressing for him. In considering and presenting the case to raise a volunteer defence force to protect Banff and the Banffshire coast, he endorsed the declarations:

Whereas we are presently engaged in a war with France and liable to the depradations of privateers landing in force, pillaging us; And whereas it is too evident that there are in some places evil-minded and designing

The YMCA Hall, Seafield Street.　　(© BODIE COLLECTION)

people who have been at the utmost pains to sow sedition and to instill principles which, if adopted, would ruin every man in the country and totally annihilate our happy Constitution...

The defence of this part of the realm was not the role of the War Office, but was rather the responsibility of the lord lieutenants of each county, reporting to the Home Office. Thus Fife, together with his deputy lieutenants, determined to raise a volunteer force of six companies numbering 60 men per company. The issue was seen as loyal subjects rallying to the defence of their sovereign and existing political arrangements:

No Private will be enlisted who has not an exceptional character, or who has ever belonged to these infamous [Democratic] clubs... It appears highly necessary to give persons of all ranks an opportunity of showing and declaring their loyalty to their King and their zeal for our happy Constitution by coming forward with the offer of personal service.

The raising of the volunteers was rapidly successful – the first company, the Banff Trades Company, offered itself for service within three months of the first call for volunteers (the first to be raised north of Edinburgh) and was properly constituted, with gazetted officers, by March 1795. Four more Banff companies followed, and in due course there were sufficient companies along the coast to form a battalion. Banff had the Trades Company, an Artillery Company, two Infantry Companies and a Town Council Company. In 1797 these merged with the corps of Macduff, Portsoy, Grange and Cullen.

The alacrity with which the Banff Trades responded to the perceived threat of invasion and revolution seems to have been due to the energy and conviction of one James Reid, deacon of the Incorporated Trades of Banff, a surveyor who, some think, designed the new prison of 1796 and proposed the new water supply of Banff in 1806. He proposed the company of 60 to be drawn from 'young men of good character in the burgh and Freemen of the Town'. The Trades Company chose James Reid as captain, Isaac Cooper (a teacher of music) as 1st lieutenant and John Smith (a cabinetmaker) as 2nd lieutenant. Reid went on to be the adjutant of the battalion when it was constituted, and appears to have given up his work in order to concentrate on the volunteers, expecting to be a salaried officer in consequence. For three years that expectation was met but, in 1800, to his great discontent, his pay was discontinued.

For eight years or so Reid, Cooper, Smith and many hundreds like them, drilled, marched, practised their shooting, conducted military exercises and lobbied the authorities for better weapons, the right to set up cavalry companies and for a permanent barracks, as they increasingly saw themselves as the military arm of the Constitution.

For all this effort, they seem to have seen very little action; there is an account of a false alarm in 1798, when the Banff companies deployed rapidly as a convoy of sails was spotted – a convoy that turned out to be friendly – and an account of an intervention in Macduff in 1800, which included the reading of the Riot Act and the issuing of ball ammunition. The occasion, often referred to as the Macduff Meal Riot, was the refusal of hungry Banff and Macduff folk to allow the loading of a ship with meal destined for Aberdeen, and their growing anger that some volunteers, mainly from Fordyce, were happy to help the owner ship his meal away from the hungry (there were public soup kitchens in Banff and Macduff that year). Stones were thrown by the 'rioters', the volunteers faced them for a day and a night, two men and a woman were arrested and referred to as 'naked vagabonds' in an official account. It is to the credit of many Banff and Macduff volunteers that they refused to protect the meal or the meal owner's hired ship or his agent, but laid down their guns and walked away.

In 1803 the volunteers were reconstructed into six companies, aggregating 480 men each, with an independent Banff company added later that year. A substantial force indeed.

The Universal Liberty Club
Amongst the threats that the volunteers were formed to counter, the spectre of internal discontent and perhaps revolution loomed large. There is no doubt that the Earl of Fife saw this threat as real. As part of his motivation to form the volunteers, the activities of a Portsoy distiller called Alex Leith played a leading role. An unlikely embodiment of revolutionary zeal, Leith commemorated the birthday of the French Revolution on 14 July 1791 by distributing quantities of free spirits, firing three rounds on a battery of five cannons, raising a flag (on School Hill) and declaring Universal Liberty in large capitals. After, at a convivial meeting in the Scotch Arms pub at which many toasts were drunk to liberty and its friends, a society was formed called the Universal Liberty Club, with Mr Leith as president. The Universal Liberty Club seems to have met irregularly at the New Inn, Portsoy, for more toasts and to debate the rights of man, the abolition of the slave trade and electoral reform in Scotland. The only record of its taking part in events is the reasonable claim that it seems to have had a seminal role in a (thwarted) plan to burn an effigy of authority in Banff on the king's birthday in June 1792. However, Lord Fife was so alarmed by this outbreak of what he saw as revolutionary zeal that he reported Leith and the Universal Liberty Club to Lord Dundas, the Home Secretary, as both dangerous in their own right and as evidence of the need for a volunteer defence force.

The Establishment for the Suppression of Begging
The Aberdeen Almanac and Northern Register of 1828 merely records the existence of this establishment and names its committee. However, there can be no doubt as to its purpose – the name could not be clearer. The seriousness with which it attended to its purposes and the weight of pressures, both spiritual and temporal, it could bring to bear on beggars to desist from their begging can be easily seen by a mere listing of the committee membership. So here it is:

The Minister of The Town and Parish, The Heritors of the Parish and Their Factors or Agents, Provost and Magistrates of Banff, The Medical Gentlemen practising in the town, Convener of The Trades and Deacon of each Incorporation, President and Masters of Mason Lodges, and Gardener, Sailor and Friendly Societies, Revd Alexander Bruce, Revd John Forbes, Revd Joseph Gibb, Two senior Elders, the Session Clerk and the Treasurer of the Parish Church, Three Gentlemen chosen quarterly from each of the five districts of the town and three from the 6th or county district of the Parish, G Cruickshank, Treasurer of the Fund, and Geo Sutherland, Police Officer.

As though to ameliorate the effects of so much heavyweight attention, the entry also notes that:

A Public Kitchen for the distribution of soup and bread (where circumstances require it) is connected with this Establishment, and under the direction of a Committee of Gentlemen, two of whom attend at the distribution three days in each week.

There is no record of how many beggars were deterred or suppressed by this mighty edifice of civic unity, but the reference to the soup kitchen being in operation three days a week suggests that there were plenty of hungry folk about.

The YMCA
An association which has left an enduring mark on the appearance of Banff in the shape of its building, close to the Castle Street corner of Seafield Street, is the Young Men's Christian Association. Now used as a drill and exercise hall by the Boy's Brigade and others and for flower shows and other community purposes, the handsome YMCA building was completed and formally opened in 1866. The young Anglican clergyman opening it, the Revd William Hay Macdowal Aitken, journeyed from London to perform the ceremony, completing the seven-year journey that the association had taken from its first beginnings locally to this, the dedication of its own purpose-built hall, with its lecture hall designed to accommodate '600 or 700 persons', drawing-room, library and reading room. It is testimony to the speed at which the association grew from its humble

beginnings as small groups meeting in the vestries of various churches (in order to avoid sectarian leanings) that it should move into such a large purpose-designed building.

The declared purposes of the association were to promote the moral and spiritual well-being of the young men of the town and its neighbourhood, to provide a focal point for young men coming to the town from elsewhere and to help prevent them being led astray into 'corrupt and sinful practices'.

The members held weekly meetings for considering the scriptures and delivering essays and, from time to time, also held special meetings and lectures:

... of a religious cast which are addressed by most of the clergymen in the town, and others from a distance, and otherwise use such means as are calculated to advance the Glory of God and the eternal well-being of the community.

In times when young men needed to be highly mobile in following opportunities for work in an era of rapid industrialisation and widespread migration from rural areas, such an institution no doubt served a vital social, as well as religious, function.

The commemorative plaque beneath the monkey puzzle tree in the castle grounds.　　(© TOMMY BOD)

The monkey puzzle tree.　　(© TOMMY BOD)

GENERAL JOSÉ DE SAN MARTIN
Charles Burnett

James Duff, later 4th Earl Fife, fought in Spain as a young man during the Peninsular War. He joined the Spanish Army and eventually was promoted to the rank of general. While there he met a fellow officer, an Argentinian of Spanish extraction named José de San Martin, who, like him, was a Freemason, and they became good friends. In due course San Martin returned to South America, where he led the movement which caused the Spanish colonies to become independent, including Argentina, Brazil, Columbia, and Peru. By then he had also achieved the rank of general and the title of 'Liberator'. The friendship continued between the Earl and the Liberator, who was not acceptable to everyone in Britain because of his actions in South America, and they were regular correspondents.

In 1824 the earl invited the general to visit Banff and acted as his sponsor with the British government. The liberator enjoyed the hospitality of Duff House, where the two veterans no doubt reminisced over their time together in Spain fighting the forces of the French Emperor, Napoleon. During the seven-day visit General José de San Martin was elected an honorary burgess of Banff by the town council in recognition of his great endeavours in South America, and signed the Banff Burgess Roll.

When he died in 1850 the liberator was buried in in the Cathedral of Buenos Aires in Argentina in a mausoleum which is permanently guarded by soldiers of the Granaderos Corps, a branch of the Army created by General San Martin. Also in the city, the Plaza de Banff commemorates the connection between the liberator and the royal burgh.

In 1950 Argentina celebrated the 100th anniversary of the death of the liberator. Banff town council, on being reminded of this, invited the Argentinian ambassador to the United Kingdom to pay an official visit to the royal burgh on 25 October of that year. The ambassador, Dr Carlos Hogan, was entertained at a formal luncheon in the Fife Arms Hotel in Low Street, now converted into apartments, where he presented the Royal Burgh of Banff with a half-size replica of the general's sword. This is now on perma-

Guard of Honour at the Plainstones, Banff, 1950, for the Argentinian ambassador, Dr Carlos Hogan. With him is Provost Thomson, and the NCO is Bailie Reid, later first district councillor after 1975.

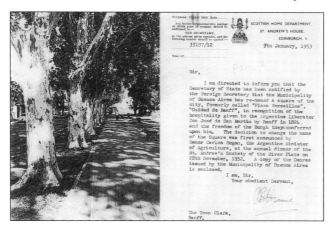

The 'Plaza City of Banff', Buenos Aires.

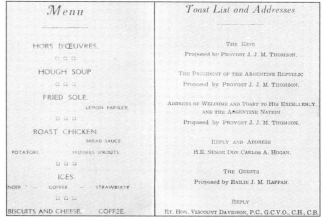

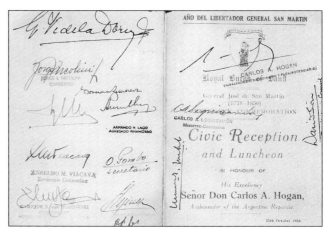

nent display in Banff Museum. After the luncheon the ambassador was taken to Banff Castle, where he planted an Araucaria tree, a native of South America, in front of the castle.

After 58 years, this flourishing monkey-puzzle tree is over six metres high. A cast metal panel beneath the tree gives the reason for planting such an exotic addition to the landscape around Banff Castle, and keeps alive the memory of the foreigner who became an honorary burgher of the royal burgh so many years ago.

Argentina cherished the link. The memorable 'Evita' Peron, wife of the President of Argentina, sent money for the old-age pensioners of Banff, and in 1964, following the footsteps of San Martin, the

Top and above: *The lunch menu from the Fife Arms with signatories.*

The arrival of Dr Hogan, the Argentinian ambassador, at the Townhouse, 1950.

world-famous Argentinian novelist Jorge Luis Borges (1899–1986) also came to the royal burgh.

ALVAH BRIDGE TREMBLED
3–4 AUGUST 1829
Jay Wilson

Soil receded from sun-bleached shrubs and withered plants, as drought squeezed the North-East coast. Smoke rose as grass and hay reduced spontaneously to ashes in their fields. Cracks in the earth gaped as if gasping for rain. Barometer needles fluctuated between unprecedented highs and lows without visible inducement, and rain finally fell on shrivelled land. Compacted, dried earth repelled the barrage of drops.

Up in the valley, the haughty new Alvah Bridge trembled. Beyond it the River Deveron had been swallowed up by a loch strewn a mile across crops in the haughs of Sandlaw. Forced to ribbon through the narrow Craigs of Alvah, water surged 40 feet up the bridge's pillars. Overwhelmed birds were dragged by a frenzied river and dashed against rocks. The bridge itself held fast as the lake discharged towards a sleeping Banff.

Agitated by a state of flux, the tame Duff House eagle bounced on its perch, rapping against the roof of its cage: watching islands form in Lord Fife's parkland; watching cattle, rats and a hare congregate on knolls left high and dry. River water spewed over the Kirkside bend embankment, claiming land, kitchens and lower rooms of the big house as its own.

Protecting Banff's south side was the great garden wall, stretching from the top of Bridge Street to the bulwark bridge. Built to support rambling roses and conference pears, it resisted pressure briefly. In the early hours of 3 August 1829 the wall was breached and flood water stole the sleep of Banffers.

Mayhem moved into Market Place as ground-floor rooms were swamped and families, half asleep, struggled, half-naked, against the torrent. Neither time nor thought was wasted on rescuing furniture or personal belongings in the flight towards higher ground. Those with two-storey buildings cowered in the upper rooms, praying that their foundations wouldn't founder.

Rescue boats were quickly launched, picking up stranded residents from second-floor windows. Winding their way through canals which had replaced streets, rescuers ferried victims to safety. By noon water had driven back boundaries and risen 10 feet above the normal level of the river; 50 houses were flooded. Seven shop owners counted costs among perishables; but neither human life nor livestock was lost. The Duff House eagle, and trout, flounder and eels removed from their natural environment and left behind by receding water, however, were not so fortunate.

Cattle perched on a parkland knoll had to stand in line when their rescuers arrived to pick them up. The hare they had shared time and grazing with leapt straight into the boat. The rats, on the other hand, refused safe passage off the island, preferring to remain until the waters receded.

Hellbent on delivering the Royal Mail, the mail coach approached town and ignored all advice to wait for the water to abate. With more to risk than a few envelopes filled with communications, its

A painting of the Bridge of Alvah by Charles Cordiner, the only Banff artist in the Dictionary of National Biography.

passengers disembarked, refusing to go further. They watched, with locals, the embattled coach being thrashed by the torrent of water pouring through the breach in the wall. Cries of horror rose with the crows as the carriage hurled against houses and the horses fought for their lives. Both the guard and the coachman abandoned the wagon. One by one, three of the four harnessed horses foundered and drowned; only one was freed by boatmen and it swam through the streets to the cheers of the crowd as the guard and the coachman clung to a lamppost.

It is not beyond the realms of imagination to believe that resonances of the previous great flood (1768) stirred as water swirled through homes and businesses in lower Banff. Human life was spared, but the remains of people whose lives spanned the years which encompass the floods are buried in St Mary's kirkyard. Christian West's headstone is quite close to its entrance. She was only three 'the year that the brig o' Banff gaed awa', and 64 when the mail coach horses perished. In the intervening years she had married a fisherman, George Watt, and had a daughter, Isabell. Both were lost to her within six months of each other. Isabell was four when she died in June 1802, and her dad was 26 years when he was lost at sea that December. Christian herself survived them both by 57 years, celebrating her 93rd birthday before she passed away.

More vivid memories of both floods could have been held by Jane Wilson. She was in her middle teens when the country feared French invasion from the sea and military bridges sprang up where rivers

slowed the movement of defending troops. Work began on Banff Bridge in 1763 and took two years to complete. Within three years, however, the forces of nature carried it off to sea. Its west side pillar had been undermined and every arch collapsed. Jane was 17 by this stage and may have seen the newly cut crops, drying in the September sun, along the length of the Deveron. When the weather turned sour suddenly she may even have cursed the violence of the rain hampering her day. She would have seen the river rise, taking with it the corn, hay and wood which dammed the arches, allowing water to build up and press against the new bridge. She would have seen the haughs of the Deveron fill with eight feet of water around Duff House.

Spates and Fatalities
Prior to the building of Banff's bridges people took their lives in their hands when they forded or were ferried across the river. It took its own toll on a whim.

1739 – In January, on a public market day, two men and three women boarded the ferry boat. It was driven downriver by the force of the current and carried out to sea. Both men and two of the women drowned. Mrs Shand, of Macduff, survived. She had been carrying a sack of wool on her back which, it is believed, buoyed her up till a boat from Doune rescued her.

1766 – In May of that year the Deveron, in spate, came to within 7 ins of the old Alvah Bridge, which appears to have had a low arch. Lord Fife's factor,

William Rose, anxiously reported that it 'stood quite well yet, but before never got such a tryale'.

1773 – Seven lives were lost in the first month of that year and the townspeople proposed holding a ball to raise funds for the children and widow of the boatmen and people of Doune who drowned. The campaign for a new Banff bridge was strengthened by the death of these seven people.

1774 – The foundation stone was finally laid for the new Banff Bridge. John Smeaton designed it. He also designed the Tay Bridge, the Perth Bridge and the Nor Loch Bridge, Edinburgh. The new bridge was build just a breadth's width up from the original one and magistrates, masonic lodges and other dignitaries were included in the celebratory procession:

Only the foundations of three middle piers and one end pier of the former bridge were standing when the new bridge was begun, but stones and material were still lying at hand.

1779 – The 11 years without a bridge came to an end; the Banff Bridge we know today was completed.

THE GREAT REFORM MEETING OF 1832
Alistair Mason

After the French Revolution the ruling classes of Britain were nervy and irritable. It might happen here. So for 40 years we had very right-wing governments, prepared to open fire on peaceful public meetings, stringing up every poacher they caught and little boys who stole handkerchiefs, and opposed on principle to any notion of change.

Given the corrupt electoral system, it is almost unbelievable that the Whig opposition ever came into power, but they did, and brought in the Reform Bill of 1832. This took away lots of rotten boroughs, gave new cities like Manchester an MP, and somewhat widened the franchise. More for its potential than anything else, the measure was widely popular, and all round the country there were mass demonstrations in its favour. The Bill passed the Commons, but was thrown out by the Lords – hence the demonstrations.

Banff had a day to remember, 24 May 1832, when they held their demonstration, the Great Reform Meeting. The only public event that could nearly match it that century would be the funeral of an Earl. Everywhere there were flags. The big one behind the stand for the speeches read 'Our King, His Ministers, and Reform'. A procession with flags and banners came from Portsoy and Whitehills. They had a banner reading: 'We've nailed our colours to the mast, and our banner is Reform'. All the trades of Banff were gathered at the Trades Hall to welcome the arriving procession with cheers. Then the Banff procession started as well, and went down Low Street and Bridge Street to the Green Banks. The procession was led by men on horseback, then a band, playing 'The Campbells are coming', then the reform committee, then the officials of the trades – the convener, the assessor, and the boxmaster – then each of the trades in turn. There is a proper order in these things, and they each had their own banner, first the hammermen, then the wrights, then the coopers, then the shoemakers, then the tailors and weavers. Then came the juvenile trades, one of whose flags read: 'From the rotten burgh system, Good Lord, deliver us'. Whitehills and Portsoy followed Banff, and then came Macduff, also with horsemen and a band, and lots of banners with appropriate mottoes. They say their procession extended from the Bridge of Banff nearly to Macduff.

Meanwhile, there was activity on the water. All the boats of Macduff sailed out in line, decked in flags and flowers – every flagstaff fringed with flowers. The leading boat, as well as a Union Jack, had a swallow-tailed flag (a burgee) aft, proclaiming 'Grey, the pilot that weathered the storm'. Grey was the reforming Prime Minister. The boats then sailed in serpentine procession to form a double line behind the speakers' stand on the Green Banks. That must have been a wonderful sight. Everyone cheered, and the sailors held their oars straight up in the air and cheered back. The meeting was convened with a bugle call and a discharge of small cannon from the boats.

The meeting itself was businesslike. They passed solemn resolutions supporting the government against the House of Lords, which had thrown out the Reform Bill:

... this meeting is certain that His Majesty's Ministers alone are capable at present of forming a Government which will possess the confidence of the country, or can preserve tranquillity either at home or abroad.

About 4,000 people took part in the business of the meeting. Many more, those who had no remote expectation of getting a vote (including women), watched from the rising ground around. We cannot tell what impact the Banff meeting had. Their local peer, the 4th Earl Fife, was already in the reforming minority in the Lords. At any rate, the king and the Lords gave way, and the Bill was passed. The MPs for Banffshire, from then on for a very long time, were Liberal. After a political statement from the town and district like that, what could they be? The other strand did continue in the town. Imlach's *History of Banff* starts with a poem addressing Banff, whose final lines are: 'The democrat, O! may we never see, Flaring his fiendish torch to smutch and smoulder thee!'

The old system was amazingly undemocratic. Like other Scottish burghs, Banff had been what is termed a 'self-perpetuating oligarchy', that is to say that whenever the time came to appoint a new town council, the only people allowed to vote were the members of the old town council. They knew what they were talking about, so they chose their successors.

When it came to choosing an MP under the old system, the rules were different for town and county. In the county, only those could vote who owned land named in a medieval list entitling the owners of these estates to vote. The towns were more straightforward. Only the town councillors had a vote, and we have already seen how the town council was selected. The burghs of Scotland were grouped into districts, sharing one MP, so Banff was one of the half-dozen burghs in the Elgin district. To become MP you had to bribe or lean on half a dozen town councils, so only families like the Fifes could afford to do it. These were the bad old days. When they passed, there wasn't such a great change locally as one might expect. Possibly Banff had slightly anticipated the likely way of doing things in the future. The last Robinson provost was in 1831, the same year that gas lighting came to the streets of Banff. A new era was dawning. However, when it came, it seemed that the affairs of the town were in a mess. Banff was very heavily in debt, and year after year they had to reckon up every one of the town's assets to see if there was anything they could turn into cash. The list included even the bibles and psalm books in the Parish Church. In 1851 – oh, the humiliation! – we had managers appointed by the Court of Session to administer the affairs of the burgh. Afterwards things got better.

Left: *Mr George Angus checks the 'Banffie' – hot from the press in the 1960s.* (© Dr David Findlay Clark ARPS)

THE *BANFFSHIRE JOURNAL*
George Boardman

Banff – and Banffshire – is fortunate to have had its very own newspaper, the *Banffshire Journal* – recording the unfolding story of the area since 1845. Fortunate, too, that the *Journal* was one of the earliest weeklies in the North East, and was a high-quality publication from the start, for although there are two other smaller and more recent Banffshire newspapers, the *Herald* in Keith, and the *Advertiser* in Buckie, neither ever rivalled the *Journal*'s ambitious policy of covering the whole county.

In fact, for much of the *Journal*'s first half-century, the paper also covered world news. News from the Royal Court shared column inches with everything from parliamentary reports on the great affairs of state to unrest on the borders of Empire, and Chicago beef prices. The *Journal* was also a serious paper on the arts. In pre-radio days, novels and 'periodicals' (magazines) filled family evenings the way that TV or the internet does now, and columns in the

Journal were devoted to thoughtful reviews of the latest offerings.

The news was written small (in terms of type size, at least) in the *Banffshire Journal* week by week. The modern reader is left staggered by the layout of these great broad pages: single column after single column of copy in tiny lettering, unbroken by headlines or photographs. And, even at the time, the *Journal* was notorious for using a small type size. But where the *Journal* has always held a unique position is in its local news. For the paper's entire history, news has flowed into Old Market Place in Banff to the two premises which have served as its home. A large staff of reporters covered the major stories and council meetings, and an army of local contributors from the farthest reaches of Banffshire submitted items about the minutiae of local life, from the state of the weather and crops to fulsome details of weddings and funerals. And for over 100 years, the quality and style of the paper were moulded by just two notable men, Dr Alexander Ramsay and Dr William Barclay.

But to begin at the beginning; William Smith, bookseller of Banff, published issue No. 1 of the *Banffshire Journal and General Advertiser* on Tuesday, 30 September 1845, at the then hefty cover price of

Above: *Staff photograph,* Banffshire Journal, *outside the office and works, formerly Banff Grammar School. Note the number of print setters.*

4¹/₂d. (about 2p). The paper was only four pages long. On the front cover there was news of trouble in America: Indian Wars and disputes between Mexico and the US. Closer to home there was concern about potato blight in Banffshire, which was also wreaking devastation on the populace of Ireland at the time. The great and the good of Banff would have noted the advert for the Banff County Ball, to be held in the County Rooms. The gentlemen's tickets were priced at one guinea (21s.), well over a week's wages on offer for the teaching post being advertised for the Academy at Fordyce. Ladies' tickets were only 5s., but presumably Banff ladies were not intended to consume much of the champagne being purveyed.

But the golden century for the *Journal* started 18 months later with the appointment of a young Edinburgh literary man, Alexander Ramsay. He arrived in this far outpost of North Britain by stage-coach, and, viewing the vista of the River Deveron and the town, the 25-year-old said to himself, 'It will do.' He admitted: 'I had no idea I was to be here for 50 years. But I began to do my work, and have been so engrossed in work ever since that I had no time to think of change.' In the event, he was only separated from the editor's chair by death in 1909, when he was in his late 80s. In the meantime, he had been awarded the degree of LLD by the University of Aberdeen for his journalism and literary writing.

Remarkably, Dr Ramsay's successor worked for the *Journal* for even longer than his 62 years.

When William Barclay laid down his pen in September 1946, at the age of 79, he had practised the craft of journalism in Old Market Place for 65 years. Add to that his father's 50-odd years with the paper as a compositor and reader, and his brother James's 30 years as a sub-editor and editor, and the Barclay family gave nearly 150 years of faithful service to the paper. The Barclays were a Banff family, and young William started work at the *Journal* as a message boy. He learnt shorthand from his father, and joined the editorial team. Under Ramsay's leadership, he rose through the ranks as reporter, sub-editor and assistant editor, and was the natural choice for editor when Dr Ramsay died. He used to teach his reporters the three crucial watchwords at the *Journal*: 'Accuracy, accuracy, and accuracy'. He was devoted to his work: one junior reporter recalls him coming back from his holidays (in exotic Cornhill) with half of next week's paper already written. Like his mentor, he too was awarded an honorary degree for his journalism and literary efforts, also from Aberdeen University, in 1941.

An Edwardian photograph of staff at the Banffshire Journal *offices.*

It seems that newspaper writing was not enough to satisfy his mind, and he wrote a number of books, much prized still in the libraries of local houses. First among those was *Schools and Schoolmasters of Banffshire*, a history of schools in the county, published in 1925. Other titles included *The Geography of Banffshire, Afternoons off in Banff, Aberdeenshire and Moray, The Moray Firth Shipping Industry*, and *The Cross of Turriff*. All that did not prevent him serving his community in other ways, as a JP and Honorary Sheriff.

The 1940s produced another crop of great journalists at the *Journal*, including the great Alec Munro, and his son Ronald. But times were changing, and the *Journal* would never again be able to hold onto its best talent. Alec Munro became the North East's foremost agricultural journalist at the *P&J*. Ronnie spent most of his career at the prestigious *Scotsman* in Edinburgh, where he rose to be night editor at the paper. Even now, the ranks of Scottish and English newpapers, radio and TV are still studded with newspapermen and women who cut their teeth at the *Banffshire Journal*.

Newspapers were changing in the 1950s. The Banffie had never looked better; there were neatly designed pages, headlines, graphics, photographs and illustrated adverts. But the international and national news was gone. Radio had put paid to that, and adverts from local electrical shops were offering the latest craze: television sets. Like many newspapers, the *Journal* was starting to tread water. By the late 1970s the technology was 50 years old and the building was crumbling.

A big staff of reporters, printers and compositors was still needed to master the clanking machinery of linotype machines, hot metal, chases, frames and the rest, but the equipment was not up to it, and the income and sales had fallen off. The paper grimly plodded on, and eventually, just as it seemed to be in terminal decline, in stepped Moray & Nairn Newspapers, publishers of the *Northern Scot*.

The *Journal*'s revival started immediately, with a level of expertise and professionalism not seen for some long time. Local ownership was gone, but the new publishers upheld the central maxim of any newspaper: they appointed an editor specifically for the *Journal*, and did not interfere with the content – a principle also adhered to by the current proprietors. But something was lost in the process: no longer would dozens of local families depend on the *Journal* for a living.

The old *Journal* could raise cricket and football

teams, and run its own golf competitions, but the paper only has staff enough now to make a whist four. The other parts of the business, the book publishing and jobbing printing, were abandoned by the new owners, along with the old printing equipment. Much priceless archive material was given away or thrown out when the original building was sold, and the *Journal* offices moved into a small office nearby, at the foot of Bridge Street, where it remains to this day (2008).

By the 1990s, word processors were used to write the copy, and eventually e-mail despatched it to the Elgin headquarters, where the pages were laid out and converted into plates for the presses. Other functions, such as accounts, circulation and production, also went to Elgin. Later, the Moray & Nairn group was itself swallowed up by the present owners, Scottish Provincial Press, one of Scotland's biggest newspaper groups. Inverness-based SPP produces no fewer than 12 titles in the North of Scotland, mostly weekly, but also including the big Inverness papers, the *Inverness Courier* and the *Highland News*. The *Journal* is now printed at their state-of-the-art colour presses in Dingwall, producing over 5,100 crisp, clear *Banffshire Journals* every week, with colour available on most pages and photo reproduction as good as anywhere. But now, the *Banffshire Journal* office looks as the same as a million others; computers, faxes and phones are the tools of the modern trade.

The centralisation of the newspaper business mirrors the real world of Banff and Banffshire. Just over a generation ago, the towns were run by their own town councils, and the county council looked after the rest. Banffshire had its own police force, education authority, health authority, and, on the national stage, she sent an MP to Westminster. All these things have gone, and although the decisions may be taken more remotely, their effects are still felt on the street we live in and the health centre we visit.

The *Journal* revival continues: as newspaper circulations drop away all over Britain, the *Journal* has been selling more copies, year on year, for at least a decade. By focusing on local news and issues, and speaking with an independent voice, the *Journal* has held on to its readership.

Worldwide, the newspaper business is facing the biggest crisis of its 300-year history. Radio and TV have chipped away at its news coverage and vital advertising revenue. Now the internet is squeezing in and hurting income hard. But, as part of a large modern newspaper group, the *Journal* has its own professionally produced electronic version of the paper, and is well equipped to compete in the electronic age. It is now possible to update the *Journal* during the week, as stories break, and to write comments on stories via the website. The future is always uncertain, but the *Banffshire Journal* intends to be part of it. All news is local news, and everyone at

the *Journal* works hard to put it into print every week.

The great figures of its past may be a difficult act to follow, but there is little time to dwell on that in the weekly race to produce a paper worthy of being under the proud *Banffshire Journal* masthead. That is surely one thing which the ghosts of Ramsay and Barclay would recognise as an unchanging part of editing the Banffie, the pressure of deadlines.

THOMAS EDWARD ALS
David Findlay Clark

In 1900, Garden Milne Hossack, Sheriff Clerk of Banffshire. read a paper, 'Some Reminiscences of a Sexagenarian', to the Banffshire Field Club. He animadverted on a number of themes in an interesting, if somewhat archaic way:

In those days… the boys had, with the sanction of the good old Earl, practically the run of the Duff House policies, since they were open and patent to all and sundry from dawn to dark, and many were the nesting parties who scoured the woods in search of eggs and anything 'unco'. When eggs or birds were discovered which were not sufficiently identified, or when any relic or curiosity turned up, a deputation of the boys with their find would frequently wait for enlightenment upon a resident naturalist and antiquarian, who had not then beyond a local fame. That naturalist was, however, Thomas Edward ALS, then a working journeyman shoemaker in Abercrombie Sheriff's back shop in the High Street almost within stonethrow of the school, but soon to be known to the literary and scientific world as one of the greatest scientists of the day. We never called in vain, for was he not versed in 'beasties and creeping things' and, like Captain Grose:

*'He had a fouth o' aul nick-nackets
Rusty airn caps, an' jinglin' jackets,
Wad haud the Lothians three in tackets,
    A towmont guid,
An parritch- pats, an' auld saut backets,
    Before the Flood'*

And his extensive knowledge was invariably good-naturedly put at our disposal, either at the back shop or in his house in the Wright's Close, and we departed wiser than we went.

This represents the mature Thomas Edward. His early days were, however, far from stable or secure. He was born on Christmas Day, 1814, in Gosport, the son of John Edward, a militiaman who had been guarding French prisoners from the Napoleonic Wars, and of Margaret Mitchell, an Aberdonian. After the war John, whose trade was that of a weaver,

Thomas Edward ALS, the Banff naturalist.

The home of Thomas Edward on Deveronside. Note the commemorative ceramic plaque on the wall.

(© Dr David Findlay Clark ARPS)

moved back almost immediately to Kettle, in Fife, and subsequently to Aberdeen. It was while there that Tam had shown an unusual interest in 'beasties' from before he was two. As he grew older, he became almost unmanageable, both at home and in school, because of this overweening propensity. He was inclined to wander almost anywhere in search of 'specimens', and seems to have been something of a 'loner' for most of his life. In the light of modern knowledge, it is probable that today he would have been diagnosed as suffering from Asperger's Syndrome. However, that was unknown in the early-nineteenth century, so poor Tam, having never been educated beyond the age of six, was left to learn how to read and write when he was adult. The pre-teen-age Thomas Edward started his first job assisting a tobacco spinner. Later, however, he began as an apprentice shoemaker, and it was at this he worked for the rest of his life.

The south shore of Scotland's Moray Firth is one of steep, high cliffs and wide, sandy beaches. The town of Banff sits on one of these bays. Its eighteenth-century gabled houses stand a street's width from the sea, and on one of these can be seen a blue ceramic plaque. And why? Because a poverty-stricken, uneducated and quite disturbed wee boy had lived and worked in that house for most of his adult life, earning a hard living as a cobbler, but eventually becoming a naturalist of high repute and an Associate of the Linnaean Society. His gravestone, raised by public subscription, stands in Banff ceme-

tery. In his night-time quests for natural history specimens, he would seek shelter from storms under other cemetery gravestones at Boyndie, a couple of miles from home. One, covered in a tomb, was a favourite.

Tam's early life in Aberdeen had been harsh. Three schools expelled him by the time he was six for bringing wild animals, birds and creepy-crawlies into the classroom. Once he was thrashed by the schoolmaster until his shirt stuck to his back in the congealed blood of the many weals, and it had to be soaked off him with warm water at home. Never at school again, he watched the animals, insects, birds and dolphins and roamed his beloved cliffs to watch the fulmars. From the age of 20, his meagre living as a cobbler working a 15-hour day allowed him almost no free time. Thus his expeditions were mostly at night, catching sleep when he could.

The long summer days of the far north were fine, but winter wrought havoc with his health. Attacked by a fox one night on a cliff, he fell to the shore and was revived from unconsciousness by passing fishers before walking several miles home in spite of bruises and concussion. He slaked his thirst at an ancient mineral well near Macduff. On the cliff tops he collected insects and small animals. His larger speci-

71

Etching of Inverboyndie kirkyard, near Banff. Thomas Edward used to shelter under its table-like graves in wet weather.

mens had to be shot and the smaller ones pocketed and boxed. There were no cameras then and he, still illiterate, taught himself taxidermy in order to preserve them. The nuts, fruits and edible plants of the wild sustained him till he reached home to his patient wife and his work. He had met and married, at age 23, a Boyndie farm girl of poor origins but of high quality; intelligent, loving and psychologically tough. She quietly tolerated his night-long absences and bore him 11 children. A Sabbatarian, he would never work or go hunting till after midnight on a Sunday – his children seem to have owed their lives to Sunday evenings! Other evenings would see him out on the moors, stalking new items for his collection. Animals, birds, insects and reptiles were included in his first collection – which, to his huge disappointment, was later utterly destroyed by cats and rats.

By superhuman efforts, he replaced it with another of over 2,000 items and showed it in Banff in 1846 and later in Aberdeen, whence it was taken in six horse-drawn carts. He hired a hall in the city, but only academics from the university showed any interest. The professors told him he was too far ahead of his time. The exhibition was a financial failure. He could recoup only by selling it off – for a mere £20.10s. Depressed, even suicidal, he was about to walk into the sea when he saw a bird he had never seen before. That set him to replacing his exhibits yet again.

Heading for home after an expedition, he would often plan all the elements of one of his displays. A week's work could only bring him in a few shillings. One daughter helped by working in domestic service, and Tam's wife too would help out while he roamed, sometimes 20 miles a night. She helped him construct the glass-fronted boxes for his larger specimens and even did some of his cobbling. His taxidermy became very expert. A fine peregrine falcon – his very first stuffed bird! – and several of his original boxed and glazed specimens remain today in Banff Museum.

Winter posed many problems. Cold, darkness and falls affected his health. Rheumatic fever limited him to studying lichens on the rocks and the sea life of the rock pools. He loved the shore and was always ready to instruct any of the young who might meet him. Everything on the shore, especially crustaceae, was noted and catalogued. Meanwhile, a local minister at Monquhitter, Revd James Smith, was teaching him to read and write so that he could communicate with the eminent biologists to whom he sent many of his sea-pool specimens for identification.

He studied all manner of tiny creatures, shellfish and crustaceans, including those regurgitated by deep sea and other fish. He actually discovered and documented 28 previously unknown and unidentified crustaceans. In rough weather he could have recourse to the inland streams and woods where everything – animals, birds, plants and insects – came under his scrutiny. By 1858 he had accumulated his third, and best, collection and had begun to contribute to national natural history publications. Then, in 1876, the philosopher and writer Samuel Smiles published his biography, *The Life of a Scotch Naturalist*, and, almost overnight, Thomas Edward became a 62-year-old celebrity. Recognition of a dedicated but deprived and hazardous lifestyle came late. Tam was made an honorary member of many natural history societies, including being made an Associate of the Linnean Society. He was awarded a generous annual pension of £50 by Queen Victoria, recommended by, among others, Charles Darwin.

Since 1852 he had been, and was till the end of his life, curator (for two guineas a year) of Banff Museum, then housed in the Doric-columned building, now the primary school. In the architecturally much duller present-day museum, some of his final collection of birds still remain on display. The sunset of his years was more comfortable than his beginnings. He often wondered what he might have achieved had recognition come earlier. He died on 27 April 1886, having lived, in his own words, as:

... a poor and illiterate working man, struggling against every sort of privation for so many years, with no other object but simply to gain a little knowledge of the works of creation.

JAMES EDWARD KYBER
Christina Ord

James Edward Kyber, who died on 11 December 1869, aged 80, was, it was said, a gentleman of culture and education, who was well known in commercial and particularly fish-curing circles, all along the shores of the Moray Firth. He worked for many years as a foreign correspondent for the firm Garden Grant & Co. As a refugee from Russian tyranny, he found asylum in Banff and became a respected and esteemed citizen of the royal burgh. Born in 1789, he was from the Baltic States, then called Livonia and part of the Russian Empire. His obituary was in the *Banffshire Journal* and there was also a follow-up story in 1869. A paper was also written some time after his death for the Banffshire Field Club. Giving a fuller account of his life, it describes how he arrived in Peterhead firstly to form links between the Baltic States and the North-East herring trade. Later he made his way to Banff, where his occupation was that of clerk.

It is said that he spent the last years of his life living in the Market Arms. He was seen on a daily basis within the bar, along with his constant companion 'Tiney', a fox terrier, as he studied.

On 8 or 9 December 1869 Kyber went to his lodgings, a single back-facing room of the Market Arms. It was recorded that this room was laid out in a ritualistic fashion. Kyber then proceeded to disembowel himself in front of the window. Some locals said they had witnessed this from the old market place. The terms used by the *Banffshire Journal* to describe his injuries was that 'his entrails were a gush'.

Mr Kyber, when taken to Chalmers Hospital, lived for two to three days, dying on 11 December. It is said he was conscious throughout this agonising time, although delirious, so no one, it is said, knew why this horrific act was carried out.

James Edward Kyber had in his possession a manuscript written by Johann Kaspar Lavater (1741–1801), the Swiss physiognomist, theologian and poet. Lavater was a personal friend of Kyber's father, a Livonian Lutheran parson, and this manuscript had a handwritten dedication to Kyber's father. As you may know, Johann Lavater tried to turn physiognomy into a science (*Chambers Biographical Dictionary*).

Kyber's father gave his son the manuscript and other articles for safe keeping, and Kyber brought these to Banff with him, as there were religious upheavals in Livonia.

About the time of Kyber's death certain gentlemen officially entered Kyber's lodgings and removed all of his possessions, along with the manuscripts and other articles. These manuscripts and other writings fell into the ownership of Mr Barclay (a well-known local gentleman), who was the owner of the bookshop/stall beside the Market Cross in Banff. James Edward Kyber was buried in Banff cemetery, in the second phase, lair 113. His occupation was recorded in the ledger as Clark/Clerk. The motive for his death remains a mystery. Was it an act of suicide? Or, considering the nature of his death, was it an act of protest?

⊶ ⚍ ⊷

THE BUSINESS OF CARRIAGE
Jay Wilson

Porters are ambassadors of their country. They are the welcoming committee to thousands of travellers arriving at and departing from airports, train stations and seaports. Transporting baggage is their business. Butting into a journey, they wrestle you as you wrestle your luggage. That they appear as they do, touting for business, is to be expected, but is nevertheless unfamiliar, and can instil suspicion and fear rather than confidence and security. You suspect that your luggage is going to be stolen, or fear that your wallet will be unduly lightened in proportion to the job in hand. This feeling of being inevitably ripped off is not, however, unique to the twenty-first century.

It seems that porters and messengers were abundant in Banff right up until the latter part of the nineteenth century, from which time they are remembered, with a smidgeon of Victorian sentimentality, as 'characters'. Just a few generations before, however, they were not to be trusted nor relied upon to do an honest turn. 'Owing to workmen's dishonesty and negligence', the local authority deemed it necessary not only to set rates of pay, and thereby curb inflation, but also to vet these characters. A panel was set up which gave authorisation to those who wished to work as porters and carriers. It would oversee the business of carriage. This may have seemed a prudent move. It isn't beyond the realms of imagination to believe that by the time the town

The Market Arms hotel, where Kyber lived and died.

(© TOMMY BOD)

council took this step (1734), a mature Robert Stewart would come in front of the panel, made up of a convener and four assessors, to be appraised and perhaps be found worthy of the position. After all, an unproven charge of arson and murder, levied 21 years before, could not have rendered Robert unfit to fetch and carry – could it? (He was one of three young men accused of burning down Inchdrewer Castle and murdering the then Lord Banff in 1713.)

A necessary ingredient in the make-up of a porter was his uniqueness. By standing out from the crowd he would be remembered and therefore patronised. For some it was their nicknames which set them apart. 'Janet' was actually Duncan, who was associated with body-snatching and revelled in being called 'Coffinback'. 'The Bishop' was a bookworm who, as a boy, was punished in school for his inability to say 'Archbishop of Canterbury' correctly. 'Hottentot' had been a soldier in Africa and, it is believed, was involved in a skirmish with some Khoikhoi nomads while there. Geordie Committi, 'The Craw', however, was the son of an Italian jeweller. Distinguished by heritage, his 'strongly marked face and foreign features, his broad bonnet and thickly set frame' made it difficult for him to go unnoticed in provincial Banff. He spent 75 years in the town and was a constant source of banter and ridicule. His fiercest rival for business was Roddie. Roddie needed no nickname. His given name sufficed: Roderick Burns Mackenzie Ryder. His family had long been associated with the old Marischal Street Playhouse in Aberdeen, and Roddie, who had fallen off the boards, was often witnessed roaming the streets, reciting Shakespeare.

Boats at Banff bridge, c.1900.　　(© BODIE COLLECTION)

Scotstown with nets drying and gantries.

(© BODIE COLLECTION)

HERRING FISHING FROM BANFF
Stanley Bruce

Since medieval times, Scots have fished for herring (*Clupea harengus*). Local inshore fisheries were first recorded on the Clyde and Forth estuaries, but only in the 18th century did herring fishing become a major commercial activity. Then, after a means of curing or preserving the fish was worked out (the Dutch had enjoyed a monopoly using their own secret method prior to this) Scotland's herring fishery expanded to become the biggest in the world in the latter part of the 19th century and early 20th century. Banff played its small part in this. The fishing followed the natural migration of the shoals of herring from their wintering grounds off the Norwegian coast down past the Shetland and Orkney Islands, the east coast of Scotland and later in the year as far south as Great Yarmouth and Lowestoft. During January to March herring could also be caught off the west coast. Scottish boats and other workers followed the shoals south, before

Fishing boats at Banff harbour, c.1910.

(© BODIE COLLECTION)

returning after a long spring and summer to their own 'wintering grounds' in harbours like Banff, Buckie, Fraserburgh and Peterhead.

Herring fishing, thanks to bounties offered by the British Government for larger boats and fish sold abroad, began in Banff around 1816, when the Lighthouse Quay was built at a cost of £7,000 by Thomas Telford, which increased the size of Banff Harbour to four acres. The number of boats in Banff peaked at ninety in 1822. The key figure was Edinburgh-born Walter Biggar, who married local

The Biggar fountain being completed. 1878. (© Bodie Collection)

A fisherwoman gives a lesson on gutting the herring. (© Dr David Findlay Clark ARPS)

lass Anne Duff and settled in Banff in 1821. He established links to sell herring to the Baltic countries, and he and his wife are commemorated by the Biggar Fountain erected in 1878 in Low Street Banff. The fountain was gifted by the Revd Dr and Mrs Blaikie, relatives of the Biggars. They were inspired to make the gift after reading the life of Banff naturalist Thomas Edward, who had said that it would be an advantage to the town to have a memorial sited on the old site of the Mercat Cross.

Herring fishing was restricted in Banff due to the want of available space near the harbour for the establishment of curing yards, and the high rates of dues. The following curers had businesses in Banff: Messrs Nesbit & Co. formerly Messrs Walter Biggar & Co., and Messrs Grant & Co formerly Messrs Grapel & Co. The house of Alexander Murray of Whitehills also transacted its business from Banff. The harbour at Macduff was better placed to take full advantage of the herring boom, and did so, becoming the commercial fishing centre, overshadowing Banff. The BF boat registration for Banffshire began in 1843, though in 1907 BCK for Buckie was established.

The cured herring were shipped to the Baltic countries in British and Prussian ships. Prussian ships were favoured by many of the foreign buyers because they were cheaper to hire; however the ships that did sail from Banff were 50/50 British and Prussian. Most of the British ships sailed to London for shipment to the West Indies; others sailed to Liverpool for shipment to Ireland. After the arrival of the railway in 1859 the cured herring was also transported south by train. The railway line ran right down to the pier south of the Lighthouse Quay. The line closed to freight in 1968. The ships would return with cargoes of grain, wool, bark, iron, hemp, flax and hides; and of course cargoes of birch wood from Norway, which was required to make the herring barrels. The town and harbour also hosted ancillary industries such as coal merchants, ship chandlers, rope, and sail makers.

The following table, relating to Banff, is taken from *The New Statistical Account of Scotland* 1845:

Walter Biggar.

Number of/date	1831	1832	1833	1834	1835
Barrels cured	1759	1959	1265	938	631
Boats employed	14	16	18	22	8
Fishermen	56	64	72	88	32
Women curing and packing	41	46	48	60	21
Coopers	6	6	6	8	4
Curers	5	5	5	6	4

The table shows a fluctuation in numbers, probably due to the herring fishing being poor in 1835. The Account also says, of the Banff Post Office, 'A very considerable portion of the revenue is derived from the correspondence with the northern parts of the continent, on account of the herring fishery'.

The Banff fishermen, like other fishermen on the Moray Firth, favoured the 'Skaffie', which was an open-decked sailing boat with a raked bow and stern and a short keel. This compared with the 'Fifie', which had a vertical bow and stern, giving it a long keel, and was favoured by fishermen from Fraserburgh and further south. In 1879 the 'Zulu' boat was developed by William 'Dad' Campbell from Lossiemouth; the first boat was named the *Nonesuch*. The 'Zulu' combined the raked stern of the 'Skaffie' with the vertical bow of the 'Fifie'. These boats, which could be 70ft long, carried two lug sails (to avoid bowsprits in overcrowded harbours) and could sail as fast as 10 knots. A wooden hulled 'Zulu' drifter, the *Research*, originally built as the *Heather Bell* in 1903 by W & G Stephen boat-builder, Banff, can be seen in the Scottish Fisheries Museum in Anstruther. Another 'Zulu' the *Hirta II*, can be seen in Macduff – it currently is sited on a dry berth at Macduff Shipyards, Union Row, Macduff.

During the 1880s and 1890s sail boats became larger. This was mainly due to the invention of the 'Steam Capstan', affectionately referred to as the 'Iron Man'. A small steam engine turned the capstan which was used to pull in the nets or hoist the sails. Much more powerful than the crew man-handling the nets and sails, this enabled larger nets to be shot, thereby requiring larger boats to hold the catch, which in turn led to larger sails on the boats. MacDonald Brothers in nearby Portsoy were famous for their capstans, said to be unique because they could also go in reverse.

During the days of sail the fishermen rowed in and out of the harbour when there was no wind. In the late 1800s a steam powered paddle tug was used to tow the fishing boats in and out of the harbour. In the early 1900s sailboats were being replaced by bigger 'Steam Drifters'. The wooden-hulled drifters built in Banff ranged between 50 and 100 tons gross, 75 to 90 feet long, with a beam of around 18 feet, and a depth of 8 to 10 feet. Banff Harbour was too small to accommodate all of these, and in any case was prone to silting, and only had a maximum depth of twelve feet at high tide, rising to fifteen feet during Spring tides. Many fishermen began to berth across the bay in the much deeper and more spacious harbour of Macduff.

Because the boats were bigger and steam-powered this meant that the fishermen could fish farther offshore and 'follow the herring' to other ports all around Great Britain. Local fishermen spent months at a time away from home, landing their catch at a variety of ports. Many of the local girls, referred to as 'Herring Lassies' or 'Gutting Quines', also 'followed the herring' travelling on ferries, trains and sometimes on a drifter to get to the next port. The lassies worked in teams of three with two gutting and one packing. They worked long hours and their fingers had to bound in 'clooties' – pieces of cotton rag – to ward off cuts, salt and infection. Banff girls, some as young as fourteen, are known to have travelled as far north as Shetland, and as far south as Lowestoft, 'following the herring.' On their travels many of the lassies lived in rather basic wooden huts supplied by the curer, or if they were lucky in a guest house.

During World War I (1914 to 1918) the admiralty requisitioned steam drifters for mine-sweeping and patrol boat duties. After the war the market for herring in the Baltic countries collapsed and many of the curers were declared bankrupt. Most of the Banff fishermen then concentrated on fishing for white fish. 1920, just over a century after it began, is said to be the last year herring was landed at Banff. Peter Anson wrote in 1930 that the harbour "is now seldom used by fishing craft for landing their fish", though between the fishing seasons it would still often be full of steam drifters. "There are now seventeen steam drifters owned here". His statement that in 1929 no herring were landed at Banff and only £59 of white fish compared to £18,522 landed in Macduff shows the terminal decline of Banff as a fishing port.

Herring fishing continues in the other Moray Firth ports, with powerful, far-sailing modern diesel-powered boats with super-efficient fishing rigs.

SALMON FISHING
John Sellar

For more than 1,000 years, in estuaries and rivers around Scotland, generations of fishers have hunted the much-prized king of fish, the Atlantic Salmon (*Salmo salar*). On the River Deveron salmon were caught in cruives (a kind of weir, or dam), by net and coble (sweep nets), and from 1825 by fixed engines (bag nets) in the sea.

Ownership of the salmon fishings in Scotland, whether in the sea, in the estuaries or in the river, originally belonged to the Crown. By the mid-eighteenth century the salmon fishings about four miles upstream, including windings and the estuary, and sea fishing to the east of the river, were owned by Lord Fife and later, in 1833, through interdict served by James, 4th Earl Fife, he managed to purchase from the burgh of Banff the sea fishings west of the Fauchie Rock, which lies at the point of the Boat Hythe just west of the Banff Lighthouse.

Prior to the rise of the herring fishing from the 1790s, the salmon fishing was the most important fishery in Scotland, mainly with salmon and grilse caught by cruives or sweep nets on the river bar or estuaries. From the mid-nineteenth century in-river fisheries on the Deveron declined in number, partly due to the growing popularity of angling as a sport, pushing fishing rents upwards and beyond that affordable by many netsmen. Also, the upper proprietors on the river complained bitterly of getting a very poor return of catches on their estates.

One can get a comprehensive report on the Deveron salmon fisheries from the *Annals of Banff* Vol. 2, which covers from the tenth century to the late 1800s.

The family of Sellar started salmon fishing on the Caithness and Sutherland coast in the mid-nineteenth century, and by the very early-twentieth century (1902) so extensive were their fishings that the company of J. Sellar & Sons formed the Scottish Salmon & White Fish Co. in Aberdeen to solely market the fish they caught. A few years later they

Nineteenth-century salmon fishers at the Wrack, Duff House grounds.
(© BODIE COLLECTION)

Salmon fishers inspecting their nets.

Fish merchant's house on Water Lane dating from 1675, later used as a salmon bothy. (© BODIE COLLECTION)

purchased the River Connon and the River Findhorn sweep-net fisheries, which allowed them to give up the rented fisheries on the north coast.

In the early-twentieth century they purchased the sea fishings at Banff and Macduff, which extended from the Boyndie Burn on the west side of the Banff links to the 'Busses' of Melrose, submerged rocks a few hundred yards west of the Point of More Head. The company, known as J. & D.R. Sellar Ltd, was operated by four brothers, and in about 1927 leased the salmon fishings of Whitehills, Portsoy, Sandend, Cullen and Portessie from the Seafield Estate – Lord Seafield.

Within the Banff and Macduff fisheries at one time four cobles fished on the coast. Each coble was 24ft in length and recognised as a four-oar or a six-oar boat. Later they were replaced by a motorised coble of around 26ft, with a 20hp petrol–paraffin Ailsa Craig engine. These cobles were built by the family at their net factory at Boddam, which had been the family seat since the eighteenth century. With the faster motor coble the company then managed to cover more of the coastline and fish more bag nets. Working methods and net design were also improved, which helped them to increase catches.

Come 1955 another generation entered the salmon fishing at Macduff, and, with a modern outlook, the old cotton bag net and leader was to be replaced by nylon nets, and likewise the manila ropes and wooden casks used to float the bag net under tension from the tide were replaced with terylene and nylon ropes and polypropylene buoys, which were lighter and not so taxing on the gear when the gales from the north-west or north-east battered the coast.

Through the '60s engines were upgraded to the four-cylinder diesel BMC Commander, rated at 45bhp. An improvement on trying to start the old petrol paraffin engine on cold mornings, these were battery started, which saved a considerable amount of time. With faster and more reliable cobles we were again able to cover more ground, and during the midsummer grilse run we used two cobles, one fishing west of the harbour at Macduff and steaming as far as Whitehills, fishing three nets east of the harbour there. The Whitehills salmon station had been closed at the end of 1949. The other coble fished east of Macduff and covered the coastline to the March at More Head. In that period salmon and grilse catches improved, and where we were catching a ratio of one salmon to two grilse through the 1950s it increased to a ratio of one to four salmon to grilse.

Fishing Banff Bay from Macduff didn't present any problem carrying nets and gear in the coble, as one could change a dirty and growthy net then return to harbour and put it ashore, then continue fishing the rest of the fleet of bag nets with little waste of time. Running east from the harbour presented a different problem, as perhaps if the weather had been bad and we missed a few days at sea we then had to carry three nets and on occasion four nets to change. Otherwise, with the distances involved, we would be steaming most of the day. Each net in the sea was changed weekly because, as the water got warmer throughout the summer, so the growth grew in the water and made the nets smelly and slimy. It was our principle that to catch salmon you had to have a clean net. With this in mind we decided to build a larger coble, so by the late 1970s the keel was laid for a 30ft boat at our premises at No. 4 Union Road Macduff. This coble was to be the largest boat used for salmon fishing in Scotland.

Once the hull was planked and framed we turned the coble over. Then we covered the hull with GRP, using the shell of the coble to act as a plug so we could make a mould for future building. This was accomplished and from then on, during the closed season of 26 August to 11 February, we produced GRP cobles and sold them to other salmon-fishing companies and individuals in the industry. Boatbuilding was nothing new to our company, as we had always built wooden cobles for bag-net and sweep-net fisheries. We also complemented the boatbuilding with net making, allowing us to keep on some of our staff during the winter months, at the same time supplying the industry with new orange or grey corylene bag nets. A GRP mould was also made for a 14ft sweep-net coble, and when we produced that size of coble we captured a market from the riparian owners of the Scottish rivers, as they were used for angling.

The early 1980s brought another generation into the company and also a bit more thought. The traditional bag net, which had gone more or less unchanged for years, underwent slight modification. Instead of the bag being at the sea end of the leader we joined two bags together and set them east and west at the end of the leader, forming the shape of the letter 'T'. The seaward wall of netting was sewn together, while the landward side of the bags had an entry left for fish to run the leader and enter either the west bag or the east bag, depending on the state of the tide. With the bags in an east–west position, they were now either head into the tide or head down tide, which made them easier to fish. We also found that they caught more fish at times but at the same time noticed that the nets to the east of a double bag didn't catch their usual fish. One drawback working double bags was when one came to change them. With twice the amount of netting, it took fully twice as long to replace it with a clean bag. Again, throughout the early 1980s we found grilse to be more numerous, but by 1986 we saw the ratio dropping back to the 1960s figures.

The company continued to fish until 1990, when the North Atlantic Conservation Trust and the River Deveron riparian owners offered to buy out the salmon-fishing rights in the Deveron area. With fishing time being restricted during the 1985–90 period, the company decided to accept an offer made by the conservation group whose intention it was to leave the Deveron area unfished. So ended the Sellar family's connection with coastal salmon fishing, which had spanned over 150 years.

<hr />

SHIPPING AND SHIPBUILDING
James A.S. McPherson

Before the advent of the railways and tarred roads, the sea was the natural carrier of goods coming into and going out of Banffshire. In about the middle of the nineteenth century the shipping industry along the Moray Firth was at its peak and employed substantial capital and thousands of men on land and sea.

Old prints, paintings and early photographs show Banff Bay and Banff and Macduff harbours crammed

The schooner Ban Righ *on the slip at Banff, 1879.*

Shipbuilding workers.

(© Bodie Collection)

The old shingle bar at Banff, with the shipbuilding yard on the left.

The schooner Gladstone, *the biggest boat ever built at Banff*

The Gowan, *built in Banff in 1878.*

Banff harbour c.1900/1910 with early steam boats and a craft being built (foreground).

(© Bodie Collection)

with ships, schooners, barques and sloops. Everything was carried in these ships, from a cask of snuff to a cargo of coal. Banff and Macduff harbours served a wide inland area. Outward cargoes comprised livestock, oats (for which Banffshire was famous), oatmeal, salmon and cured herring. Imports included timber, coal, salt, bones for bone-meal and general cargo.

An indication of the activity is illustrated in issues of the *Banffshire Journal* of August and September 1850, which noted that a total of 37 vessels entered Banff harbour during those two months, and on one occasion no fewer than 26 schooners were berthed within the harbour.

The Moray Firth sailing ships were not confined to coastal waters. Some of the larger ships, owned in Banff and Macduff, seldom saw their port of registration. They were employed largely on foreign service – breaking records on a voyage from China with the new crop of tea, or in the emigrant trade, leaving Banff direct for Melbourne or Quebec with cargo and passengers.

It is recorded that on one occasion there met in Archangel the *Sovereign* and *Consort* of Banff and the *Lass o' Doune* of Macduff. Others found themselves as far away as Australia. But the majority of the ships were engaged in the local coastal trade, carrying coals from the Tyne or shipping grain, cattle and salmon to southern ports or cured herring to the Baltic. The volume of trade was such that a Custom house was established in Banff as early as 1790.

In the mid-nineteenth century the shipping industry in Banff and along the Moray Firth was in its heyday, and many fine vessels carried the BF register around the world. In 1857 the Mercantile Navy List, prepared by the Board of Trade, credited Banff with 142 ships.

Side by side with this tremendous shipping industry there also thrived a shipbuilding industry which was second to none for the quality of the vessels it turned out. Shipbuilding yards were established in practically every port. The largest concentration of yards in the Moray Firth was at Kingston and Garmouth, at the mouth of the Spey, which, in the 100 years or so of their existence, produced more than 600 ships, some of which were still in operation well into the twentieth century.

Both Banff and Macduff had yards building mainly schooners for the coastal and Baltic trade. The best-known builders were Geddie, Watson, Dick and Walker in Banff and Anderson, Duncan and Hutcheon in Macduff.

Inevitably the passage of time brings many changes, and the advent of steam power, the coming of the railways and developments in local commerce which no ship owner, however resourceful, could resist, heralded the end, within a few short years, of the merchant sailing ship era, which had flourished for more than a century.

As Dr William Barclay, editor of the *Banffshire Journal*, explained in his booklet *A Lost Industry – Banffshire Sailing Ships*, reprinted in the *Banffshire Journal* in 1906:

The arrival of the railway and the growing use of steamers extending to every corner of the land, accompanied by very largely altered business conditions helped to seal the fate of the sailing merchant vessel, and we have seen the disappearance of what used to be a great industry, which provided a large and at one time highly profitable field for private venture and enterprise and which as a nursery for brave and hardy seamen was of national importance.

By 1906 only one sailing ship remained, the schooner *Alice of Macduff*, built in 1873 at Watson's yard in Banff.

Although all the commercial sailing ships had vanished, there remained a shipbuilding trade which retained the finest traditions of quality and craftsmanship handed down over several generations, and this was directed towards providing vessels for the developing fishing industry.

Following the small undecked 'Scaffies', 'Fifies' and 'Zulus' came the steam drifter, and when war broke out in 1914 Banffshire had no fewer than 306 drifters and more than 4,500 fishermen, many from Banff and Macduff. These local fishermen, who were among the first to adopt the seine net when introduced in 1921, showed themselves just as ready to exploit other new fishing methods and gear over the years.

In 1965 the Macduff Boat Building & Engineering Co.'s shipbuilding and engineering business and premises were acquired by Messrs John Watt & Sons of Gardenstown, who had been building boats at Banff for some years. Operating in 2008 as Macduff Shipyards Ltd, they are major fishing-boat builders and enjoy a reputation for good design and high standards which is respected throughout the fishing industry, both in the United Kingdom and abroad. The range of facilities they offer is impressive. A full service for designing, building, repairing, converting and modernising is provided, together with craneage, transport and quayside support for repair work.

As from 2008 the new upgraded slipway facilities at Macduff, accommodating larger steel boats, will be available. At Macduff harbour the company has two fully fitted building halls, one for construction in wood and the other for the construction of steel-hulled vessels.

A modern design building at the harbour is also, at the time of writing, nearing completion. Their reputation for style, reliability and commitment to quality and customer satisfaction is well known, as is evidenced by a full order book, and it is generally accepted that future prospects for shipbuilding in this area are bright.

FARMING
Alan A. Meldrum, Retired Executive Secretary
Banffshire Area, National Farmers' Union

Before we take a closer look at farming in the immediate vicinity of Banff, let us start by having a look at Banffshire in general.

The old county stretches from the top of Cairngorm some 80 miles south-west of Banff to the shores of the Moray Firth. That South West part of the county is hill and moorland, with no farming as such, and populated by red deer and grouse, with some coniferous plantations in places up to the tree line at around 1,800 feet.

The land slopes down to Glenlivet and Inveravon, where we find in the valleys soil of excellent quality, crop production only limited by the fact that the height above sea level gives a shorter growing season. This land has been improved since the late 1950s by sheer hard work by the local farmers, aided by government assistance, started during and after the war to bring more land into production. The application of lime was of particular benefit.

The farming practised here is largely the breeding and rearing of livestock. The area is renowned for the production of quality cattle, reared then sold on to farms in the lower part of the county – Moray and Aberdeenshire – for fattening. Many go on to be prize-winners at local and national shows. As is the case elsewhere, the traditional black Aberdeen Angus cattle have, to a considerable extent, been replaced by the faster-maturing continental breeds, such as Charolais, Simmental and Limousin, although the

black cattle have made a comeback, with a premium being paid for the quality beef. Sheep farming has always formed a large part of the income of those upland farmers, with flocks of ewes being kept on the lower grounds until after lambing then put out to the hill. The lambs are sold in late summer for fattening down-country and further south.

From the hills and glens of Upper Banffshire the county broadens into the middle belt, where upland-type farming is still practised, but nowadays with an increasing amount of cereal production – mainly barley growing, along with cattle and sheep breeding and fattening. The land here is of mixed quality, with some good land in the Grange valley but with poorer land in the hillier parts.

As we get nearer to the coast, we find the arable and fertile land – some of it amongst the best land in Scotland, fetching around £4,000 per acre for the top quality. With the less harsh climate of the coast, a wide range of crops is grown, much of the cereal production going to feed the livestock fattened in the area. Barley, the predominant grain crop now, fetches high prices at the present time, with a premium for barley of malting quality for our 20-plus distilleries in the county, and further afield. Oats, once the main crop, are grown to a much lesser extent, despite the fact that there is a large modern meal mill at Boyndie.

In the 1960s around 50 per cent of the Scottish pig herd was in the North East, much of it in the Cullen, Banff, Turriff area, with farms of all sizes keeping either breeding or fattening pigs. The number of farmers keeping pigs has fallen dramatically, with only a few units now keeping large numbers.

Canal Park and the Princess Royal Park as farming land.

Grampian Food Group, which had its origins in Banff in the 1970s, has extensive pig herds around Banff, and the group is also an important purchaser of cereals for pig, cattle and poultry feed, through the local mill at Brydock.

As was the case with pigs, poultry production is now being concentrated in fewer hands. Every farm used to keep hens, the farmer's wife depending on the eggs produced to pay the grocer's bill. Nowadays the rearing of chickens for supermarkets is the main poultry enterprise, but there are still a number of larger-scale egg production units.

Potatoes are grown on a considerable scale around Banff, mainly seed potatoes for export and for growers in the South. This being a specialised business, it has again been concentrated on fewer farms. Some local farmers do, however, grow ware potatoes for local demand, such as the farmers' market held monthly at Banff/Macduff.

I can remember when there were at least 14 dairy farms in and around Banff and Macduff – in 2008 there are only two, with only one other in the whole county. The dairy herds, until after the war, were mainly smaller herds with up to around 20 cows, but now herd sizes are much larger, running up to 400 cows, with the milk going off to centralised depots for distribution rather than individual farmers having their local milk round.

There is a limited amount of vegetable growing, mainly carrots and brussels sprouts, with the bulk of the crop sold through producer groups or middle men to the supermarkets in the south. A few local farmers still grow on a small scale to supply local shops and farmers' markets.

Having covered types of farming and range of crops produced around Banff, it should be mentioned that there has been a very significant change in the ownership and size of farms in recent years. While the Seafield Estate still owns a considerable number of tenanted farms to the west of Banff, the estate has taken more of their land in hand, mainly for cereal growing and with new woodlands being planted. Fife Estate owned much of the land around and to the south of Banff. In the early 1960s the estate sold off the farms, mainly to sitting tenants who were able to buy at favourable terms, certainly compared with the price of land today.

Traditionally most farms in the area were family farms, ranging from around 80–200 acres, but since the '60s the size of the average farm has increased substantially to around 400–500 acres, with some of the larger farms well above 1,000 acres. This has resulted in there being far fewer farmers, and coupled with the introduction of costly larger modern machinery and the increased use of contractors, there has been a severe reduction in the number of farm workers employed, leaving the countryside empty of people compared with days gone by. The knock-on effect has meant closure of rural schools and shops, and no longer do we see the bakers' and butchers' vans winding their way through the countryside. One can also notice the increasing size of fields, with old stone dykes, fences and hedges removed to accommodate the modern large farm machinery. Unfortunately, some of our old small deciduous tree woodlands have also disappeared.

There's always one!

(© Dr David F Clark ARPS)

Such is progress, but the landscape of much of the North East could be improved by the shelter provided by more woodlands and hedges. It is quoted that in the nineteenth century: 'From Culbirnie [a hill in the Ord district] to the sea, you may walk from tree to tree.' Nowadays barely a tree exists in that landscape.

Up until the last war, Banff could have been described as a market town, but no longer. Although the economy of the town still depends to a fairly large extent on the prosperity of farming, there is now very little direct involvement, apart from two modern mills, one at Brydock, the other at Boyndie. The closure of Grampian Food Group's chicken processing factory at Banff marked the virtual end of farm-related industry in the town.

Going back over the years, the scene was somewhat different. The town boasted a livestock mart, a slaughterhouse, a knackery, a large foundry famed for its range of farm machinery, an egg-packing station and several grain merchants. The harbour saw a fair trade in handling grain exports, while also handling imports of feedstuffs and fertilisers. The Banff harbour railway station also handled farm produce, including milk consigned daily to Aberdeen creamery.

Changed days indeed, but the farming scene in and around Banff reflects the scene throughout the county as a whole. I have often remarked over the years that Banffshire is very much Scotland in miniature, with the emphasis on the quality of our local produce, whether it be whisky, cattle or fish. That reputation should stand Banff and the old county in good stead in the years ahead.

RAILWAYS
Alexander Colley

Today the traveller to Banff without a car or other means of private transport has only one choice, the bus. It was not always so. For a period of about 100 years covering the later part of the nineteenth century and the earlier part of the twentieth, one could travel from Aberdeen to Banff by train. Not only that, but there was a choice of two routes, although a train travelling on one of them deposited the traveller on the slopes above the east side of the River Deveron at the station known as Banff Bridge.

Neither route, however, formed a direct link with Aberdeen and the outside world. Even if they had, it is extremely doubtful if they would have survived to the present day with comfortable road travel available.

But one must remember that in the 1850s and 1860s, when the lines opened, the only alternative way of travelling overland was horse powered, and it

Banff Bridge Station.

Banff Harbour station, c.1910, with the cholera hospital on the skyline (top left). (© BODIE COLLECTION)

was this that caused the two lines to be considered, authorised and built.

The route actually terminating in Banff was the longer of the two. A journey from Aberdeen went by way of Cairnie Junction, a few miles east of Keith on the main line to Inverness, then approximately north to Tillynaught Junction before heading east towards Banff – some 64 or so miles. Having to change trains was also the norm. Even on arrival at Banff the station was somewhat less than convenient for the town centre, being situated at the foot of the brae at the end of Castle Street. Little can now be seen to identify the site of the station, though as one walks along the shore towards Banff Links the elevated track bed can be seen. Passenger trains on this line ceased in 1964. Goods lingered a few years longer. Looking at photographs of the last day, one might conclude that rail traffic was popular and wonder why the line was closed, but such pictures give a false view. As with many rural lines in the land, it was only the threat of closure that produced any real interest.

The other line was the more direct, but still some 50 miles, leaving the Inverness line at Inveramsay, to the west of Inverurie. That line went by way of Rothienorman to regain what might be regarded as the direct Aberdeen to Banff route at Fyvie. Turriff was then passed before the Banff passenger reached Banff Bridge Station. This was not quite the end of the line, as the terminus was a quarter of a mile away in the town of Macduff. For the industrial historian there is much to see of this line, perhaps surprisingly, since passenger traffic ceased as long ago as 1951. The station building at Banff Bridge was converted to a private dwelling, and both the station and engine shed at Macduff have been adapted for commercial use. The station building at Macduff has, unlike many country termini, an overall roof. This afforded passengers a degree of comfort and shelter from the elements. Banff Bridge, on the other hand, is typical of many wayside stations, with an exposed platform. Banff Harbour Station, like that at Macduff, was covered. But remember, if looking at remains, these are in private ownership, they are not public museums.

A question that is often asked is: 'Why did railways take circuitous routes?', and to this question there is no single answer. Intermediate traffic was important if a line was to make a profit, so it was worth making a deviation to tap a source of potential revenue. Construction and land acquisition costs also had to be considered.

The direct route would have involved some 40 miles of new line. The route to Banff via Cairnie Junction only involved some 16 miles, and some of that was shared with the line that eventually reached Elgin by way of the coast. Even the more direct line to Banff Bridge only involved some 20 miles of new construction. Topography is also relevant. While the landscape is hardly mountainous, there is some serious climbing between Oldmeldrum and Turriff, and what one has to remember is that a 1 in 50 slope was a challenge to Victorian trains. It was only with the advent of electric traction that the hills were flattened, so to speak. Also, many Victorian lines were constructed by small local companies with limited finance. These lines were no exceptions. In fact there was a number of years' delay between the railway reaching a station on the south side of the Hill of Doune outside Macduff and its ultimate terminus. The aim often had to be to connect to the national rail network at minimum cost.

Both lines ultimately passed into the control of the Great North of Scotland Railway and, following the First World War, became part of the London and North Eastern Railway. They became part of the nationalised system in 1948.

In conclusion, it is perhaps easy to be romantic and mourn the passing of the lines, but with advances in road transport, a system that served people well in its time had outlived its usefulness. One has only to look some 35 miles to the east. Even a town as large as Peterhead, with all its potential fish- and oil-related traffic, could not hold onto its railway. But should the oil supplies run out, who knows? As was once said of a country line, perchance it is not dead, it only sleeps.

THE FOUNDRY
Alistair Mason

The Banff foundry grew out of a smithy. In 1827 William Frazer, a local blacksmith, installed an industrial forge. The device needed to create a permanent draught was worked by a horse – not very advanced technology. There was a demand for farm machinery, and also, as we are on the coast, for

Mr Hutcheson, who owned the Foundry.

Inside Banff Foundry, showing the forges. This stood on the present site of Tesco, on Carmelite Street.

Machinery inside Banff foundry.

marine equipment. The firm changed hands several times, however, and scarcely prospered until it was taken over by G.W. Murray in 1863. Murray was a trained engineer and a typical Victorian entrepreneur. His portrait has been handed down, and he looks the part. Apparently they had to use sand from the Thames, because Deveron sand was the wrong sort.

For all its history, the foundry was in the heart of old Banff. Underneath were medieval remains. Murray's foundry was destroyed by fire in 1894, but was rebuilt on the same site by the Watson brothers in 1897. They had been fish curers, and the emphasis shifted to the marine side of the business. These were the days of steam drifters, and the foundry prospered making parts for boats. In the First World War, naturally enough, every foundry flourished, and the Banff Foundry had as many as 150 employees. There was a slump in the fishing industry after the war, and in the 1920s the firm changed hands again. Most people who do remember the working foundry will have known it under the management of the Hutcheson–Grant partnership, which lasted until 1951.

The emphasis went back to farm equipment. Some of the brand names from the Banff Foundry were known far and wide. If you are from a farming background, do you recognise any of these names: the 'Scotch' plough, the Jubilee Manure Distributor, the Spring Tine (or American) Harrows, the Victory Reaper (back delivery), the 'Colonial' wire strainer, and indeed the 'Tiny' hand threshing machine? They were all made in Banff, and there were lots more.

In 1951 the firm was taken over by Mr J.L. McRobert, who had great schemes for expansion, brought in such new models as the McRobert potato sorter and planned a new showroom across the road. Sadly, his plans came to nothing, and the foundry was closed in 1954.

THE 'ROPERIE'
THE BANFF ROPE AND SAILWORKS
Coralie Campbell

Henry Munro, my ancestor, worked as a rope and sailmaker at Seatown, Banff. He and his wife, Helen Gerrard, had 12 children and the third child, also Henry, took over and expanded the Roperie on the death of his father. Around 1870 the family moved to Ropeworks Cottage, at the junction of Coldhome Street and St Catherine Street. The ropeworks ran from the side of Ropeworks Cottage to the Battery Green, behind the houses in Campbell Street, which were built after the ropeworks were established. Henry had other business interests, having part ownership of three ships, and was provost of Banff between 1896 and 1902. The provost's regalia – the chain made for the diamond jubilee of Queen Victoria, which he attended with other northern provosts, can still be seen in Banff Museum. Henry's oldest son, Alec, and his third son, William (Bill), worked along with their father. In 1902 Henry took a back seat in the business, moving to Gellyhill Farm to indulge his passion for breeding cattle. Alec and Bill continued to run the Roperie until the First World War, Alec running the business and Bill in charge of the sail loft. Tents were also made at the Roperie and some were made for the World Fair in Chicago. In 1914 Bill joined the Gordon Highlanders, leaving Alec to carry on the business until it came to an end in the 1940s. Henry himself died at Gellyhill in 1919.

Parts of the original walls are still visible – from the seaward wall at the bottom of Bartlett Place, the length of the 'walk' can be seen between the back gardens of Bartlett Place and Campbell Street up to St Catherine's Street.

My mother, Christine M. Campbell, wrote, in 'Easter on the Braes', *Banffshire Journal*, 12 April 1955:

The office was a wonderful place. It was the only place I knew which had a telephone, and there was a machine for cutting double holes in paper. There were also two telescopes, through one of which I remember seeing,

The men and boys who worked at the Roperie.

Provost Henry Munro, owner of the Roperie.

when very small, a thing like a seagull, which turned out to be some intrepid airman flying round the British Isles. Another time on looking through, I heard my father say to my uncle in a cheery voice, 'Thar she blows', and then I saw a whale in the bay.

Then too the tar boiler was going full blast and sending its healthy aroma over that part of the town. One couldn't fall in. One could only throw oneself into it.

Then we had a look at the hemp shed, where a kindly old man was teasing the hemp; we went on to the sail loft. I think that I can smell it yet and see the sail makers busy with their palms, greasing the sail twine with beeswax and hear the whirring of the sewing machines and the joking voices ringing in the raftered ceiling. To reach the loft we climbed a precipitous outside stair. McBeath, Cameron and White were the names of three of the sailmakers. The last named gave his life for his country. To get an order out in time, the men would work sometimes on a Saturday afternoon, though this was rare. It was quite gloomy in the winter afternoon light of the sail loft. As the men worked, they talked. Stories were told of the time when they sailed as sailmakers in the sailing ships. As you walked through the long ropey-smelling building, each section was partitioned off. In the first division were the balances for weighing the ropes, and in another section there was a thing like a giant top.

DISTILLING AROUND BANFF
Michael J. Roy

The history of distilling practice goes back into the mists of time, the process being discovered by the Persians over 2,000 years ago in their quest to realise the alchemists' dream of turning lead into gold.

The first record of distilling in Scotland was made in the Scottish Exchequer Roll of 1494–95, when '8 bols of malt were given to Friar John Cor to make aqua vitae'. Nearer to home, the parish records of King Edward Church of 1794 record that:

Banff distillery at Inverboyndie in the early-twentieth century. (© BODIE COLLECTION)

The small whisky stills of the neighbourhood which afford a good market for barley and supply us with good whisky of a quality greatly superior to what we have from the large stills in the southern districts.

Undoubtedly illegal distilling was widespread, as there are a number of references to this in parish records throughout the north. Several attempts were made to control the practice, until the government passed the Distilleries Act in 1824.

It was in that year that James McKilligan established a distillery at Mill of Banff, just outside Banff. James Simpson and his son, James, subsequently purchased the distillery in 1852. Presumably because of the lack of sufficient water, the Simpsons relocated the distillery in 1863 to the site as we know it, at Inverboyndie.

The distillery enjoyed a chequered existence; it burned down in 1877, was rebuilt on a more modern plan by James junr, and went bankrupt in 1932.

It was taken out of bankruptcy by Scottish Malt Distillers, now Diageo, and operated successfully until 1983. The change of ownership did little to change its luck, as it was again damaged by fire in 1941, when a German bomb, which caused extensive damage to a warehouse and whisky stocks, hit it.

The spirit produced was considered by the trade to be of good quality, and most of it was used for blending through the licensee Slater Roger. The capacity of the distillery was 200,000 proof gallons (772,000 litres/alcohol) per year.

By the late '60s and early '70s, the whisky industry was extremely buoyant and plans were drawn up to relocate the distillery, on a much-expanded scale, to the Inverboyndie Industrial Estate. Unfortunately, before the plans could be implemented, the industry went into one of its cyclical downturns and the plans were abandoned.

For various reasons the plans were never resurrected and the distillery finally closed in 1983, with most of the buildings being demolished in 1985.

Bottles of Banff malt whisky are currently still available but are increasingly difficult to find.

The establishment of another distillery in the Banff area was proposed and researched in the '50s, by the then town clerk, Bertie Cumming. Mr Cumming had interests in the whisky industry through his ownership of Scapa, Pulteney and Balblair distilleries. He persuaded a group of Glasgow businessmen, George Crawford (builder), Brodie Hepburn (owner of Red Hackle Whisky), Morty Dyke (whisky broker) and James Stirrat (solicitor) that a suitable and adequate source of water was available locally on the Duff House estate. Coincidentally, the Duff House estate was about to be sold to pay off death duties. The embryo company was the first to purchase part of the Duff House estate, on which they developed Macduff distillery. It was among the first of the new distilleries to be built since the Second World War.

The distillery was designed by Delmey Evans, a notable distilling architect and engineer, and contained a number of revolutionary features, i.e. Cortone steel fermentation vessels instead of Oregon pine and horizontal shell and tube condensers instead of worm tubs. The stills were heated by steam instead of by direct firing and, most unusually, the pots of the stills were completely lagged. The lagging was significantly reduced in 1990.

The distillery went into production and filled the first cask on 16 June 1960, for Mr R. Cumming of Balblair.

Because of the innovative features, Macduff was visited by the great and the good of the trade, who copied and adapted the innovations, so they are now standard specifications throughout the industry.

The distillery was a great success, so much so that in 1964 a consortium of local businessmen drew up plans to build another distillery near the Wrack, with the process water coming from a spring near Alvah. Unfortunately, due to the death of one of the principal partners, the project was dropped.

The original consortium sold the distillery in 1964 to Block, Grey & Block, wine merchants, whose principal brand was The Speaker. They immediately expanded the distillery from two stills to three, and then again in 1968 from three stills to four.

In 1970 the company obtained permission to convert one of their warehouses into a bottling hall, and

Left: *A copper still from the Macduff distillery.* (© DR DAVID FINDLAY CLARK ARPS)

was at that time one of only two distilleries to have the facility to bottle on site. At that time the distillery employed 36 people.

The distillery was sold again in 1972 to a company called Clan Munro, a subsidiary of Martini & Rossi. This was subsequently changed to William Lawson Distillers. A further change took place when Martini & Rossi merged with Bacardi to become Bacardi–Martini.

A continual programme of improvements was embarked on, with the installation of equipment to convert the effluent into animal feed in 1976, a new cooperage and cask filling facility, which was heated by waste heat from the distillation process, in 1984, and a further expansion of production capacity and redevelopment in 1990, taking its production capacity to 2.5 million litres of alcohol per year. Rationalisation of the warehouse facilities took place in 2003, with all maturation now taking place off site.

In 1998 William Lawson was successful in purchasing John Dewar & Son from Diageo, and the company adopted the more famous name of Dewar's.

The distilling industry has brought Banff international recognition through the success and worldwide prominence of locally produced whisky in such brands as Banff Single Malt whisky, Glendeveron Malt Whisky and Wm Lawson's and Dewar's range of blended whiskies.

THE WAR MEMORIAL
Norman Tonner

The Banff War Memorial, which is Category B listed, stands in Castle Street at its junction with Seafield Street. The stone of the cenotaph is polished pale grey granite ashlar. The plaques on the chequered granite wall bear the names of those from Banff and its surrounding districts who died in the First and Second World Wars.

The foundation stone for the War Memorial was laid by Her Royal Highness the Princess Royal on 27 May 1921. The memorial lists 143 men who died in the First World War on the central panels and 36 men and three women who died during the Second World War on the two outer panels. The following are names of families represented more than once:

Asher	Badenoch	Campbell
Cormack	Chalmers	Crawford
Donald	Duncan	Dustan
Falconer	Forbes	Hadden
Hutcheon	Ingram	Johnston
Kennedy	Mair	McGregor
McKay	Milne	Munro
Murray	Ogg	Pirie
Reid	Robb	Ross
Scott	Slater	Smith
Stephen	Stewart	Thom
Tocher	Watt	Webster
Wilson	Wood	

Of the men who died in the First World War, most were members of the armies which fought in France and Belgium. Included are men who enlisted in the Australian and Canadian Armies and were born or had family connections in and around Banff. The Canadian regiments represented are of many of the country's provinces, including Ontario, Manitoba and Quebec.

Of the men of the British Army listed, most were Gordon Highlanders. Of the regiment's battalions, the majority of casualties were borne by the 1st, 4th and 6th battalions. The blackest day of the war for

Alexander Davidson, builder, Banff, handing the gavel to HRH Princess Louise, the Princess Royal, Duchess of Fife, at the laying of the foundation stone of the war memorial, 1921.

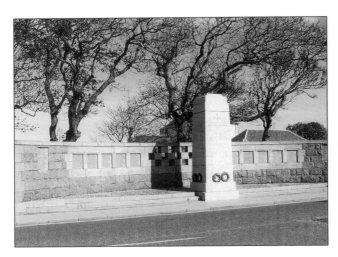

Banff War Memorial. (© NORMAN TONNER)

Banff was 25 September 1915, when seven Gordon Highlanders died in the Battle of Loos. On that day, the first day of the battle, the 15th (Scottish) Division captured the Lens Road Redoubt, a German strong point. The Gordons fought on the Western Front throughout 1914–18 and their names can be seen on memorials associated with the main battle arenas at Ypres, Le Touret, Loos, the Somme, Vimy and Passchendaele.

Of the marine forces, many men were merchant seamen or members of the local fishing community who were part of the Royal Navy Reserve. Most were lost at sea.

Of the 39 members of the Forces who died in the Second World War, three women are included, one a nursing sister in the Queen Alexandra's Imperial Military Nursing Service, another a Leading Wren of the Women's Royal Naval Service. The men who died represented all of the elements of the Armed Forces and include men of the Gordon Highlanders, merchant seamen and members of the Royal Air Force Volunteer Reserve.

The memorial maintains its open and prominent position facing west towards the broad expanse of Seafield Street and is, in its stark, simple majesty, a striking reminder of the sacrifice made by those who died in the twentieth century's two world wars: 'At the going down of the sun and in the morning, we will remember them.'

'DR' WALFORD BODIE
David Findlay Clark

The late-nineteenth and early-twentieth centuries were times of showmen and charlatans. Throughout the UK and the USA, ventriloquists, illusionists and tricksters filled the halls and constantly invented 'new and wonderful' attractions to intrigue and puzzle the crowds. Walford Bodie, born in

'Dr' Walford Bodie in academic dress (which he was not entitled to wear).

Aberdeen in 1869 but raised in Macduff and frequently in Banff, was one of these.

Samuel Bodie, as he was originally named, the son of a baker, was quite clever at school, and it was thought he might one day follow one of the professions. However, he found work first as an employee of the Scottish National Telephone Co., where his deep interest in electricity and magnetism could be indulged. He had also read much about hypnotism and ventriloquism, and soon practised both to a degree whereby he felt able, even as a teenager, to present a show on stage at Stonehaven. In fact, he first met Jeannie Henry, the lady who was to become his wife and stage helpmeet, at one of his shows in Banff. Jeannie actually came from the neighbouring town of Macduff, where Bodie was later to build a home. Bodie regularly employed his extended family on his stage shows, Jeannie as Princess Rubie, his niece Mary as Mystic Marie, and another sister, Isabella, as La Belle Electra. The last two named unfortunately died young, but Bodie also found jobs for their younger sisters, Louie and Kitty. At one point he also gave a job to Harry Lauder – who would later become famous in his own right and who, in due course, was knighted.

Something of Bodie's meteoric rise to fame and the questionable methods he used, embellished and promoted by his skills as a cartoonist and self publicist, are encapsulated in the following paragraph from this writer's book *Chancer* (Leopard Publications, 2008):

In 1897 Sam Bodie was working as a theatre manager at the Connaught Theatre of Variety in Norwich, but although the general ambience associated with such work suited him, Sam was driven to seek his fame on the stage in his own right. His early skills in ventriloquism, hypnosis and magic tricks were honed and in due course supplemented by his famous electrical tricks and demonstrations. They were also bolstered by his considerable prowess as a self publicist. He was soon to be described as 'the least modest man in the world', and quickly enhanced his prestige by garlanding himself with degrees of one kind or another, including those of MD, PhD, DSc and others. Not only did he append these to his name, but he also presented himself in the trappings appropriate to a learned professor or academic. Samuel Murphy Bodie did not quite have the ring of eminence he thought appropriate to his image, so about this time he changed his name to Dr Walford Bodie. His brother-in-law, whom he held in some regard, was called Walford, so he simply appropriated his name. When, in 1905, he published The Bodie Book, *its front pages illustrated this transition from baker's son to illusionist perfectly.(p12)*

These 'qualifications' were later to land Bodie in court, but he published in 1905 his own book, *The Bodie Book*, outlining his special skills not only as a showman using electricity and illusion but also as a healer and 'physician'. Such was his stage success that in 1906 he was able to build a house for himself and his family in Macduff designed by the famous architect Alexander Marshall MacKenzie, the architect of Aberdeen's Art Gallery, and also a swimming pool for the locals. For the next 20 years he made his way not only on the stage throughout the UK, but also in the world of property. A cutting from *The Performer* of 1932 tells of how he was then the owner of two hotels, six guest houses and another house in or around London, as well as a boat on the Thames, the *Cigarette*, described as 'a palatial houseboat'.

The stage success that had allowed Bodie to accumulate such riches had not been without incident. In 1914 Bodie was already 45 and the Military Service Act of 1916 limited the conscription of men older than 41. Too old, then, to be called up in the First World War, Bodie, seeking the answer to the Indian Rope Trick, went out to India to give shows. While he was there he narrowly escaped harm when it was found that a length of railway line had been removed from the track while he was on the train heading for another of his show centres. Later he went to Ceylon (now Sri Lanka) but there fell ill with malaria. On his way back to the UK the ship carrying him, his wife and all his stage properties and apparatus was torpedoed and sank. All his staff and Jeannie and himself were picked up and rescued, though not together, and he and Jeannie were separated for some weeks. They were later put aboard another ship, and when that too was torpedoed in the Mediterranean, they

were rescued again and taken to Malta. It is quite likely that had he been called up, his life might have been less adventurous than it turned out to be!

One of the core elements of the Bodie shows was an electric chair into which he would strap one of his assistants. Then, with high drama and serious preamble, he would pass high voltages of electricity through the subject with accompanying flashing lights and sparks. The essence of this act was that because he (Bodie) had hypnotised his subject, he or she would be able to remain undamaged and untroubled by these high voltages. What the audience did not know was that the electricity was at very low amperage and that his usual collaborator in the chair, James Wright, from Blackburn, near Aberdeen, had schooled himself to accept these shocks for suitable cash rewards. The fact that he wore a specially designed and wired suit also helped. There is some doubt as to whether the chair he used in his act was an actual electric chair from Sing Sing Prison, gifted to him by Houdini, or a copy fabricated by Bodie himself. The doubt only enhanced the mystery.

There is no doubt, nevertheless, that Bodie was indeed a very competent hypnotist. He had for years studied the work of Coué and Mesmer and, of course, many of the effects of hypnotism were less well known in these days. In *The Bodie Book* Bodie declares, quite without irony, 'There is no power so dangerous as that of hypnotism in the hands of the unscrupulous.' Earlier (on p.19) he had declared:

I myself am both a hypnotist and a mesmerist. I employ both methods, and combine electricity with them. But for the sake of simplicity I style myself an electrical hypnotist, and under that name I practise both the methods of Mesmer and Braid.

In the reface to *The Bodie Book* the good 'doctor' writes with his usual modesty:

It is now nearly 20 years since I first appeared before the public as an exponent of the marvels of hypnotism and electricity. During that time I have visited every important town in the British Isles, and in every town there are at the present day healthy and happy people who owe their health and happiness to me. Before I treated them they were victims of paralysis in one or other of its forms, and burdens to themselves and their friends. Since then they have been free from that dread disease, and are able to take their share in the great battle of life.

I do not say this boastingly. It is a plain statement of facts set down as my main reason for writing this book. In effecting these cures I have only been the instrument of higher forces, and in my public appearances I have always endeavoured to make this clear to my audiences, and in some measure to explain the nature of these higher forces.

Bodie, on his part, did everything he could to

enhance his power and prestige before his audiences. He would wear dramatic black clothes, sometimes of academic style, and even walking about Banff and Macduff he would affect a black cloak and elaborate hat. His waxed and pointed moustache, black hair and piercing eyes did more than impress people, they frightened some, who believed his powers were supernatural. Many thought that he had a strange aura about him. Even my mother was somewhat in awe of him, and described him to me when we saw him in Banff one morning in the 1930s as 'Dr Bodie, the famous hypnotist'.

It was his academic pretensions, however, which got him into trouble with the law – and for using the degree letters of MD (Doctor of Medicine). He avoided big trouble on that occasion by stating simply that MD stood only for 'Merry Devil'. In 1909, however, another case was brought against him on the basis that he had been (falsely) demonstrating that he could personally tolerate huge resistance to electricity. In the course of the trial, Bodie's apparatus, called the Death Cage Experiment, was actually set up in the London court where the case was heard. He lost the case and the cost of the action, reckoned by some to have been nearly a five figure sum, a lot of money in those days. Undeterred, and still the showman, he then commissioned a lithograph of the trial as an advertising ploy.

In November of that year, the undaunted Dr Walford Bodie, self–described, with his usual modesty, as 'The Most Remarkable Man on Earth', came with his show to the Coliseum, Eglinton Street, Glasgow. There had been, for some time, murmurings of annoyance, especially among the medical fraternity, with Bodie and his claims and antics. It is thought that the events of that week were not wholly spontaneous but rather fully orchestrated by university medical school staff and students. Be that as it may, the theatre was fully booked, largely by students and medical staff from Glasgow, and possibly elsewhere, so that when the curtain went up on the first night all was well until Bodie himself came on stage. Then he was subjected to a riot of barracking, and vegetables and other objects were flung at him to such an extent that the show had to be abandoned. Bodie, who really saw himself as a kind of healer, was very disturbed by this outcry and retreated for a time suffering from stress, then described as 'neurasthenia'. He travelled less thereafter, but still took his shows round even quite small communities throughout Scotland. If the events in Glasgow had chastened him, he still saw himself as a healer and physician with special powers. At the end of *The Bodie Book* (p.193) he wrote:

... although I elect to appear on the stage, I should be equally at home in a private consulting room in Harley Street. Yes, at home in every respect save one; I should be cut off from the poor, and the poor are, and always

have been, my especial care – the beginning, middle, and end of my extensive practice.

Many residents of Banff during the years immediately before and after the Second World War will remember that Albert, Walford Bodie's grandson, ran a successful photographic business in the High Street. Major Bodie, as he was at the end of the war, always seemed to me, when I talked of his grandfather, a little ambivalent about how to regard him. That was probably true also of many who remember the mysterious but potent self-styled doctor. Walford Bodie was indubitably clever and mixed technical and showmanship skills in furthering his cause. But he was, too, a caring man who really believed in his 'powers' and, according to his lights, tried to help many and showed his sense of civic responsibility by such things as his gift of a swimming pool to the people of Macduff and his presence at the opening of their golf course at Royal Tarlair. The roles of charlatan and benefactor became irretrievably confused, both while he lived and subsequently. His family tomb stands in the cemetery at the Macduff Parish Church.

THE PRISONERS OF DUFF HOUSE
David Findlay Clark

Towards the end of 1939 and in the early weeks of 1940, the people of Banff, accustomed to walking freely through the policies of the Duke of Fife, past Duff House and out to the Bridge of Alvah, suddenly found themselves seriously restricted. 'KEEP OUT! MILITARY PROPERTY' notices prevented our intrusion into the new domain of scores of Royal Engineers and Pioneer Corps soldiers. They were busy felling many exceptionally fine specimen trees,

Duff House before it was bombed.

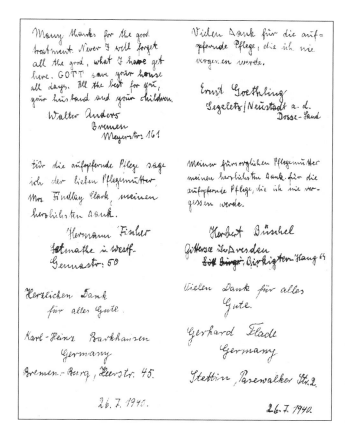

Messages from wounded German PoWs imprisoned at Duff House to their nurse.

digging up beds of snowdrops and bluebells, pouring concrete foundations for Nissen huts, and, most significant of all, building a great double barbed-wire fence, part of it electrified, about 50 metres away from and all around the house. Supported by pine poles nine or ten feet high and punctuated by raised strongpoints where soldiers with machine guns and searchlights could be posted, the many, many strands of wire, and especially the insulator-borne electrified wires, looked formidable enough to us small boys who sneaked close enough to examine it all. There was one main gate at the south-western corner with a small guard-house, and soon several dozen Nissen huts, with their strange half-cylindrical shapes and camouflage paint, nestled among the remaining trees of Duff House grounds, all the way from the Barnyards Cottages to 'The Big Gates'. Duff House had become a prisoner-of-war camp.

Generally, once the house was functioning as a PoW camp, local people were discouraged from getting too close to it and its high, forbidding fences. I was fortunate in that my father was appointed Military Officiating Chaplain both to the British guards and to the German prisoners. He himself spoke reasonable German and he was keen that I should get an opportunity to learn some German before it was taught me in school. Consequently, I was privileged to accompany the padre when he

presented himself to the sentries at the gatehouse, and to enter Duff House and speak to both guards and some prisoners in the main hall while my father went about his business.

Some of the prisoners, mainly officers, still wore their own uniforms, but most were in issue kit made up of dark brown, navy blue or khaki battledress with large, brightly coloured round, diamond or square patches stitched to the backs and fronts of the garments. The popular view of these was that they were put there to act as targets for the guards in the event of an escape or attempted escape, but in reality they were there only to be conspicuous. Mostly, 20 or 30 of the PoWs would be exercising or playing football on what, in happier days, had been the tennis courts in front of Duff House. Most were survivors of destroyed U-boats or other Nazi warships, but some were infantrymen and a few were Luftwaffe crew. Some of the officers were clearly confirmed Nazis and behaved accordingly, claiming, for example, that the war would be over and they would be free by Christmas (1940). They took a rather scornful view of their guards and of myself. Most, however, were much more like their guards and ourselves, half glad to be out of the conflict but sad and worried about their relatives and girlfriends back in Germany.

When I got a chance to speak with them, the inevitable response was, 'Hier hab' ich ein Bild – meine Frau, mein Sohn usw.' ('Here's a picture, my wife, my son, etc.'), and from that starting point they would get round to asking for cigarettes or chocolate, neither of which I had. Some of the guards got a bit tetchy when I seemed to be engaging too eagerly with the Germans, but that all stopped rather dramatically after only a few weeks, when the place was bombed by a German Heinkel 111 bomber.

My mother, who was a nursing sister, worked with Dr Smith, the local surgeon and GP, in the theatre at Chalmers Hospital, where the injured from the bombing were taken. Some days later I was taken to see some of the wounded Germans in the ward, where I was encouraged to present the Hohner mouth organ I had just been given for my birthday a month previously to one Walter Anders, who could play it better than I could. He played the tune 'Die Lorelei', and I was not far from tears, not at the loss of my instrument but at the sheer pathos of the situation. Most of us had been propagandised into considering all Germans as Nazis and fiends, who ate children for breakfast, and here were some of them, shattered and in pain, listening to tunes of home with tears in their eyes. That was the first time I saw Herbert Büschel, from near Dresden. He was swathed in bandages from head to toe. He had been blown into the disintegrating boilers, and my mother and Dr Smith took 365 pieces of shrapnel and glass from all parts of his body on the day of the bombing. He was not expected to live, but he did.

I am fortunate still to possess the autographs of several of these prisoners in my mother's autograph book for these years (see previous page). They tell of her unremitting care for these men, regardless of nationality (for she nursed British casualties as well), and of man's common humanity in the face of other men's inhumanity.

After the bombing, the house was insecure because of the damage, and the prisoners were moved to other PoW camps before some were transported by sea to Canada. It is believed that some of these unfortunates, having been bombed by their own men, were later torpedoed in mid-Atlantic by some others of their erstwhile colleagues. War is so wasteful.

THE BOMBING OF DUFF HOUSE
David Findlay Clark
(Originally written for Friends of Duff House)

From my earliest years I have been a poor riser in the morning. Several stratagems were in regular use to allow me to go on reading in my room until midnight and after, but the inevitable consequence was that I was last up for breakfast. I was not indulged and often had to eat cold porridge as a result.

That was still the case one summer morning in July 1940, when Tom, my young brother, appeared in my bedroom to tell me that there was a 'Jerry' plane buzzing about over Macduff, and – he thought – he had seen smoke and heard bombs! I pulled on some clothes in spite of being in the unwashed state of most small boys of that, and other, eras, and dashed to the big window of our parents' bedroom, from where we could see both Duff House and much of the surrounding area. The window was, of course, criss-crossed with stuck-on pieces of tape to prevent the glass flying in the event of bombs and explosions, but through the untaped areas of about nine or ten inches square we could clearly see what we instantly recognised as a Luftwaffe Heinkel 111. Tom said he'd seen it flying over the back of Macduff but, as we watched, it approached from over the Hill o' Doune (on top of which two members of the local Royal Observer Corps were dancing around in their sand-bagged emplacement in a state of high excitement and frustration, trying to persuade RAF Dyce that the Germans had an interest in Banff) and seemed to come straight at us at no great height, perhaps 1,000ft. We could clearly see the black crosses on the wings and fuselage and a swastika on the tail.

A column of black smoke was already rising from behind Macduff, but no resistance seemed to have been mounted so far and the air-raid siren had been silent. As the bomber approached we could see the bomb doors open and, just as it crossed over the Hill

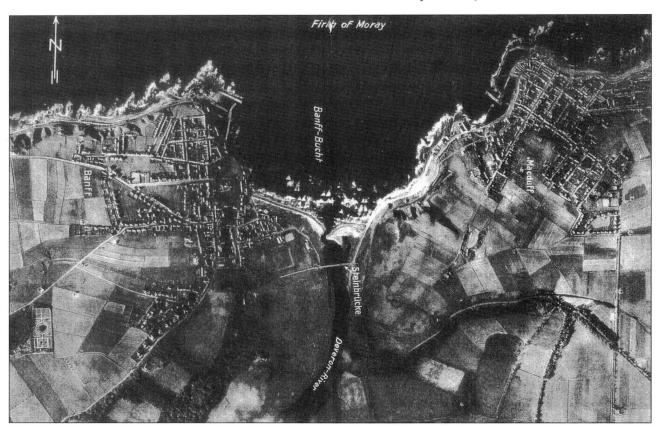

German Second World War aerial map of Banff. (© J. ROBERTSON, MACDUFF/BANFFSHIRE MARITIME HERITAGE ASSOCIATION)

o' Doune several dots (five or six, I think) appeared underneath it and gradually increased in size as the bombs fell towards the golf course, the house and, of course, us. We were fascinated, like rabbits before a weasel, and continued to look as the Heinkel flew straight over our house.

At that point, our father rushed into the room and pushed us to the floor. 'Get down, you boys!' he bawled, almost simultaneously with four or five loud bangs as the bombs exploded, and everything shook violently as pictures on the wall and ornaments in the room hit the floor well before we did. I can't actually remember whether father hit the floor with us, but as soon as we found the house had not been hit we were at the window again and then saw great clouds of steam and smoke rising through the trees from Duff House. The trees prevented us from seeing exactly what damage had been done, but at that point the air-raid siren (rather redundantly) began to wail and a minute or two later, Army ambulances and the local auxiliary fire service converged on the grounds. The Heinkel was heading out to sea, into which it was shot down by the reluctant Dyce Spitfires half an hour later.

My father hastily finished dressing. During the raid he had shot into the bedroom half shaved and Harlequin-like in his black trousers, white vest and half his face covered in shaving soap. Now he was off to Duff House, where he felt his duty then lay. He was the officiating chaplain to both British troops and German prisoners. A few minutes later, the telephone (of which there were only about 200 in the whole town – ours was Banff 107) rang to order my mother, who was a Red Cross nursing sister, to Chalmers Hospital immediately. It was the first time we boys had seen her in uniform, and we were quite impressed.

The public were immediately, and for some time, officially excluded from the site, but we boys quickly found a vantage point by walking (i.e. running) along the river, across what was left of the golf course and creeping through the long grass near a machine-gun post, by that time silent, the remains of which are to this day quite visible at the side of the 13th fairway. We could see that most of the wing on the east side of the house had been destroyed and was on fire. Firemen and soldiers were moving about amid the smoke and steam, and we later heard that one, possibly two, of the bombs had made a direct hit on the kitchens and boiler room of the house, killing six German prisoners and two British soldier cooks and severely wounding many more. Two of the bombs fell on the edge of the 17th fairway and another on the 5th fairway. The barbed-wire fences were, however, still intact, and many of the German prisoners were helping amid the wreckage. The whole wing of the house was, of course, later razed to the ground. It seemed that my German lessons had come to a full stop.

THE BANFF AIRMEN
David Findlay Clark

Some time about the middle of 1942, Banff echoed to the sound of heavy earth-moving machinery such as the citizens had never seen. Huge scrapers, bulldozers and tipping trucks with wheels higher than the tallest man, bright yellow and carrying such names as Wimpey and Caterpillar, worked on the shingle bar in Palmer Cove and moved it, in a few weeks, from the clutches of the sea to cement mixers at what became Boyndie aerodrome – RAF Banff. In nearly 70 years the sea has never quite replaced it.

The airfield was opened on 21 April 1943 and was originally used for training aircrews in Airspeed Oxford and Avro Anson twin-engined planes. They too were in brilliant yellow livery. Almost inevitably, some crashed with the loss of young lives, but casualties were much heavier when, in early September 1944, the Training Wing was replaced with battle-hungry Mosquitoes and Beaufighters. These were then part of Coastal Command, and the intention was to destroy or interrupt enemy coastal freighters and defence ships off the Norwegian coast and deep in the fjords. The anti-aircraft defences in the restricted flying space of the fjords were formidable and this writer, as a boy, watched badly shot-up aircraft struggle over the cliffs to crash land at Boyndie. Four or five squadrons were based at Banff, including the famous 333 Squadron of Norwegians who, using their local knowledge, acted as pathfinders for the multinational other squadrons.

Many wives and girlfriends of the pilots and other aircrew lived in and around Banff. They could often be seen anxiously counting in the planes – usually around 5p.m. – as they straggled back over the town after a raid. The crews themselves enjoyed some free time in the town. They were welcome in pubs and homes alike, and many people would do with fewer rations to give meals to airmen and WAAFs alike, regardless of rank. The writer's own parents held open house for flyers and ground crews alike, and I still have the autographs and thankyou notes from many. Frequently there would be as many as 20

An Operations Room briefing at RAF Banff, 1944.

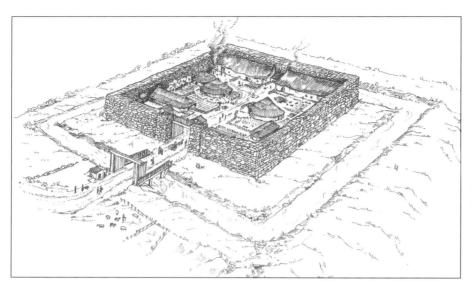

Roy Chillingworth's impression of Banff Castle in the early Middle Ages. The remaining walls are to the right and top of the drawing.

Above: *Remains of a medieval gateway at Banff Castle.*

(© Tommy Bod)

airmen and airwomen in our house for snacks, even meals, and usually games of cards or just relaxed chat. They led tense and dangerous lives.

The commanding officer of RAF Banff was Group Captain Sir Max Aitken DSO DFC, son of Lord Beaverbrook and a fearless and distinguished flyer himself, not averse to leading a 'strike' in his own red-spinnered Mosquito. Because of his personal friendship (and frequent bridge battles) with my mother and father, Revd Dr D. Findlay Clark, I was given the thrill of my young life when Sir Max took me for a short flight one day in his own aircraft with the famous red spinners. After the war, my father baptised Sir Max's children in London, and during the war married several of the personnel from the base, frequently to local girls.

From time to time the pressure of constant stress and dangerous flying told on crews. On one notable occasion a squadron had enjoyed a stunning victory over Nazi torpedo bombers, shooting down nine out of 18. A certain amount of drink had been consumed on their return, and by late evening the town pubs had to turn them out. In high spirits, one might say, some tore off the protective chicken-wire stretched over a huge EWT (Emergency Water Tank) at the foot of Institution Terrace and went for a swim – fully clad. Others gained the Parish Church steeple and proceeded to ring the bell – an activity then reserved solely to announce a German invasion. RAF and local police descended on them in numbers, and several revellers finished up 'in jankers' back at the base. It put the lie to the much repeated: 'Nothing much ever happens in Banff'!

As schoolboys, we watched the strike-force 'formate' over the town, usually before lunchtime, with the steady roar of as many as 80 or 100 Rolls-Royce Merlin engines (each aircraft had two) shaking the school. They would then dive to just above sea

level for the North Sea crossing before climbing to attack an hour and a half later. They wrought tremendous havoc with Axis shipping, but suffered relatively heavy casualties themselves. Such attacks were carried out almost daily till the end of the war, when the base was closed down in June 1946. A deserved memorial to all who gave their lives flying out of RAF Banff stands just outside the town by the road to Portsoy, only a mile from the old runways, now a wind farm.

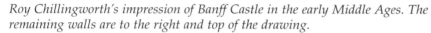

BANFF CASTLE
Ronald Lees, Julian Watson, Alistair Mason

The Building of the Ramparts

The date of the first Castle at Banff is not known. However, with the arrival of the Normans in the late-1100s the castle would have been fortified. King David I (1124–53) probably stayed there.

It was in the mid-1200s, during the reign of Alexander III (1249–86), that the northern coastline was under threat of a possible invasion by Haco of Norway. The royal castles of Aberdeen, Cullen and Banff were further fortified. The two remaining castle walls, in all probability, date from this period. This was a Scots Norman Castle, a simple square court enclosed by strong walls surrounded by a ditch. This was spanned by a drawbridge defended by outworks, with towers either side of the gateway.

Hammer of the Scots

Edward I (Longshanks), Hammer of the Scots, King of England, was to visit Banff Castle on three occasions during its occupation through the Scottish Wars of Independence. In 1291 the castle of Banff was delivered up to the English with all the other royal

96

The walls of medieval Banff Castle.

(© DR DAVID FINDLAY CLARK ARPS)

Banff Castle, built 1750. (© DR DAVID FINDLAY CLARK ARPS)

Pipe band Banff Castle, 1983. (© DR DAVID FINDLAY CLARK ARPS)

Castle Street outside the castle gates during the Prince of Wales's visit in 1883. (© BODIE COLLECTION)

fortresses. The Englishman appointed governor of the castle was Robert de Grey. After the battle of Dunbar in 1296 Edward I made a triumphal progress through the kingdom, staying at Banff Castle on 22 July. There he received the surrender of the castle and submission and homage of the local barons. Edward's army at that time amounted to 5,000 armed horse and 30,000 footmen.

Following the successful battle of Stirling Bridge (1297), under William Wallace, the English garrisons retreated.

Edward I returned to Banff for a second time on 4 September 1298, after the defeat of William Wallace at the battle of Falkirk on 22 July. The English were to remain at Banff Castle for the next 12 years. The king's final visit was in 1303 to hold court when he was on the way to Kinloss. William Wallace was betrayed and captured the following year.

The castle was still held by the English during the famous razing and laying waste of Buchan, the neighbouring Comyn province, in 1307 by Robert the Bruce. Provisions of corn, peas, beans, malt and wine were being ordered by Edward II in 1309. The castle was still being supplied by sea as late as 1310. When the English left prior to 1314 is unknown, but it was the last English stronghold held north of the Grampians. The fact the castle remained in English hands for so many years reflects the strength of the fortress at the time.

So in winter, when walking by the walls, treat the castle with care lest Longshanks, the Hammer of the Scots, should come striding out of the mist!

Royal Visitors

When David II, with his queen and sisters, visited in 1342, the town council spent 10s.9d. on entertainment. In 1470 Margaret, queen to James III, stayed, as did James IV in 1494. Mary of Guise, regent, held justice courts at Banff in 1556, and in 1557 she excused Banff from military call-up as the town was an easy landing place for the English. Her daughter, Mary Queen of Scots, was the last royal visitor to stay in the castle in 1562.

The Sheriffs of Banffshire

As sheriffdoms were instituted in Scotland, Banff castle became associated with the Sheriffs of Banffshire. The first recorded Sheriff of Banff is Henry Prat in 1242.

The surprising lack of references to Banff Castle in later years leads one to conclude the castle was no longer of significance, or militarily had effectively been dismantled. Robert the Bruce had fought a guerrilla style of warfare, destroying most of the castles in Scotland to stop the English using them as power bases. Sir Andrew Murray, Guardian of

First Minister Alex Salmond and singer Sandi Thom (right) opening the first ever Coast Festival in the grounds of Banff Castle, 2008. (© TOMMY BOD)

Scotland in the 1330s, had successfully resorted to the same campaign style against Edward III. Banff is not mentioned during the invasion of 1336, when Edward III caused destruction as far as Elgin and burned the city of Aberdeen. The castle remained the seat of the Sheriff of Banffshire. The office of sheriff was controlled by powerful families: Hugo Ross, Walter de Leslie, Patrick Ogilvie and James Stewart, Earl of Buchan. The building remained an administrative centre. In 1642 the walls are described as in ruins, with a small house within.

The Days of the Sharps

After the Earls of Buchan, first the Ogilvie and then the Seafield families took over as sheriffs. In practice the county was run by the sheriff deputy, based in the castle. One deputy, Mr Sharp, was in residence in the mid-seventeenth century, and his son James, born there, grew up to become Archbishop of St Andrews.

Archbishop Sharp (1618–79), one of the best-known natives of Banff, was probably not as bad as he was painted. Many people thought he was a rascal. Thus Oliver Cromwell said the man was an atheist, and, if we are to believe Bishop Burnet, King Charles II, even though he made him an archbishop, thought him 'one of the worst of men'. These two were men over whom Sharp had no power. What people under him thought is sometimes difficult to find out. He persecuted Presbyterians, and grumbled when the king issued royal indulgences to stop this persecution. Presbyterians generally saw him as a traitor, because at the Restoration he had been sent to London to represent them and had somehow ended up leading the other side.

On the other hand, it was simple common sense to see that the king was set upon a restoration of the bishops, and the church settlement in Scotland was not as harsh to dissenters as was the one in England. The rulers of Scotland then were a rough bunch, and the archbishop looks moderate beside them. Poor

Archbishop Sharp, in any case, was murdered in cold blood by a party of Covenanters on Magus Muir in front of his daughter.

His colleague, the tolerant and truly saintly Archbishop of Glasgow, Robert Leighton, had no joy whatsoever in his dealings with Covenanters, so probably Sharp's failings, though they didn't help matters, were not the root of the problem. These bishops were confronted with bigoted religious extremists. Sharp was not the first worldly prelate to be at least a competent administrator.

Banff had a positive view of Archbishop Sharp. He left money to the poor of the town. The big monument on the old kirkyard wall, backing onto Church Street, is a Sharp family tomb. Cramond points out acidly that almost every fact on the nineteenth-century plaque about the family added to the back of it is unreliable. The archbishop's own tomb in Holy Trinity, St Andrew's, makes the case for him at length in flowery prose.

Banff's Resident Countess

The hereditary sheriffdoms were abolished in 1748 as part of the response to the Jacobite Risings. The Earls of Findlater and Seafield left standing two of the outer walls of the old castle, and in 1750 built the Banff Castle of today on the cleared ground inside, a Georgian mansion-house by John Adam. Mary, Dowager Countess of Findlater and Seafield (1720–95) was the first lady of Banff in the second half of the eighteenth century. There was no rival countess at Duff House, as the second Earl Fife's marriage had broken up and he was indeed never there. There was tragedy in the Countess's own life: her husband killed himself in 1770 and her only son, the last Earl of Findlater (the Seafield title passed to a cousin) had to live abroad because he was gay. (He helped spread the taste for Adam-style neoclassical houses like Banff Castle in Germany.) As the next Earl of Seafield, who died in 1840, was a bachelor too, there was no question of the family needing a dower house when the Countess died. In any case, the Seafields loved Cullen rather than Banff.

The Castle in Modern Times

At about the same time as the new house was coming into use, the whole site was reconfigured to fill in most of the moat and to produce the fine lawn, but thereby, unfortunately, also to cover over the extensive archaeology which is surely associated with a large medieval Scottish castle. It was thought by the archaeologist most expert on the site that under the lawn may be the remains of several structures, probably including a substantial gatehouse.

Thereafter, the house was leased to a succession of tenants – local ministers, lawyers, etc., but eventually came into the possession of Mr T. Barton, the last private owner of the house, in the early twentieth century.

During the Second World War the building was requisitioned by the military as an administrative centre, and when hostilities ceased it was bought from the trustees of Mr Barton's estate by the Banff War Commemoration Fund to be a tangible memorial to those who took part in that conflict.

The present use of the building, under the Banff Castle Community Association, is as a community facility accommodating the needs of many small local groups and charities.

DUFF HOUSE
Charles Burnett

Unquestionably the finest building in Banff, albeit unfinished, is Duff House, located just south of the town on the west bank of the River Deveron.

William Duff of Braco, first Lord Braco, and then Earl Fife, commissioned the architect William Adam in 1735 to design a new residence to suit the status of a wealthy earl. He had a home in Banff, the old Ogilvie Lodging, long since demolished, but there is one heraldic reminder, a carved stone panel.

Unfortunately, the relationship between Earl Fife and his architect broke down, there was a lawsuit and the house was unfinished and left uninhabited by the earl. The architect intended the house to consist of a central main block with flanking curved wings terminating in two-storey pavilions.

The quality of the exterior carving and decoration of Duff House is quite outstanding; there is nothing else to compare with it north of Hopetoun House, near Edinburgh. It was the 2nd Earl Fife, James Duff, who completed the interior of the house, and made improvements to the Duff House estate. He caused the building of the Bridge of Alvah to connect his estates on either side of the River Deveron and he transported the remains of his ancestors from other places of burial to a mausoleum he built in the grounds. This is near the ice house, created for the storage of ice from the winter for use in the summer. The ice house consists of an egg-shaped brick structure sunk within a mound of earth with a top hatch through which ice was deposited. There is a side door for the removal of the ice.

Among other improvements, the earl had a temple built on Doune Hill, which overlooks Banff on one side and Macduff on the other. The latter was founded as a Burgh of Barony by the 2nd earl in 1783. After Banff Bridge was completed in 1779, the earl constructed a boundary wall between his estate and the town, along with two lodges and gates at the west end of the bridge. The 2nd earl was conscious that Duff House lacked full accommodation without the wings, and he commissioned plans in 1764 for wings of a different design from those of William Adam. The wings were never built, and it was not until 1870

A gardener in the vinery at Duff House in 1890, located in Airlie Gardens. (© BODIE COLLECTION)

A memorial stone for the Duke of Fife's dogs, Bevis, Tip and Barkis, in the Wrack Woods. (© TOMMY BOD)

that a new kitchen and bedroom wing was added to the east side of the house.

The new wing came into its own when the house was filled with a party of 19, including the Prince of Wales, from 13 to 17 November 1883, and they and their servants had to be accommodated. Balls, shooting expeditions and entertainment were all arranged by the 6th earl. This may have been part of the plan which came to fruition six years later, when the earl married the Prince of Wales's daughter, Princess Louise, and became the Duke of Fife on the morning of his wedding.

The duchess was not overly fond of Duff House; she found it rather damp and too close to the town,

The dovecot at Montcoffer.   (© TOMMY BOD)

and as a result the duke rebuilt Mar Lodge on Deeside, which then became the Fifes' principal residence in Scotland. The Mar estate had been purchased by the shrewd 1st Earl Fife after the Earl of Mar had been forfeit for his part in the 1715 Jacobite Rising. Mar Lodge was for shooting originally, but became a lavish Edwardian country house with its own chapel and ballroom. The 1st duke and duchess are buried in the chapel. For some as yet unexplained reason the duke began to sell off most of his land holdings in Moray, Kincardineshire, and Banffshire, retaining only the Mar estate in Aberdeenshire.

In 1907 he gifted Duff House and over 100 acres of surrounding land to the burghs of Banff and Macduff for the mutual benefit of the two towns. All the contents were removed except for a very large mirror in the north drawing-room.

Since 1907 the burghs and their local government successors have gradually sold off the land or turned it from grass-land to sports grounds and a play-ground. In 1908 the house became a hotel, making much of the fact that the Prince of Wales had once been a guest there. As part of the new facilities added to the house for the benefit of guests was a nine-hole golf course, laid out on the east side between the house and the River Deveron.

The hotel was never a huge success, but in 1913 Duff House was leased as a high-class sanatorium. This was to prove very successful. The staff consisted of a senior physician, two assistant doctors, three chemists, a consulting bacteriologist, a dental surgeon, a radiologist, and a matron with ten nurses. Duff House Sanatorium provided the scientific treatment of disorders of the metabo-

lism, such as gout, diabetes and obesity. The sanatorium was fully equipped with such up-to-date facilities as laboratories, radiography machinery, sun-ray rooms, a massage room, special bathrooms and a kitchen where specialised diets could be prepared. The sanatorium proved so successful that a request was made for permission to build an extension to the house. The Duff House trustees decided this would not be suitable, with the result that in 1923 the sanatorium was moved to Ruthin Castle in North Wales. Several of the Banff-born staff also went with the doctors to the new location in the south.

Once again, having been the residence of a duke, a hotel and a hospital, Duff House was ready for another role to play.

The trustees decided to lease the house to a hotel company, so once again rooms were altered to suit the new role. Former laboratories became bedrooms, but the main public rooms, vestibule, drawing-room, dining-room and billiard room remained as they were. Further changes were made to improve the facilities, including new parquet floors in the vestibule and drawing-room on the second floor. This enabled the latter to be also used as a ballroom. The hotel became the location for much of the social activity in Banff, and competed with the Fife Arms Hotel in Low Street, which had originally been constructed by the 4th Earl Fife as over-flow accommodation for Duff House in 1843. It replaced the former Black Bull Inn, which had stood on the same site. Behind the Fife Arms Hotel was the large vegetable garden which served Duff House during its several functions as residence, hotel, hospital and hotel.

Duff House Hotel continued to operate until the outbreak of the Second World War. It was requisitioned by the government and initially turned into a centre for the reception of aliens – Germans and Austrians who had fled from Nazi Germany.

However, by the beginning of October 1939 Duff House became a

Left top: *Fishing temple on an island on the River Deveron.*   (© TOMMY BOD)

Left centre: *Folly on Mount Carmel, Duff House grounds. The story goes that the medieval mound was built with stones carried for penance.*

Left bottom: *Dovecot with Banff's market cross on top (Sandyhills).*

100

prisoner-of-war camp. Certain items have been found under the floorboards of the house which remind us of those troubled times. Those who were born after 1950 may not appreciate that food, clothes, petrol, confectionery and even furniture were rationed during the war because Great Britain was besieged by German submarines and many goods came by sea. Citizens were supplied with ration books which contained pages of tear-off coupons. Food and other necessities could only be purchased when the appropriate number of coupons were given to the shopkeeper.

In July 1940 a German bomb badly damaged the east wing of Duff House, killing six of the German prisoners and two of their guards. Soon afterwards, the prisoners were removed from the house. British soldiers were billeted there for a while, then the Polish 6th Lancers Reconnaissance Regiment arrived in 1942 to help guard the Banffshire coast against a possible German invasion. Evidence of their occupation of the house can be seen in the stencilled signs, which state 'No Smoking' or 'Fire Point' in Polish.

When the war ended poor Duff House stood empty and unloved for several years. In 1952 there was a suggestion that the ground floor be turned into a swimming pool, an alternative idea being that the house be demolished and the materials sold for the benefit of Banff and Macduff. The house was offered to the Duff House Royal Golf Club for use as the club house, but this was turned down.

Eventually, in October 1953, the house was gifted to the forerunner of Historic Scotland, along with 7.5 acres of land immediately surrounding it. Historic Scotland had to replace broken windows, renew lead which had been stolen from the roof and take down the horseshoe staircase balustrade for repair and replacement of missing parts. Gradually, the house was made wind- and water-tight and by 1975 visitors could view the rooms during summer months only. In 1977 the six lead statues at the top of the house were removed because of their deteriorating condition and replaced with fibreglass replicas.

An attempt was made to bring the house alive for visitors by placing plaster figures in some of the rooms. These looked like ghosts, and some people found them unnerving. By the end of the 1980s many people came to realise that Duff House was an underused facility which could become the magnet to draw tourists to the Moray Firth coast. Led by Historic Scotland, encouraged with enthusiasm by Timothy Clifford, director of the National Galleries, and supported by Grampian Region and Banff & Buchan district council, a legal consortium was founded on 21 July 1992 to draw up a plan to turn the house into a first-class tourist attraction.

Historic Scotland arranged for a researcher to go through the Montcoffer Papers in Aberdeen University to gather information on the construction history of the house and to discover which rooms

The Bridge of Alvah, Banff.   (© Dr David F Clark ARPS)

Duff House as William Adam visualised it.

were used for what purpose. The papers had been gathered by the Fifes' factor, William Rose. The sum of 2.5 million pounds was allocated by Historic Scotland to restore the interior of the house, to insert a new electric power supply, to fit central heating and to install, for the first time in a Scottish historical property, a complete fire alarm and fire suppression system.

A system of close-circuit cameras was installed to provide security throughout the building, and a new tearoom and kitchen were added for the convenience of visitors, along with lavatories and a shop. Paint scrapes were taken in the main public rooms so that the original schemes of decoration could be replicated. The National Galleries of Scotland agreed to provide pictures and period furnishings for the house. Fortunately, a collection in Fife which had not been seen for many years was provided on long loan. Many of the pieces from the Dunimarle Collection required extensive conservation before they could be displayed, and all the clocks had to be repaired before they could once more tell the time. By 1995 a transformed Duff House could once more adopt yet another role as a country-house gallery, providing a venue for cultural and other events. HRH the Duke of Rothesay officially opened the house on a beautiful sunny 28 June 1995. Since the opening, a summer and winter programme of events has taken place consisting of exhibitions, musical evenings, talks and demonstrations. In 1997 the first wedding since the house became a hotel was held in the great drawing-room, and many more couples have taken their vows there since then.

BANFF PARISH CHURCH
Alistair Mason

Banff has been a parish for more than 1,000 years, for half of that time as part of the undivided church of the west under the Pope. After the Reformation Scotland took some time to settle on a form of church government, and some generations had bishops and others didn't. There were not two denominations alongside each other, but just the Church of Scotland, sometimes Presbyterian, sometimes not. A modern Episcopalian would find the Church of Scotland when it last had bishops very Protestant indeed, with extempore prayers, long Calvinist sermons, stern church discipline and black

Banff Parish Church in the nineteenth century.

(© BODIE COLLECTION)

Banff Parish Church and the Collie Lodge, c.1880.

(© BODIE COLLECTION)

gowns. Sharp eyes at the time could see differences: the church under bishops used the Lord's Prayer and the Creed. When the parish minister of Banff reported in 1683 that his parish had few Papists, no Quakers and no fanatics, the people he called fanatics would, within five or six years, be the ministers who ran the Church of Scotland instead of the bishops. After the Revolution of 1688 Banff was only nominally Presbyterian until 1716.

The first Presbyterian minister in that year encountered a riot. This was quite usual, and normally the story would go that after years of patient work, he won them round. We are not told this about Mr Innes. The rival Episcopal chapel flourished, while the Parish Church fell further and further into disrepair. His successor in 1753, Dr Trail, did better. The rival chapel had been destroyed by Cumberland's army, and Dr Trail was learned and articulate. Banff struggled in vain to keep him when he was promoted to a divinity chair at Glasgow in 1761. His successor, Andrew Skene, was there for 30 years, and at last had the church rebuilt on a new site, its present one. He had a tremendous struggle getting the money out of the heritors, who were either devout Episcopalians or mean with their money. Mr Skene was a typical Moderate minister, the sort of person whom heritors normally liked, trying to make the world a better place by simple Christian morality and by common sense. A trained doctor, he published a 'Serious Address to the People on Infectious Fever'. Many ordinary lay people at the time called this 'a clatter o' cauld morality'. They wanted high-flying evangelical preaching; how we are all sinners, and it is all God's grace. So a rival chapel was set up for the seceders of the Relief Church. But most people, looking back on Mr Skene's ministry and his fine new church, thought he had done a good job.

The next minister was Abercromby Gordon (1793–1821). Everybody liked Mr Gordon. Even the Relief Church minister came back into the Church of Scotland. Mr Gordon came from a county family, and could mix with anyone. He was the first minister

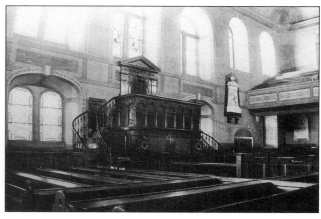

Banff Parish Church former layout and pulpit, pre-1920s.

Revd Dr Bruce.

At the Disruption the minister and half the congregation walked out, to set up a Free Church congregation. As often happens in church documents, nothing is said about this in the Parish Church records of the time. They pretended nothing had happened, and moved to appoint a new minister. They had to find a good number of new elders, and there was a legal protest about this, but the ringleader of the protest turned his energies to raising the money at last to build the steeple on the Parish Church. This was obviously a statement from the Auld Kirk that business was as usual, or even better. The steeple was finished at 7.45 on the morning of 11 August 1849.

There is no doubt that the Established Church in Banff was weakened by the Disruption. Nevertheless, they had two distinguished Victorian ministers, Dr Bremner (from 1845) and Dr Bruce (from 1873). Dr Bremner was much travelled, and lived in some style in Banff Castle. There is a *Life of Dr Bruce* in the local library. He was the centre of a literary and theological circle, and had a great reputation. In his time the church introduced an organ and stained-glass windows. Sometimes the impression is given that the Auld Kirk is the continuation of Moderatism, and dislikes religious exuberance, but Dr Bruce welcomed the Moody and Sankey campaign which brought American revivalism to Scotland. Was there ever any other event in Banff than Moody's preaching in 1874 that brought an audience of 15,000 at once? When Sankey sang in Banff Parish Church the whole congregation broke down; the choir were so moved they could not sing the next piece, and every single one of them 'that night gave their hearts to God'.

From the 1920s, there was a great scheme to beautify Banff Parish Church. Everything had focused on the pulpit, high up on the south wall with a great curve of galleries around it. They did not need all these seats; perhaps they never had since the Disruption. The galleries were removed and a High Presbyterian chancel built to the east. Very expensive materials were used, and the best stained-glass artist of the day employed. A new suite of halls was built alongside the church. The money came from three ladies, the Misses Katherine, Helen, and Susan Martin of St Catherine's, in Banff. Their father had made his money in Africa, and married there, and we must hope that the ladies' generosity bought them the social acceptance that sadly could not be guaranteed in Britain for people of mixed race between the wars.

In the twentieth century, the Presbyterian churches had come together by 1929 in one denomination instead of three. The Parish Church became St Mary's and the United Free became Trinity. Churches of the same denomination, they still each had their own ethos. A memorable ministry at St Mary's was the wartime one of Dr Findlay Clark. It

to have a drawing-room and a lively social life. Some of the stories of Lord Byron's childhood are set in the manse, because this was the sort of manse where young noblemen were visitors. The manse then was at the foot of Water Path, facing Ingleneuk. In a time of war and social tension, it may be there were great issues the Church of Scotland did not face. The Moderate party in the church, which had been the voice of good-humoured openness, became conservative along with the ruling class, confronted with the threat of revolution. Mr Gordon's Christianity was good-humoured paternalism.

The next minister was Francis Grant. As was customary, the town council challenged his appointment, because they thought they should appoint, not the patron, the Earl of Seafield. The issue of lay patronage had divided the church for a century, and certainly the Seafield trustees did rather tend to appoint men called Grant. The strange thing is that when the church split at the Disruption in 1843, Mr Grant went out. He gave up his job on the question of conscience, protesting against a system of appointing that he might have been thought to have benefited from. Mr Grant was a busy minister of the new style, led by the Evangelical party of the church. Banff now had (and all these were novelties) a Sunday school, Bible classes (male and female), a weekly prayer meeting, a parish library, a communicants' class, a minister's hour and a fund-raising association. Also moving with the times, the Parish Church had gas lighting, and so they moved the afternoon service to the evening.

is cheerfully recaptured in his son, David Findlay Clark's, book, *Remember Who You Are*. It was not just that he was dealing with German prisoners of war and Norwegian and British troops, but he seemed to have a more naturally public role than later ministers could easily achieve.

In 1994 the two parish churches united in St Mary's, which had been the original Parish Church, so there is once more someone with the historic title of parish minister of Banff. At the time of writing his name is Alan Macgregor.

◦─━✦☰✦━─◦

ST ANDREW'S CHURCH
Alistair Mason

St Andrew's Scottish Episcopal Church on the High Street is the third St Andrew's Chapel on the same site. The first was built in 1722, so no other congregation in Banff has met in the same place for so long.

After the Revolution of 1688 the Church of Scotland became Presbyterian instead of Episcopalian; that is they threw out the bishops who had been ruling the church and their followers. This was not a popular move in the north-east of Scotland, and in quite a number of parishes round here the Episcopal ministers remained in place. But Banff was a county town, so the minister and congregation conformed to being under the Presbytery, and when he died, his successor, William Hunter, was instituted as a Presbyterian minister. However, over the years it became apparent that he, like most of his congre-

gation, was quietly hoping for a return of Episcopacy, and, in particular, for a return of the Stuart kings. The Episcopalians were called 'Nonjurors' because they would not take the oath of abjuration, which renounced the royal house of Stuart.

In 1715, with the first Jacobite Rising, Mr Hunter

St Andrew's Episcopal Church, High Street.

(© BODIE COLLECTION)

Episcopal church Sunday-school outing.

(COURTESY OF MR J. MORGAN)

showed his true colours as a Jacobite so was deposed by the Presbytery in 1716. As soon as they dared, his followers built him the first St Andrew's Chapel. The chapel was built by the incorporated trades of the town, facing their own building on the other side of the High Street, and the trades used to process across the street into their own loft in the church. All the statistics suggest that a very large part of the congregation of the Parish Church moved up to St Andrew's. The old Parish Church was damp, unloved and falling to bits; the Episcopal chapel was a very fine piece of workmanship. They had to add new galleries as the congregation grew.

It was the first church north of Aberdeen to have an organ. Presbyterians didn't believe in organs, but Episcopalians did, and the organist was a focus for the musical society of the town. When Andrew Murray succeeded William Hunter, there had been some query about oaths to the king, but it looks as if the town council had let sleeping dogs lie.

Then came the 1745 Rising. Mr Murray was not a Jacobite hero, and when the Rising failed, he quickly took the oath to the House of Hanover. Little good it did, because Cumberland's troops destroyed the chapel in any case. Again, as soon as they dared, after a period of taking services in private houses, the chapel was rebuilt in 1752. This time it was a 'qualified' chapel. There were fierce penal laws, saying that no one ordained by a Scottish bishop could take services. The 'qualified' chapels sent young Scots down to England to be ordained. The congregation was the same people, trying to rebuild the St Andrew's chapel as it had been before, on the same site, with everything as it had been before. Only before outsiders called it 'the Jacobite chapel' and now they called it 'the English chapel'. A large part of the congregation disliked having to send their minister to England to be ordained, and after a time, in 1778, the Bishop of Aberdeen set up a rival Scottish Episcopal chapel on the Braeheads. Poor Mr Cordiner, the minister of St Andrew's Chapel, saw his congregation slip away to the real Scottish alternative.

In 1788 Charles III or the 'Young Pretender' died, and the Scots Episcopal Church decided that they had done their duty by the House of Stuart, and agreed to pray for King George. There was thus no longer a reason for two Episcopal chapels in Banff, and they united in St Andrew's, the bigger and better building.

These were Scottish ministers and people, under a Scottish bishop, but St Andrew's had been, in some sense, an 'English church'. There had been English regiments stationed in Banff, there were incomers from the south and some genteel Scots wanted to be in an 'English church', so a certain Captain Cuming took St Andrew's to court for daring to recognise the Bishop of Aberdeen. He tried and failed in court to prove that St Andrew's, Banff, was an English church. Litigation is misery whoever wins, and the church was nearly bankrupt in winning the case. St Andrew's has a verdict in a court of law to prove it is not an English Church, but the name has stuck.

The church was rebuilt in 1833, again on the same site, by one of the great architects of Aberdeen, Archibald Simpson. Anyone who has seen the west front of St Andrew's Cathedral on King Street, Aberdeen, also built by Simpson, will see the family resemblance. Like the majority of Episcopal churches in Scotland, St Andrew's is an elaborate little jewelled casket with memorial windows to wealthy Victorian donors. Because of a fire, it has lost the wonderful chandelier presented by the 5th Earl Fife, but it has still a window in memory of him. In 1913 a new chancel was built, with a useful hall underneath. The church had its own primary school from 1864 to 1921. Several of the priests have been in the Anglo-Catholic tradition, so, for example, people are likely to talk about Father Haines. Most of the twentieth-century clergy learnt their Anglicanism in England, as did some of the congregation, and so, quite naturally, St Andrew's has many English ways.

Numbers fell in the twentieth century. In 1957 the congregations of Banff and Portsoy were put together under one priest, and the little church in Macduff was closed. Later, Portsoy was given to Buckie, and Banff to Turriff. There has been no resident priest since 1970. In 2008 the priest-in-charge lives in Buckie. Most services are led by a local ministry team. A retired priest, Canon Haines, and a lay reader, Pam McLennan-Brown, live in Scotstown. It is surprising how resourceful a small elderly congregation can be.

<hr>

TRINITY AND ALVAH CHURCH
Alistair Mason

For 100 years the Free Church of Scotland has been the 'Wee Frees', a small, stern body, predominantly Highlanders. But from 1843 to 1929 the Free Church (from 1901 the United Free) was the alternative church in Scotland, with a church in every parish in the land. At the Disruption in 1843, more than a third of the Church of Scotland walked out, and it was the eager and generous ones who went. Every overseas missionary of the church, all the Church Extension charges, and the parish minister of Banff, with a large part of his congregation, went into the Free Church. Actually, the North East of Scotland, apart from the city of Aberdeen, where every minister went out, was not fertile territory for the Free Church, and over the years the established Church (the 'Auld Kirk') worked its numbers up again. The Free Kirk in Banff, looking back, would say that Mr Grant led half his congregation out; the Auld Kirk would say there were only 11 left the next

The Free Church, later Trinity and Alvah, now closed and its future in question. (© TOMMY BOD)

Banff Choral Society and Primary School Choir in Trinity Church, 1983.

Sunday, and look how they had built up since then.

The Free Kirk, after all, in every parish in the land, had to build a new church, and a manse, and pay a minister, and often set up a school. The Auld Kirk had largely depended on tithes, which were a tax on the heritors. Free Church congregations were wonderful fundraisers, so if you didn't want to be pestered for money, you were better at the Auld Kirk. In Aberdeen, where work has been done on who belonged to each congregation, it seems that people going up in the world, new money, joined the Free Church, while old money and the poor stayed with the Auld Kirk. The work has not been done to compare the congregations of Banff. Certainly Banff Free Church had some sheriffs and provosts, but the

chances are that primarily it exemplified the hard-working virtues of the Victorian middling sort.

Until they had a church, the new congregation met in the Congregational Church, but within a year the present handsome building was in place. After Mr Grant's death, the minister from 1857 to 1864 was Archibald Smellie. He coincided with the 1859 revival all along the coast, led by James Turner of Peterhead, which helped the meeting-halls and the Methodists, but also the Free Church. They said that he was 'more frank than discreet in his notice of secular events of the day' – probably an ardent Liberal. After him was the long ministry (1864–1904) of John Watson Geddie. One has the feeling that Mr Geddie was out-manoeuvred by Dr Bruce of the Parish Church. The Free Church in 1873 wanted to change the time of public worship from 12.00 to 11.00, and sent a delegation to Dr Bruce to propose it. Strange they felt the two churches had to coincide. They got no answer. Then, in 1876, the Free Church was being refurbished and arranged to use the Seafield Street Hall. The Church of Scotland then very graciously offered the use of the Parish Church, and the Free Church was made to appear narrow in refusing.

This was the age of temperance. The Free Church actually refused the Total Abstinence Society the use of their church in the 1850s, but as the century progressed the Protestant churches became sterner about drink. When the Prince of Wales visited Banff in 1883, the Free Church fitted out their schoolroom as a 'temperance refreshment room'. One cannot imagine the Prince patronising it!

Presbyterians had a long-standing suspicion of organs. The Parish Church introduced a harmonium in 1877. The Free Church had a vote on an organ in 1897, 137 for, 67 against, and the Kirk Session decided that not enough had voted for out of the congregation to justify the change. However, in 1900, without another ballot, they changed their mind, though the big bazaar of 1913 was to help pay for the not-yet-introduced organ. A democratic church, they had another ballot in 1911 to introduce individual communion cups.

In 1901, with the union with the UP Church, Banff had two UF congregations, the Free being called the High, and the UP on Seafield Street being Trinity. In 1914 they united in the one building, just called Banff UF (the Trinity church building was moved bodily to Whitehills), and from 1929 it was a parish of the United Church of Scotland, called Trinity, keeping the name of the vanished church. In 1961 the church was united with the little rural parish of Alvah, formerly linked with Ord, and then in 1992 with its neighbour in King Edward.

In 1994 the two parishes of Banff, with Alvah and King Edward, all united as Banff Parish Church. Given the realities of geography, population and finance, it was a typically sensible decision of the modern Church of Scotland. But years afterwards one meets nostalgia for Trinity and Alvah, which must have been a very warm and friendly 'belonging' sort of congregation. The last, very popular, minister was Harold Steven. No use has yet been found for the building, though the county played with the idea of turning it into the public library, and the Harvest Centre, using the old suite of halls to the full, would be very happy to take over the church as well. If there were the money, it would make a delightful concert hall.

OTHER CHURCHES
Alistair Mason

Let us begin with the Methodists. John Wesley (1703-91) was the greatest preacher of the Evangelical Revival. From 1742 to his death he travelled round Britain preaching, covering thousands of miles on horseback. Often he encountered angry mobs, urged on, sad to say, by the local clergy. In his later years he was a national institution; the societies he set up became the Methodist Church.

Wesley passed through Banff in 1764, but didn't preach. By 1773 there were Methodists in Banff. In May 1776 Wesley re-visited Banff, and was here two or three days, preaching first on the Battery Green, and then at the Grey Stone (at the top of Strait Path). He lodged in the house of a Mrs Allan, at the foot of Strait Path, now called in his honour Wesley House. The social establishment of Banff was very interested, and he had dinner one evening at Lord Banff's house on High Street, and the next at Admiral Gordon's (now the Carmelite Hotel) on Low Street. Mr Cordiner, the minister of St Andrew's Episcopal Church, invited him to preach on the Sunday in his chapel, where Wesley had "an elegant and crowded congregation". He preached there again on a flying visit in 1784 and Lady Banff gave him a chair, still treasured by the Methodists of Aberdeen.

The early Banff Methodists met in a rented room at the top of Strait Path. In 1820, with help from Lord Fife, they built a chapel on Reid Street, still there. It was a cramped site, liable to flooding, and they abandoned it in 1848, for a new chapel (opened in 1851) on Castle Street. Methodism prospered in the revival of 1860, which swept the fishing communities of the Moray coast. The present church was built on Seafield Street in 1878.

The early Methodist tradition was to move their ministers on quickly, working in "circuits" of churches. The last minister resident in Banff, Peter Jessup, left in 1969. The congregation now share a minister and a full-time lay pastor with the five other Methodist churches on the Moray coast. The Banff church has lately been agreeably refurbished, with comfortable chairs and a convenient meeting room behind. They have a fine little history of the church, called *Marching* (Burch and Borrowman 2007).

The Catholic Church was the church of all Western Europe until the Reformation. Banff saw occasional Catholics for the next few centuries. A Jesuit was imprisoned here briefly on his way to Aberdeen, then Edinburgh, then transported to the Continent with fierce threats of what would happen if he ever came back. The parish minister reported a 'few papists' in 1683, and in 1700 Adam Gall was up before the Kirk Session for getting Priest Dunbar to conduct his wedding. The continuing Catholic districts of Upper Banffshire and the Enzie were not so far away, so quite early in the nineteenth century a chapel was founded. It was a tiny building with a small congregation, up near the ropeworks on Coldhome Street.

Relations between Catholics and Protestants in the North East of Scotland had none of the tribal animosities of the industrial belt. It is not quite clear why there was a close called after Bishop Kyle, who certainly never lived in Banff. The town was proud of its fine new Catholic Chapel of Our Lady of Mount Carmel, built in 1870 on the smart Sandyhill Road. The architect was Alexander Ellis of Aberdeen, who also built St Mary's Cathedral in Aberdeen. Banff has retained its elaborate Victorian marble altarpiece, and a fine series of paintings of the stations of the cross. The parish priest from 1872 to 1890 was Aeneas Chisholm, who was obviously very gifted. He went on to be head of the seminary at Blairs, and then Bishop of Aberdeen. In Banff he was a leading light of the Town and County Club, and a founder of the Banffshire Field Club.

After something of a decline, Our Lady of Mount Carmel now has a packed church, because of the Polish and other Eastern European immigrants.

These churches have been part of Banff's history for hundreds of years. The other church in the town is the Harvest Centre, which has just celebrated its twenty-fifth anniversary. For most of these 25 years it met in Macduff, in a school hall. The flourishing Harvest Centre is part of the Riverside Church, a network of three congregations in Elgin, Buckie and Banff. To place them in a wider context, their leaders are part of the Fellowship of Scottish Charismatic Church Leaders, and they recognise the apostolic authority of David Brown, based at the King's Church, Aldershot, to whom they are accountable. They base all they do on the Bible, so if they clap and shout, lift their hands, dance, speak in tongues, or (like the other churches in Banff) play musical instruments, they have a verse from the Bible giving the precedent. They understand their mission in very Biblical terms: 'Will you help me find the people whose names are already written in the Book of Life?' They have Impartation Meetings and Healing Hours (not the only local church that does), and a 6.00a.m.

Ladies Early Morning Prayer Meeting. The people of Banff have been delighted to see the halls of the old Trinity and Alvah church beautifully fitted out for the Harvest Centre. One wonders what a history written in 100 years time would report of them and the other churches in Banff.

Visitors to Banff noticed in the eighteenth century how well the people of the various churches got on together. This may well be a continuing theme in the religious history of Banff, and the Banff Churches Together are evidence of happy co-existence.

CHURCHES OF THE PAST
Alistair Mason

Some closed churches represent congregations that simply moved. There are the ruins of the old Parish Church in St Mary's Kirkyard. If you look closely at the house on the opposite side of North Castle Street from the hospital, you might be persuaded that the tall window is evidence that it was indeed once a Scots Episcopal chapel. There was a Roman Catholic church up beside the rope works, and a Methodist one on Castle Street. Medieval Christianity quite often had little shrines, so the story that the Fife mausoleum is on the site of an older chapel may be true. There was a late-medieval chaplaincy of the Holy Rood, with some hint of a site around George Street, but the documents describing the actual endowment would fit better with a side altar within the Parish Church.

Our main concern here is with Christian denominations that once had followers in Banff and now have gone. It might make more sense if one suggested that there was a small, eager minority who could not abide the established church and in each generation tried something else. In the late-eighteenth century, with a Moderate minister in the Parish Church, a group seceded and set up a Relief Church. The Relief Church (for the 'relief of tender

The UP (United Presbyterian) Church in Seafield Street, which was relocated stone by stone to Whitehills.

(© BODIE COLLECTION)

consciences') was for people who wanted gospel preaching but didn't say that everyone else was damned, as sterner Seceders might. They were the first Presbyterian church to sing hymns and not just metrical psalms. When there was a change of parish minister, the Banff minister and some of his people went back into the Church of Scotland, but the rest bought the old Relief building and set up an Independent or Congregationalist church in 1808. The Congregational Union of Scotland grew out of the missionary preaching of the Haldane brothers. In 1797 James Haldane preached to large and interested crowds on the bank of the Deveron at Banff. Congregationalists give great power to the local group, the gathered flock, and perhaps some of their members from the Seceding tradition thought this went too far. At any rate the congregation split in 1820, and one half became a church of the United Associate Synod, one of half a dozen little Seceding Presbyterian churches. The point at issue was 'a case of discipline', and the Congregationalist minister, Mr Gibb, later emigrated to America. The Banff United Associates probably were what was called 'New Light' (who had more taste for revivalism than the 'Auld Lichts'), and the tradition evolved, after uniting with the Relief, into the UP (United Presbyterian) Church, one of the three big churches of nineteenth-century Scotland.

The Congregationalists continued in Banff, and John Murker, minister here for 50 years, was, within that tradition, very well known, famous enough to have his life written. The 4th Earl Fife sent Mr Murker sermons he had been reading for his comments, so not only Congregationalists listened to him. Their church was in the Seatown. After Mr Murker died in 1879, the Congregationalists migrated to Macduff, and flourished there for a time. It was an up-to-date Congregationalism, quite sure that it had moved on from Murker. The original UP church, the Associate chapel, was on the corner of Carmelite and Reid Street, where Tesco's stands at the time of writing. It was replaced in 1880 by a fine building on Seafield Street, built by the architect Alexander Ross of Inverness (there are few towns in the north without a Ross church). UP congregations were always happy to move their churches to a nicer part of town. The UP church exemplified the joys of a free market in religion. They didn't believe in a state provision of religion, just let people get on with it. When the two non-established Presbyterian churches, the Free and the UP, came together nationally in 1901, they didn't need two churches in Banff. So, with a happy resourcefulness, the UP church was moved bodily to Whitehills, where it is now the Parish Church. Imlach reports on a small Baptist congregation, meeting in a hall, in the 1860s. The map in the official history of the Baptists in Scotland shows a temporary preaching station.

Along the Moray coast, wherever there is fishing

there is revival. This has an impact on almost all the churches, but one visible strand left behind from revival are the Brethren meeting-houses. Banff had less of this tradition than Macduff, but there were meeting-houses, now gone. In the 1880s there was a Brethren meeting using the Town House, so they obviously had no hall of their own then. The Harvest Centre is probably the natural home for the Brethren tradition in Banff now.

St Mary's Kirkyard
Harry Mantell

The kirkyard on Carmelite Street is one of great antiquity and national significance. It appears that, according to Imlach, the old church within the kirkyard was rebuilt in 1471 by the town council. According to one source, a Carmelite chapel originally occupied the site, but this may simply be speculation. By 1749 the old church was in a 'ruinous way' and was finally demolished in 1797. It was replaced by the present Banff Parish Church, located on High Street. The only part of the original church remaining today is the recently restored Banff aisle.

The aisle was erected in 1580 by Sir George Ogilvy of Dunlugas as a memorial to his father and mother. It opened off the south side of the nave of the original St Mary's Church. Dr Mahood, in his 1919 book *Banff and District*, describes it as opening off:

> ... the South side of the nave by a moulded Gothic Arch resting on dwarf fluted columns with moulded capitals. The walls of the aisle were for the most part rebuilt by the last Lord Banff, who died in 1803. The pointed window is said to have been made of various stone mouldings from the Old Church. The moulded round-headed doorway was probably part of an earlier church.

The old church must have been an imposing building, measuring 94ft 3ins x 24ft 8ins internally, with a magistrates' loft reached by an external stair. Between 1664 and 1714, galleries were put up by various trades and individuals, including Lord Braco. By 1749 the church was, as mentioned above, in a 'ruinous way', and in 1761 the bells and clock were removed and part of the steeple taken down. In 2001, after years of neglect, Aberdeenshire Council, aided by Historic Scotland funding, carried out restoration and conservation work to the aisle. This work included the installation of a screen in the north side lancet-headed opening to prevent unauthorised entry into the interior and the installation of a slate roof to protect the otherwise unprotected vaulted stone roof.

The kirkyard has a wonderful collection of interesting and sometimes, to us, eccentric gravestones and tombs. These have been recorded in varying degrees of detail by a number of interested parties in the past.

Aberdeen City Archives, where the royal burgh of Banff records are now held, has in its possession what is described as a 'Plan of Churchyard' dated 1819. This is, in reality, a handwritten book numbering the lairs, and noting the names of those with rights to the lairs. This was drawn up after the old St Mary's kirk was demolished when considerable work was carried out to repair and secure the kirkyard and generally tidy it up. It was improved

Banff Aisle, Saint Mary's Kirkyard.

(© Dr David Findlay Clark ARPS)

Skull and crossbones memorial stone in Saint Mary's Kirkyard.

(© Tommy Bod)

Masonic memorial stone in Saint Mary's kirkyard.

(© TOMMY BOD)

with 'gravel walks, flower pots and shrubs'. Some years later it was described as being 'very tastefully laid out'.

In the mid-nineteenth century, Andrew Jervise (1820–78) collected epitaphs and inscriptions from burial grounds and old buildings in the North East of Scotland. In his book of that name, Banff is not mentioned. He had, however, unpublished material relating to Banff. These manuscripts are held by the National Museums of Scotland in Edinburgh. William Cramond in fact consulted them when he was researching the churchyard section of his *Annals of Banff*, published by the New Spalding Club in 1893 in two volumes.

James Imlach, in his *History of Banff* of 1868, chronicled the old churchyard of Banff, although William Cramond says of this:

Mr Imlach's copy of the inscriptions is very inaccurate, and has not been utilised [for Cramond's transcript of inscriptions in the Annals] *but his notes have been found serviceable.*

A.L. Nicol's *Banff and Neighbourhood*, a popular handbook of 1879, gives a general description of the churchyard and some of the more interesting stones.

The most detailed chronicle of the contents of the old churchyard is, not surprisingly, given in William Cramond's wonderful and meticulously compiled *Annals of Banff*.

The churchyard section includes an astonishing 568 descriptions of gravestones. In 2007, Banff Preservation & Heritage Society, with help from Aberdeenshire Council, published a booklet reprinting this section from Cramond's *Annals of Banff*.

Cramond's compilation was referred to in Alan Edward Mahood's *Banff and District*, published in 1919. In it is a rough map of the churchyard giving a useful cross-reference between his notes and Cramond's notes on some of the stones.

Town council and church records mention the kirkyard from early days.

In 1664 the magistrates ordained that the inhabitants of the burgh were liable for 'putting up the kirkyaird dykes', and in 1676 'the heritors to be stented £40 for building the kirkyaird dykes'. In 1682 there is a reference to a 'stent of £93 for melioration of the kirkyaird dykes', and in 1683 it was reported that: 'The fabrick of the church and kirkyard dykes are found to be in very good order.'

By 1749, however, the church was, as mentioned previously, in dire condition, and in 1750 the presbytery found that a sum of £814.15s. Scots (approx £81 sterling, or £8,000 at today's value) would be necessary 'for reparation of the kirk of Banff and kirkyaird dykes' – a considerable sum of money in those days. A new gate to the kirkyard was put up in 1772 at a cost of £3.4s.2d., but by the end of the century it was apparent that construction of a new church was inevitable.

In 1792 the town council appointed a committee to consider a proposal:

... made by the heritors for giving off the roof and materials of the old Church, upon condition that the town and community take the burden of upholding the dykes of the churchyard.

About half a century later, a council committee reported on 7 April 1841 that the walks, etc., of the churchyard 'are in a bad condition, but are being now repaired, and that the map of the Churchyard and book of reference had been discovered after having been lost.' Was this the 1819 'Plan of Churchyard' book now in the Aberdeen City Archives? By 1853:

The churchyard and burying ground had got into a very ruinous and confused state, and that there is no proper means of ascertaining what spaces are properly available for interments.

The provost was requested:

... to wait upon the Minister with the view of getting him to convene a meeting of the Heritors and Magistrates, for the purpose of taking into consideration the condition of the churchyard generally, and of

adopting measures for the improvement and regulation of it in the future.

In the same year, the possibility of providing a new cemetery rendered necessary by the crowded state of the old one was being considered. (Mahood reports as many as 40,000 bodies were buried over the years in the kirkyard.) The latter was finally closed for burials in 1862 when the present Sandyhill Cemetery was opened.

In 1863 an Extraordinary Head Court meeting recommended to the council that 'the freedom of the burgh be given to Lord Macduff in gratitude to the Earl of Fife for giving up his houses adjoining the Churchyard for its improvement'. Earlier in the year a letter to the council from the factor for Lord Fife's trustees, Mr Hannay, formally offered to grant to the provost and magistrates the old houses lying on the west of, and contiguous to, the churchyard. They had to undertake:

... to see that the improvements specified by Lord Fife should be carried out, viz, to demolish the old buildings and continue the wall and railing now in progress round the other parts of the Churchyard.

The grant was accepted and thanks of the council were offered to 'His Lordship'.

In 1873 William Farquhar of Sruan Cottage, near Aberdeen, bequeathed to the town £400 for maintaining the kirkyard and for looking after his family's tomb. Cramond reports, 'the sum was not paid in full [19s. per £1] his property in Gibraltar not having been realised.'

This was not the only legacy recorded for the churchyard. In 1654, for example, an Alexander Craig 'mortified 100 merks to the kirk' (a merk was 13s.4d.); in 1869 Miss Margaret Strachan of Cortes bequeathed the sum of £50, and in 1884 Miss Cruickshank, Bridgend, Fyvie, bequeathed £17.9s.2d. for keeping in order her burying ground in the old churchyard.

The Aberdeen City Archives hold an interesting 'Cash Book of Alan Farquhar's Bequest for Keeping Old Churchyard'. Entries start in 1873 and end in 1932. The cashbook shows, for example, that salaries were paid to the following people appointed to look after the churchyard:

1873–83 John Kynoch
1883–98 Charles Greig
1898–1917 William Duncan [sexton]
1917–21 William Rennie
1921–32? Robert Greig [the book ends in 1932]

John Kynoch was also the beadle and church officer. Church records show that when he resigned in 1882, Charles Greig was appointed 'in his room'. His duties were to include 'to keep the grass and grass

walks in the old burial ground in proper state'. The cashbook records expenses for buying implements and materials from local shopkeepers like Peter Lyon (scythe), Raeburn & Sons (plants), A. Cameron & Sons (tree supports and ropes), I. & A. Munro (wheelbarrow) and George Cumming (Blacksmith), etc., and repairs are recorded to gates, railings, locks and masonry.

Payments for repairs included to the heirs of Charles Cook for painting railings, and the Farquhar tomb railings and gravestones in 1878; to William Lawrence, mason, for 'repairing gable of Old Church' in 1895, possibly a reference to a part of the old church adjacent to the Banff Aisle still standing at that time; to Watson Bros. for repairing a lawnmower in 1925, and to a town council mason for driving shingle to the churchyard in 1926. Works recorded included repairs to items 'broken by boys', removing rubbish thrown into the churchyard by slaters and rebuilding the arch and gateway to the old churchyard 'shattered by wind'.

Many of the gravestones are now difficult to decipher, worn and moss and lichen covered as many of them are. Banff Preservation & Heritage Society has, however, embarked on a project to record and photograph the stones as they are to be found today. The kirkyard, nevertheless, remains an important feature in Banff, as well as providing a peaceful and tranquil refuge away from the bustle of the streets around.

BANFF ACADEMY – INTO THE TWENTY-FIRST CENTURY
Donna Scott

Formal education was underway in Banff at least 500 years ago. At first glance the educational experience of the average Banff Academy pupil today may seem to bear little relation to that of their sixteenth-century predecessors. The academy provides a comprehensive, nondenominational education for over 1,000 pupils, the vast majority of whom actually live outwith the town of Banff. Pupils

An Edwardian view of Banff Academy.

(© BODIE COLLECTION)

Sandyhill Road with former 'Jannie' Robertson's house and old school building at the foot of Bellevue Road.

(© BODIE COLLECTION)

undertake a broad range of subjects, from the arts, sciences and humanities to lifestyle, technology and computing. As a New Community School, other agencies such as community education combine with teaching staff to provide an education in the broadest sense for young people in the local area. In addition, the Curriculum Support Unit ensures no one is excluded because of learning difficulties or physical disability. However, on closer inspection, it seems that no matter the century, there are always unruly pupils, debates over the curriculum and the perennial issue of funding to contend with, as this tour through the history of the school will show.

The earliest records show that by 1544 a grammar school had been established and was being run by Dominie William Clerk. In 1585 continued educational provision appears to have been assured when Bishop Cunningham granted a charter for the long-term provision of a grammar school in the town, to be presided over by a rector. This arrangement was confirmed by James VI in 1592, and a tenth of the King's rents from certain lands were earmarked for the maintenance of the school. However, these funds were never drawn, and the original charter was only rediscovered in the early-nineteenth century.

It seems remarkable that this kind of oversight could have occurred given that educational funding, then as now, was a major policy issue in post-Reformation Scotland. John Knox's vision of 'a school in every parish' was a popular one, but the real struggle would be over who was going to pay for it. In 1616 a Privy Council Act required that local landowners provide for a parish school 'where convenient means may be had'. This duly provided a useful loophole for unenthusiastic heritors. For the rest of the seventeenth century, repeated attempts were made to compel landowners to meet the educational needs of their area, but most education was provided privately, as was the case at Banff Grammar.

In common with the rest of seventeenth-

century Scotland, the most affluent residents of Banff were clearly keen on sending their children to school. In 1632 the school, which was housed in Gledisgreen on Carmelite Street, required 'bigging of seates', which the town council funded. However, George Chalmers, who was appointed schoolmaster in 1620, must have proved an asset to the local community; in addition to his school duties, George also read Common Prayer and Chapters in Banff kirk every morning and evening, and also fulfilled the roles of the precentor and session clerk. By 1693 the entire school was being run on a budget of £185 Scots. The schoolmaster's salary was £120 and the precentor's £50, leaving the remaining £15 for general maintenance.

By the early-eighteenth century, Banff town council were committed enough to providing a quality education that they consulted one of the top Latinists in the country, Thomas Ruddiman, on the question of appointing suitable rectors. Perhaps this was wise, as in 1698 Alex Syme had demitted his office as rector after 'several of the scholars have rebelled against their former maister and wer incouraged to do so by their parents'. Bad enough when the pupils 'break the glasses windows and cut, braek or abuse the dasked [desks]', but quite another when their parents encourage them!

Any lessons learned from this, however, seemed to have been forgotten with the appointment in 1773 of Robert Alves, whose: '... simplicity laid himself open to the jeers of his roguish pupils... nothing would induce him to punish them with the rod... so they defied his authority altogether.'

Some of the 'rogues' even hid fireworks ('crackers') in his jacket while he was wearing it, and lit them using a trail of gunpowder. Understandably, a long period of absence followed for Mr Alves, but at least on this occasion there was punishment for the culprits – a flogging by the town drummer. However, by the time Robert Alves left it was felt that the school 'which used to be an ornament and convenience to the town had dwindled away to nothing...'

Fortuitously, Dr George Chapman LLD, a local boy originally from Blackton in Alvah, was invited to become rector in 1786. The town council had built a new school near the old site. Chapman had been very successful in running Dumfries Grammar and he was asked to take over in Banff. Chapman's approach to education reflected a changing Scotland. In the industrial age it would be developments in physics and chemistry that would enable Britain to emerge as 'the workshop of the world', but traditional grammar schools in early modern Scotland had been well named, as they largely provided only a

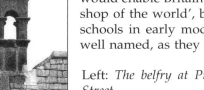

Left: *The belfry at Pirie's Free School, Clunie Street.*

(© TOMMY BOD)

Pupils outside the old Banff Academy, now the Primary School, with 'Jannie' Robertson (on the left) *and headmaster McKenzie* (far right), *1930s.*

classical education, with emphasis on Latin and Greek grammar as well as religious instruction. This suited the sons of upper-class lairds, but the embryonic middle classes, the merchants, required many more vocational skills, such as bookkeeping and foreign languages, and therefore found this traditional curriculum largely irrelevant. Surprisingly for us, even the elementary skill of writing was not always guaranteed to be taught well, or even at all, at a grammar school. In 1792 the *Old Statistical Account of Scotland* remarked that Latin was 'taught well' at Banff Grammar, but many pupils attended other institutions for the remainder of their subjects, including writing.

Chapman, though, was a champion of the introduction of new 'scientific' subjects such as algebra and practical geometry, and proceeded to turn Banff Grammar into a model of modern education. All the public schools of Banff were brought together into a new 'Academy', and a wider curriculum offered mathematics, French and English, along with the classics and principles of rhetoric. Chapman, who had already produced such influential educational works as *A Treatise on Education* and *Hints on the Education of the Lower Ranks of the People*, succeeded in establishing a thriving institution. The *Statistical Account of Scotland* observed in the 1790s that: '... the plan of instruction which Dr Chapman laid down has

Pupils from Banff Academy leave Banff Bridge Station for their trip to France in the early 1950s.

been strictly adhered to by the different teachers and has answered the expectations of all concerned', adding that 'the seminary is currently in a flourishing state'. Indeed, by August 1797 there were

180 regular pupils and the rector was aided by four assistant masters.

The high academic expectations of George Chapman were safeguarded by the next incumbent to the post of rector, John Cruickshank. He sent his pupils out into the world equipped with 'the sinews of high education and firm discipline', taking his responsibilities so far as to insist to the town council that 'strolling players' were most unwelcome in the community as 'anything of that kind would very much unhinge the youth who attends the school here'. The town council were duly convinced of the danger such thespian diversions could pose and banned travelling actors, citing them as 'prejudicial and hurtful to younger members of the community'. The importance of the theatre as a valued extra-curricular activity at Banff Academy would clearly have to wait until the late-twentieth century, in the golden age of the school pantomime.

Such was the demand for education in the Banff area in the late-eighteenth century that in 1805 records show that an extra storey was to be built onto the school. Rector Cruickshank had warned as early as 1797 that the buildings were overcrowded. Despite various extensions and improvements, by 1835 it was still noted that the school was 'unhealthy and subject to frequent inundations', a situation probably not helped by the presence of a neighbouring slaughterhouse.

A contribution from a generous benefactor meant Banff Academy could address this problem. James Wilson, a Banff merchant who had made his fortune in Grenada, left £6,567.6s.1d. in a 'charitable trust'. The provost, bailies, dean of guild and the treasurer decided to use the funds for an ambitious programme. The Grammar School would be rehoused and the architect, William Robertson of Elgin, was to design the new Grecian Ionic building, the façade of which can still be seen at the beginning of the High Street. The poorer residents would also be served by the establishment of an 'institution for moral and religious instruction of labouring poorer classes so as to fit them to become useful members of society'. However, should any of these Wilson's Institution pupils prove to be particularly able, they could avail themselves of bursaries for the Grammar School itself.

The town council also felt an infant school could be established by employing the 'Madras' or monito-rial system of tuition. Older pupils would pass on the information they learned to other pupils, allowing for a cost-effective system that could give a basic education to large numbers of children. This system was very much disliked by the teachers of the Grammar School, who felt that this pupil-led approach minimised the importance of the teacher as an expert professional. It is interesting to note that in the early-twenty-first century 'peer education' has again become popular, and the concept of the teacher as a 'facilitator' of education rather than simply a provider of knowledge has again gained currency, although, happily, for proven educational benefit rather than reasons of financial economy. Finally, the town council were pleased to provide a museum, which remained as such until 1902, when a new museum was built; the school used the old one as a central hall.

However, not all of Banff's citizens could afford to send their sons to such a prestigious institution as the Grammar School. This did not mean that the lower classes were content to sit back and neglect their children's education. Church schools existed in the area, funded by poor relief and voluntary donations. Charity schools also operated, such as Pirie's Free School, founded in 1804. However, by far the main provider of primary education in the eighteenth and nineteenth centuries was the private sector. A small fee was paid daily or weekly, but a lack of money and a need for child labour at home meant it was likely that less than half the pupils on the roll attended regularly for six months or more.

Educational standards in the average 'adventure' school were also pitifully low. Only the two Scottish R's (reading and religious education) were tackled, and usually addressed together by using the Bible as the main teaching text. Writing, even for the purposes of producing legible handwriting, let alone as a medium of self-expression, was not seen as essential, and in the worst schools the teachers themselves did not even have this basic skill. Jean Horn held classes in Wright's Close and 'she could not write. Her reading exercises were from the Bible with all the "big" words left out of the narrative.' Vocational activities such as knitting, needlework and spinning were taught instead. These dame-schools, run, as the name suggests, by older females, were, on the whole, more effective as providers of basic childcare than of education. For many of these teachers, education was only one of many ways to earn a living; Jessie Guthrie, who taught in Clunie Street, supplemented her earnings with a profitable sideline in white pudding and toffee ('plonky').

There was also the thorny issue of female education for the better off. The four ancient universities of Scotland did not bestow degrees on women until 1896, so perhaps Banff Academy was actually ahead of its time by admitting female pupils 30 years prior to this. Before 1866 middle-class female educational needs would have been attended to by institutions such as the Misses Mitchell ran in Reid Street. The nineteenth-century view of the limited intellectual capacities of women meant that girls' schools like the 'Boarding School for Young Ladies' run by the Misses Martin in St Katherine's, disproportionately concerned themselves with achievements like deportment. Mattresses were exchanged for hard boards and one unfortunate pupil was made to walk the length of the drawing-room with a pile of books on her head every day for a week to redress the heinous 'crime' of being caught with her elbows on the table. However, although it took 22 years of coeducation at Banff Academy before the first girl, Miss Annabella Leith Lumsden, became dux of the school in 1888, it appears that by 1925 the girls had very much settled in, as that year all five major school prizes were won by female pupils.

By the late-nineteenth century the educational climate was changing again. The landmark 1872 Education (Scotland) Act ensured elementary education for every child in Scotland between the ages of five and 13. The school-leaving age was then raised to 14 in 1884. In 1918 the official leaving age was raised again to 15, although with the difficulties of the interwar period, this wasn't fully implemented until after 1947. In response, in 1883, all branches of the school were combined into 'Banff Burgh School', and underwent an official name change again in 1903 to 'Banff Academy'. Structural extensions were added in 1898 by Marshall Mackenzie, an architect from Aberdeen, at a cost of £3,000, and in 1911 a new block was added at a cost of £6,000. A fire in 1921 gutted the entire central block, leaving only four classrooms, the janitor's house and the front façade, and it was 1934 before the replacement primary school was finally completed.

In the aftermath of the Second World War, the battle to slay 'Ignorance' as one of the 'Five Giants' of post-war Britain would continue to be fought in Banff, as elsewhere. Secondary education in Scotland had had a two-tier system since the 1920s, with the more academically able pupils attending different schools. Selection of pupils for the more prestigious Senior Secondaries would now take place at the end of primary schooling. Those children who didn't make the grade could expect a more vocational and practical education in a Junior Secondary school. The *Third Statistical Account of Scotland* in 1961 did note that Junior Secondary schools in Banff still provided classes in history, art and science. It also mentioned that 'this process of classifying children by ability has not been willingly accepted by all parents'. Acceptance for a Senior Secondary school was not an automatic guarantee of the attainment of prestigious qualifications either; the *Third Statistical Account* reports that, although a quarter of children in the area received Senior Secondary education, only nine per cent of all pupils achieved a leaving certificate, with only five per cent reaching the standard required for university entrance.

On 12 November 1969 Banff Academy finally moved to the present site on Bellevue Road. Built at the cost of £712,000, it was the first purpose-built comprehensive school in the North of Scotland. It ushered in an era when pupils of all aptitudes and abilities would learn together. This culminated in the introduction in the 1980s of Standard Grade exams for S4 pupils, whereby pupils of different abilities

followed common courses. The Curriculum Support Unit was also developed in the late 1990s to include all young people in the school community, regardless of learning difficulties or disabilities, and officially opened in November 2002.

It can be seen, then, that Banff Academy has been a central part of the local community for well over 500 years. From a small institution for the local elite to a New Community School providing integrated services for all young people in the area, it has grown in ways that the earliest recorded Rector William Clerk would have found hard to imagine. Nevertheless, despite the passage of time, the actual business of education has remained the same because what to teach young people, how to motivate them and how to pay for it are eternal considerations that the Academy will always have to address.

BANFF MUSEUM
Dr David M. Bertie

Banff Museum, founded in 1828 by 'The Banff Institution for Science, Literature, and the Arts, and for the Encouragement of Native Genius and Talent', is the oldest museum in Scotland north of Perth to have had a continuous history since its foundation. Only Inverness could lay some claim to an older museum, but its original museum, founded in 1825, was extinct by 1834, and the present Inverness Museum was founded in 1877.

The origin of the Banff Institution and its museum lie in the discovery of a bed of fossils following a rock fall at a mill lade at Gamrie in the winter of 1826/27. James Christie (1774–1854), solicitor in Banff, investigated this discovery in early 1828 and forwarded a small collection to the Geological Society of London, where they were identified as fossil fish. In August that year Christie, along with John Pringle

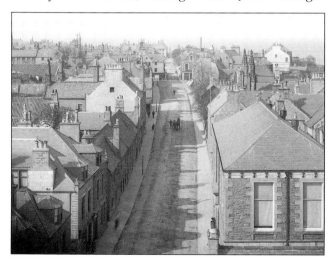

Aerial view looking along High Street, with the museum building in the foreground. (© BODIE COLLECTION)

(1785–1853), who had been Sheriff-Substitute of Banffshire since 1821, and the Revd James Smith (1800–53), mathematical teacher at Banff Academy since 1823, founded the Banff Institution. The Institution's very first lecture was by Christie on the Gamrie fish fossils.

The Institution had a fairly lively existence until the early 1830s. Monthly lectures were presented, though half of these tended to be given by the three founders. Many of Christie's lectures were based on his geological interests. Three lectures given by Dr Robert Wilson (a graduate of Marischal College, Aberdeen; Marischal Museum has a collection of material brought back by him from the Middle East), who had been a notable traveller in Egypt, the Middle East and India, reflected the prevalent nineteenth-century interest of Western Europeans in Turkey – the so-called 'sick man of Europe'.

The museum received a stream of donations, both locally and from Banff residents abroad. Among the latter donations was a large collection of shells from Java, presented in 1835 by James Milne (who was made a burgess of Banff for his generous donation), together with other material from the East Indies. He also presented a model of a Molucca vessel, made entirely from cloves; this is the oldest surviving item in the museum's collections today. One of the most significant early additions to the museum's collections was the Deskford carnyx, an Iron-Age war trumpet found about 1816 at Leitchestown Farm in Deskford parish.

The museum's first home was in Banff Townhouse, and this continued to give the Institution a physical presence when the society became somewhat moribund during the mid-1830s. When the new Banff Academy was built in 1838, the Revd James Smith, by now rector of Banff Academy, ensured that the central hall of the building was given over as the new home of the museum. This led to a renewed phase of activity in the Institution which lasted until the Disruption in the Church of Scotland in 1843. The social splits which the Disruption induced in the Banff populace seem to have ushered in another phase of dormancy in Institution life.

A growing interest in cultural affairs in Banff during the late 1840s and early 1850s was engendered to a great extent by the new editor of the *Banffshire Journal*, Alexander Ramsay (1822–1909). He instigated four series of public lectures in Banff and Macduff between January 1848 and March 1852. This led, in part, to the revival of the Institution in February 1852. The monthly series of lectures was re-established, new members were elected and donations to the museum were made. The museum was overhauled and a salaried sub-curator, Thomas Edward (1814–86), appointed. Edward had become known to the people of Banff over the previous decade as a notable naturalist, despite his humble

occupation as a shoemaker, with the *Banffshire Journal* regularly calling on his expertise. As well as holding lectures and reorganising and improving the museum, the Institution became active in promoting local educational initiatives. One key success was in encouraging Banff town council to establish an elementary school of design in the burgh in 1853.

Among the more active members of the Institution at this time were Dr Alexander Leith Emslie and David Grieve, Collector of Customs. Both these men had strong geological and natural-history interests. Emslie came to Banff about 1844 and collected fossils at Blackpots tile works at Whitehills and at Gamrie. He claimed to have found graptolite fossils at Gamrie and presented one to Hugh Miller when that geologist visited the area in 1847. (That fossil was shown in 1973 to have actually come from Peeblesshire.) During 1852 Emslie published in the *Banffshire Journal* a series of lists of flowers to be found in Banffshire. Grieve gave six lectures on natural history to the Institution between 1852 and 1854, most of which appear to have been based on actual research. A highly original lecture was given in August 1852 by Alexander Rae on 'The Stereoscope'. Rae, a druggist, had begun taking daguerrotypes in Banff in 1850, only eight years after the first such studio in Aberdeen. He was Banff's principal photographer all through the 1850s, and won a medal at Aberdeen in 1853 for his callodio-calotype portraits. In 1858 he took one of the earliest photographs of an eclipse of the sun.

The Institution's three founders all died within a matter of months of one another: Smith in January 1853, Pringle in December 1853, and Christie in August 1854. In the same period, Emslie left Banff in September 1853 for Auchtermuchty (he died in March 1854), while Grieve left for Dover in early 1854. This loss of key active members appears to have affected the Institution badly, and by 1859 it was virtually moribund.

In contrast, developments in the museum took on a new dynamism as two Institution members, Thomas Edward and the Revd Walter Gregor (1825–97), carried out pioneering research into the marine fauna of the Moray Firth. Edward and Gregor were making discoveries not only of species new to Banffshire, but of species new to Britain. The ultimate accolades came when two of their discoveries were named after them: the crustacean *Praniza edwardsii* in 1858 and the sea anemone *Gregoria fenestrata* in 1860. While their work was only occasionally reported in the form of lectures to the Institution, the list of their donations to the museum bears testimony to their practical achievements. This dynamism faltered after Gregor moved from the Banff area in 1863 to become minister of Pitsligo parish (Gregor's research interests turned thereafter from marine biology to folklore), but Edward continued to act as curator to the museum. In 1866 Edward was elected an Associate of the Linnaean Society in recognition of his natural-history work.

Donations to the museum during the period following the Institution's re-establishment were a mixture of natural history, geological, archaeological, and ethnographical material. Some natural-history specimens were purchased from Thomas Edward; this had been at the suggestion of David Grieve. Grieve had also been responsible for ensuring Edward got the job of stuffing a number of Banffshire bird specimens given by various Institution members. In July 1853, when the Revd James Smith's private museum was being sold off at after his death, the Institution bought a number of foreign and British birds for the museum. One of the most significant archaeological donations was that of the Gaulcross hoard (Pictish silver chain, armlet and pin) from Sir Robert Abercromby in December 1853. A number of items relating to the Banffshire astronomer James Ferguson (1710–76) were purchased in 1864, including the clock owned by Ferguson which had been previously owned by the American scientist Benjamin Franklin.

The Banff Institution was dissolved in 1875 and its museum handed over to Banff town council. Five years later, the Banffshire Field Club was formed with Thomas Edward as one of its founding members, and for some years this new body assisted the town council with looking after the museum. Edward continued to act as curator until his death in 1886. When the Free Library Act came into force in 1899, it was decided to build a new museum and library in High Street on the site of 'The Turrets'. The new building was completed in 1902 and the museum moved there from Banff Academy.

Additions to the museum during this period included a collection of rock specimens donated in 1885 by John Horne, one of the most outstanding Geological Survey geologists in Scotland. The pieta dug up in the churchyard of the old Parish Church in 1860, the only known example of a stone pieta found in Scotland, was presented to the museum in 1886. The 1st Duke of Fife presented a collection of arms and armour, including a rare amber- and ivory-handled carver set made in the Baltic region in 1600. The set of standard weights and measures that were made in 1707 for the burgh following the Union of Parliaments was purchased from Banff town council by the Banffshire Field Club and presented to the museum.

The Banffshire Field Club continued to assist in looking after the museum until the 1920s. The museum then entered a long period of near-dormancy during the mid-twentieth century. A number of key archaeological items, including in 1947 the Deskford carnyx and in 1962 the Gaulcross Pictish silver, were removed from Banff Museum to the National Museum of Antiquities of Scotland (now National Museums Scotland) in Edinburgh,

ostensibly to provide greater care for these items. Sometime during the 1960s Banff Academy took over the supervision of the museum. During this period a number of items were unfortunately dispersed from the collections.

Banff Museum became part of North East of Scotland Library Service in 1975, part of North East of Scotland Museums Service in 1984 and part of Aberdeenshire Heritage in 1996. The last quarter-century has seen the museum provided with more direct curatorial care than received since the nineteenth century. The room above Banff Library was developed as a local-history room, while the museum's ground-floor room became the focus for a natural-history display. The natural-history display was renovated in 1987/88 and went on to win a Glenfiddich Living Scotland Award in 1988. A significant development was the concerted effort between 1975 and 1996 to build up a representative collection of Banff silver, resulting in the acquisition of examples of silverware by almost every known Banff silversmith to have marked silver. The most recent acquisition of Banff silver was that, in 2004, of one of the pair of communion cups made in 1720 by Patrick Scott for Boyndie Parish Church.

Aberdeenshire Heritage had a new central stores and workshops complex built at Mintlaw in 2004. The reserve collections of the museum are being housed there and completely redocumented. While the new building is intended to be accessible to the public by appointment, public access to the reserve collections is being aided by the creation of an online catalogue on Aberdeenshire Council's website.

Since the early 1990s there has been considerable discussion within local government circles as to the future location of Banff Library and of the museum, and of how to best meet changing public needs and demands from these two services. A decade and a half later no firm decision has as yet been taken by Aberdeenshire Council, and the museum still continues to occupy its third home in Banff's High Street, a home which it has occupied for 106 years of its 180-year history.

Bibliography
The only primary sources for the Banff Institution are the two following printed papers:
Report of the Council of the Banff Institution, Banff 1830.
Regulations of the Banff Institution, Banff 1852.

No previous detailed history of the Banff Institution or its museum has been published, and much of the above account is derived from the author's unpublished museums diploma thesis:
Bertie, D.M. (1996) The early history of the Banff Institution, 1828–59 Unpublished Graduate Diploma thesis, University of St Andrews, 124pp.

The back numbers of the Banffshire Journal have been the source of many of the details noted above, while the books by Nicol (1879), Cramond (1891, 1893) and Mahood (1919) have added various snippets of information. A more recent publication is: Bertie, D.M. (2004) Hugh Miller's graptolite revisited. The Geological Curator, 8 (2), 43–45.

THE BANFF POLICE OFFICE

In 1815 the Commercial Bank bought the building on High Shore, now known as 'Shore House' (one-time property of Lord Byron) and it became only the second bank to be established in Banff. 'Shore House' was vacated by the bank in 1869, at which time it became a 'Stamp and Tax' office.

In 1869 the Commercial Bank erected next door what is now the Police Office, Banff. The bank occupied these premises until the late 1930s, when it moved to new premises at the top of the Strait Path, Banff, where it has remained to the present day, although it is now known as the Royal Bank of Scotland. Evidence of this building being used as a bank can still be found today in the fact that two 'strong rooms' can be traced to what is now the Sergeant's Office. It is also borne out by the fact that the exterior doors and windows are protected by heavy metal shutters.

From 1938 onwards this building was used as the headquarters of the Banffshire Air Raid Protection.

During 1949 the former police forces of Aberdeenshire, Banffshire, Kincardineshire and Moray and Nairn were amalgamated to form the then Scottish North Eastern Counties Constabulary. The Joint Police Committee had to choose the site of the new headquarters, and, by a majority of one vote, Banff was selected in preference to Aberdeen. The High Shore building was purchased and became the headquarters of the Scottish North Eastern Counties Constabulary. The first Chief Constable of Scottish North Eastern Counties Constabulary was George I. Strath, Chief Constable of the Banffshire Constabulary at the time of amalgamation.

This building remained police headquarters until 1964, at which time it transferred to new, purpose-built premises at Bucksburn, Aberdeen. Following the transfer of headquarters this building became a sub-divisional office, with an inspector in charge, until 1986, when the station was upgraded and a chief inspector was appointed subdivisional officer responsible for the policing of the Aberchirder, Banff, Buckie, Cullen, Cuminestown, Fyvie, Keith, Macduff, Portsoy and Turriff areas.

Prior to occupying these premises, the headquarters of Banffshire Constabulary were in the building adjacent to that occupied in 2008 by Grampian Kitchens on Carmelite Street. At that time the burgh sergeant resided in the premises later occupied by 'Chapter and Verse', Low Street, Banff.

The police cells and court were situated in what is now the Town House. The cells, still in existence, are used as storage areas at the time of writing.

On 15 May 1975 the Scottish North–Eastern Counties Constabulary and Aberdeen City Police were amalgamated to form what remains to this day Grampian Police.

BANFF FIRE BRIGADE
Brian Lamb

For over 100 years an organised fire brigade has been provided by local citizens living and working in Banff, and the community spirit that characterises our local fire brigade remains a distinctive feature within the modern fire service.

In the early 1900s the Banff fire brigade was a far cry from the modern service we have today. The 'fire engine' was a simple cart filled with hose and water mains fittings and pulled to the fire by hand or, in the better-off fire brigades, a horse. The fire station at this time was situated at the market close beside Low Street, but there is also mention of a station in Castle Street.

In the mid-1930s Banff eventually entered the mechanised age with the acquisition of a petrol-engined trailer pump. These versatile fire pumps could be towed behind any vehicle and it was not uncommon for private cars, taxis and even hearses to be requisitioned to get the pump and the firemen to the fire.

As war with Germany approached in 1939 an auxiliary fire service was formed and Banff acquired a second trailer pump. These pumps could be manhandled over rubble and bomb craters and proved to be the ideal solution to scarce fire-fighting resources, as they could be mass-produced in a short time.

In 1941-42, as the country recovered from initial deficiencies in equipment at the start of the war, Banff was allocated a Home Office Austin K2 auxiliary towing vehicle for their trailer pump, and it was soon put to use when the Inverboyndie distillery was bombed, sending thousands of litres of whisky into a local stream. The worst that happened was that several head of cattle were later found to be drunk and incapable.

In 1941 the National Fire Service (NFS) incorporating the local and auxiliary fire service, was formed. This new service standardised training and equipment throughout the UK and remained in place until 1948, when control was passed back to the local authorities. In particular, the standardisation of fire fighting became the backbone of the British fire service.

With the demise of the NFS, the North Eastern Fire Brigade was born and provided fire protection

Banff fire brigade on the Plainstones in 1897 on the occasion of Queen Victoria's diamond jubilee.   (© BODIE COLLECTION)

Banff fire brigade with a new fire engine. Left to right, back row: *C. Stewart, L. Alexander, leading fireman W. Still;* front row: *J. Urquhart, W. Scott, R. Laing, W. Mair, sub-officer G. Duffus, A. Taylor, G. Reid.*

Banff purchased this water pump in January 1936.

for the area that we today recognise as 'Grampian'. By this time the fire brigade in Banff were housed in a simple hut on Boyndie Street. During daytime hours firemen were alerted by a siren that all the town heard and during the night by a bell in their homes.

In the aftermath of the Second World War there were few cars and none of the chemical industries that we see today, and fire service training was all about handling ladders and operating pumps.

Because of the lack of training facilities at the Boyndie Street fire station, firemen could regularly be seen at Banff Primary School, Banff links, and the Wrack at the Deveron practising their skills.

As today, the fire station complement was ten firemen with up to six crewing the fire engine.

Investment in the fire service has been continuous since 1948, and in 1955 the first all-metal body fire engine in the shape of a Commer QX/Carmichael with a built-in pump arrived at Banff.

Further improvement took place on 25 April 1974 when the current fire station at St Catherine Street was opened. The difference over previous facilities cannot be overstated; for the first time physical training could be carried out on the station, and technical instruction to meet the changing needs of the community could be carried out in a purpose-built

119

environment. Following regionalisation of the Grampian area in 1975, the North Eastern Fire Brigade became Grampian Fire Brigade.

In 1995 Banff was one of six fire stations in Grampian being considered for closure, but a successful campaign mounted by the serving personnel and local community members saw this being withdrawn. Today the fire station is an important resource within the fire service structure in Grampian, and continues to develop its services in response to community needs.

Unique in the UK, Grampian's fire engines are white rather than the traditional red. The decision for this colour change was based on extensive research that concluded white was the colour most visible to other road users, and exemplifies one of a number of initiatives by the service to improve road safety.

For the first time in 2003 Banff fire station became the winner of the Arbuthnott Award Scheme. This closely contested award, involving all Grampian fire stations, requires station personnel to demonstrate the highest levels of skill, efficiency, dedication and community service.

The legislative basis for the provision of a fire service was the Fire Services Act 1947, and although it had served the service well for over 50 years it did not reflect the role and responsibilities that the service was required to develop to protect the community, such as fire education and road traffic collisions. The Fire (Scotland) Act became law in 2005, and with it Grampian Fire Brigade became Grampian Fire and Rescue Service. Not entirely to leave behind our origins, the new service badge incorporates a depiction of fire, water and the Scottish thistle.

LADYSBRIDGE HOSPITAL
David Findlay Clark

Prior to the middle of the nineteenth century, little attention was paid in Scotland to the care and treatment of the mentally ill and handicapped. Royal asylums in Aberdeen and Montrose were the main institutions where such persons were segregated. Banff District Lunacy Board was the statutory body tasked with finding out who and where were all its 'pauper lunatics' and how best they could be hived off to the care of (or more likely locked away in) the large national public asylums. Even then, local authorities were not keen on spending money!

However, the Banff Lunacy Board eventually decided to build its own asylum, and in 1860 purchased land from the Earl of Seafield, borrowed £12,000 from the Aberdeen Town and County Banking Co. and for just under £10,000 built the Banff Lunatic Asylum on the west side of the town. On 1

May 1865 the asylum was opened. The annual rate of board was set at £23.10s. per patient. Patient numbers quickly increased to over 100, which compelled the board, under the legislation then in place, to appoint a resident medical superintendent. Dr G.M. Bell was appointed as the first such, and a fine villa on the edge of the estate was built to house him and his family. 'Asylum' then literally meant a place of safety and succour for the mentally ill. Many also suffered from chronic physical diseases such as typhoid, pulmonary tuberculosis and epilepsy, and accommodation had to take account of this, with many verandahs and provision, too, for those patients who were perpetually bed-bound. Active treatment with drugs or by psychological methods was then little known or attempted, but Dr Bell became an innovator of new methods and attitudes, which eventually led to his leaving to take up a similar post at Dingleton Hospital in South Scotland where, against old prejudices, he instituted an 'open door' policy for which he later became nationally and internationally famous.

Fortunately, successive medical superintendents, Dr Tom Dymock and Dr Peter Sykes, were both forward-looking psychiatrists who began to lead their nursing and ancillary staffs to break free of the traditions of custodial care which prevailed up to and immediately after the Second World War. In the late 1940s Dr Dymock and his team cared for about 288 patients, many of whom were psychotic and suffered from other physical illnesses. Insulin therapy and electro-convulsant therapy were almost the only therapeutic regimes available. In the early 1950s a new type of drug (the phenothiazine group) was discovered which revolutionised psychiatric care and treatment, and it became easier to settle very disturbed patients, whether mentally handicapped or psychotic, to a condition which allowed for a wider range of therapeutic activities and psychological treatments. The hospital then ran its own 250-acre farm with a farm manager, grieve and other staff, and several patients of rural background began to work on it during the week rather than just be confined to the wards. Female patients could work under a sewing mistress or take on laundry duties.

Then, in the 1960s, a century after the hospital was founded, a wind of change began to blow through the psychiatric world, and particularly through the traditional institutions. Films such as *The Snake Pit* and books like Erving Goffman's *Asylum*, Professor Alan and Anne Clarke's *Mental Deficiency – The Changing Outlook* (to which this writer contributed over 100 pages) and those of other contemporary psychologists all began to offer new vistas of patient care, training and behavioural therapy, which began to reduce dependence on heavy drug dosages which themselves had placed limitations on the individual freedoms of patient groups. Nursing staff, many doubly qualified as state-registered mental as well as general nurses, physiotherapists and occupational therapists, as well as social workers and skills training supervisors, quickly became aware that custodial care was not enough. Grampian Regional Health Board also took the innovative step of appointing a consultant clinical psychologist, whose brief was to research and develop new training and treatment methods for both staff and patients, but to introduce these in such a way as to convince the many grades of staff that they themselves were the initiators. That was a bold project strongly supported by the consultant psychiatrists in post, such as Dr Harold Ross and Dr Alan Cook, medical superintendent at that time, and it also required a complete rebuild of the physical hospital at a cost of over £1.4m – a far cry from the original £9,848!

Behind the original asylum building (which was itself much modified and incorporated into the new establishment) rose a very fine modern hospital, purpose-built to accommodate the new principles of care and treatment, and consisting of six two-storey ward blocks and six single-storey wards to accommodate more disabled patients. There was a main structure housing a hall, activities rooms, occupational therapy, staff dining-room and a kitchen for the whole hospital which at one time was capable of serving over 2,000 cooked meals a day to both staff and patients. In part of the old building was the clinical psychology research laboratory, the dental surgery, a small school for younger patients and the physiotherapy department. A small 25-metre swimming pool was built adjacent to that. The new Ladysbridge Hospital was opened on 25 November 1966 by the Rt Hon. William Ross MBE MP, Secretary of State for Scotland.

From then on, Ladysbridge set out to provide a modern template for all that was best in the care and treatment of mentally ill and mentally handicapped patients, not only in Scotland but throughout the world. Dr David Clark, the consultant clinical psychologist mentioned above, was invited to lecture on his work at Ladysbridge not only in the UK but also at universities and hospitals in Canada, the USA and India. He and his colleagues formed a powerful team for change through which patients not only experienced a very high level of clinical care but also found that they could develop practical and social skills, a range of human relationships and a diminishing of their symptoms. By dint of huge efforts from the nursing staff, their living conditions moved from large open dormitories to individualised cubicles, affording some personal privacy and places for personal bits and pieces. Programmes of occupational as well as recreational content were fully developed, and more and more patients had opportunities to experience the world outside hospital. Patients had their own dances and cinema, church choir and sports events, some even competing in the Special Olympics. By this time the hospital had

Banff Lunatic Asylum as it was in 1960.

(© Dr David Findlay Clark ARPS)

One ward and the main building at Ladysbridge Hospital, Banff, 1968. (© Dr David Findlay Clark ARPS)

expanded to some 550 beds and a similar number of staff of all professions.

Normalisation of the daily life of patients, many of whom were not now acutely ill, was developed. They were considered to be residents rather than patients, and modern cognitive behaviour therapies and token economies were increasingly developed. Effecting those very significant changes in practice and regime was not always without difficulty, since some, mostly older, staff were reluctant to change time-honoured methods. However, nursing staff numbers had increased with new, keen young recruits to complete their nurse training, and other departments expanded appropriately. In 1970 a brand new occupational therapy block was completed and a house was taken over to allow training in normal domestic skills for patients increasingly likely to be discharged into the open community. By this time too a children's and adolescent unit was developed, together with a school teacher appointed by the local education authority. It all added up to an air of optimism and high morale among the staff.

Unfortunately, Mrs Thatcher's government did not appear to be sympathetic to the enormous development that had been engineered in the very best hospitals such as Ladysbridge. It was still influenced by the very poor conditions for both patients and staff that prevailed, even then, in many psychiatric hospitals south of the border. She had set in train a process through which, in 1991, Parliament passed the Community Care Act, whereby small community units would replace the larger hospitals, with all professions redistributed from the hospitals to multi-disciplinary teams based largely in social work departments. Many felt at the time that the whole plan was not so much a plan for the better care of patients as a plan to shift expenditure from the national exchequer (NHS) to local authorities and the rates. It certainly became a very expensive way to ensure that each patient had a level of care less rich in activities and less professionally supported. The hospital began to run down from 550 beds to a mere 100 in 2001 and it finally closed in 2003. Staff resigned, retired or were redeployed as community services developed. Some ex-patients did very well under the new conditions, but one effect of the change was that very little high-quality published research was subsequently done on the kind of patients Ladysbridge Hospital housed. The years between 1960 and 1985, coinciding with the years which found Ladysbridge at its peak performance, probably saw the greatest psychiatric and psycholog-ically research-based developments in the care of the handicapped ever, both in Britain and the USA. In more recent years many handicapped people have had to be cared for by long-suffering relatives when in the past they might have enjoyed a more actively therapeutic and satisfying life in a hospital with the advanced and enlightened ethos a hugely competent staff brought to Ladysbridge.

In 2008 the hospital now stands empty and rather forlorn in its spacious grounds, being progressively vandalised while awaiting development as a commuter village.

THE GREENBANKS
David Findlay Clark

Between the bridge over the Deveron and the seashore of Palmer Cove lies an ever-narrowing strip of grass with sandy patches, usefully flat and fenced off from the road running alongside it. The Greenbanks, as it is not unreasonably known, is today barely half of what it was 70 or 80 years ago. Some of it has become a travellers' caravan site and a car park, both of the latter now defended from the ravages of the sea by a great sea wall. Happily, what remains is still open to walkers breathing the fresh sea air and, from time to time in summer, the pitches of funfairs and roundabouts. The latter are hard put to survive commercially in the face of competition from TV, computer games and the blasé attitudes of a modern younger generation.

But 'twas not ever thus. Before the Second World War saw the greensward fenced off with barbed wire to keep folk off what became, for five years, a mine-field and a base for huge concrete cubic tank traps, the Greenbanks was the regular site used by the great circuses of the early-twentieth century – Roberts's Circus and Sanger's Circus among the regular hois-ters of the big top. Billy Smart's circus was a much later entrant into the ring. The day the circus came to town had us all a-buzz with anticipation. Huge gaily painted trucks towed huge gaily painted trailers and cages. The latter would contain fine horses, white, palomino and black; a bear or two, several lions and occasionally tigers. Best of all, from a small boy's point of view, were the elephants – great, peaceable, softly shambling giants with their turbaned trainers, or mahouts, astride their necks or walking alongside.

The whole caravan would park itself in a great oval so that the vehicles formed a secure barrier, with solid sides to the outside and the caged parts to the inside, with steel mesh walkways for the animals to get into the Big Top. The locals would gather to watch sweating and skilful men swinging mallets and hauling at the ropes as the huge tent went up the night before the big show. In the circuses of those days nearly all the men travelling with them in their fine caravans would fulfil several functions. One might be a trapeze artist, electrician and animal trainer. Another might be a clown, cook, engineer, bandsman and even ringmaster. Attractive and athletic young ladies, when not on the high wire or in the ring with tigers, would be costume managers, babysitters or announcers.

Tiered seating was erected in the tent and the approach to the main entrance would be lined with

Local children with a circus elephant, Canal Park, 1992.

stalls offering shooting, candyfloss, the hairiest woman in Europe (no trace of political correctness in the circus!), an especially talented fortune teller (the fact that her talent was in extracting cash from the gullible was not declared!), and 6d. could be paid to see the 'biggest rat from the sewers of Belgium' – later discovered to be a coypu! But most families, and they were families, who frequented the circus, were happy to suspend disbelief for a couple of hours and in turn to wonder at the daring and skills of the trapeze artists, the jugglers and the animal trainers. For a week, the Greenbanks would come alive – and in a night, as if magically spirited away, all would be gone to be replaced by a game of football, a few salmon fishers adjusting their rods and lures (for salmon abounded in the rivermouth then) or a few old folk just strolling along the shore.

Further along, towards the Low Shore, these self-same walkers might well have cut off onto the road rather than get too close to what was well named as the 'Stinkin' Lochie'. At one time an arm of the river that had been cut off by accumulations of shingle and sand, it became a stagnant pool and the repository of nameless and generally unpleasant bits and pieces which inquisitive small boys might explore – usually incurring their mothers' displeasure. It is the one part of the Greenbanks which most were glad to see disappear under concrete. What remains as greensward should be protected as long as possible. It carries its own little history and is part of the town's heritage.

ON THE STREET AND IN THE MART
David Findlay Clark

As a small boy I lived in a large house on Sandyhill Road. Before, and for some years during, the Second World War I would sometimes be allowed to stay out of bed and watch the world go by from my bedroom window above the front door of the house. There was no 'political correctness' then (1930s and '40s), so it did not seem strange to me when, on some of those occasions, the maid who looked after me would say, 'Look, Davie, here's the dafties!' They formed only one of the several processions which passed by.

On a fine weekend evening, the authorities who ran Ladysbridge Lunatic Asylum (as it was then called) would encourage several nurses, or 'warders' as they were often called, to escort 20 or 30 patients on a long walk for exercise. These walks started from the hospital, up the road called the 'currie bog', past Wardend Farm and down the main road from Huntly through Banff and back to Ladysbridge. The 'warders' impressed me because there were long chains to hold their keys which hung below their

blue serge jackets and some of them wore peaked caps like the janitor at school. Even the headmaster could not sport such an authority symbol! Some of the patients were quite disturbed or had bizarre behaviours and tics. They hallucinated and postured. There were no phenothiazine drugs to calm them then. I was somewhat disturbed by our maid's open laughter at them, which seemed to me a bit insensitive, even callous. It may well have determined in some part my later professional calling to try to be more understanding.

Another parade of some regularity which traversed Sandyhill Road and other town streets would take place early on Monday mornings – and some other days when the mart was held. The mart stood just where Somerfield's store now stands. For a large building, it was strange to find it built entirely of red-painted corrugated iron. It had a curved roof like the later Nissen huts of the war years and was virtually surrounded by wood-fenced pens for the segregation of cattle, pigs, sheep, lambs and so on as they went under the auctioneer's hammer. To get them there from the farms, however, required the services of drovers who, with sturdy sticks, a rich though largely obscene vocabulary and other sounds of command known only to them, drove the small herds/flocks of beasts to market. Two of the best known drovers were 'Princie' and 'Lordie' Hay, brothers of small stature but (one was led to believe)

Auctioneering at the mart.　　(© Dr David Findlay Clark ARPS)

A matter for serious consideration.

(© Dr David Findlay Clark ARPS)

more regal origins. They certainly bore very strong facial resemblances to the Prince of Wales, later King Edward VII, who had visited Duff House in 1883. Suffice to say that hardly any of the locals could remember their original Christian names. They lived in Wright's Close when at home but were often away, as they seemed to have a reputation as good drovers. I personally, in all the time I observed them, never saw them lose a cow or a steer into any of the local gardens or shops, or lose control over their charges as they negotiated the streets of the town. In their way they played an important part in the town's economy so long as the mart remained a going concern. Their origins are still the subject of much local speculation, but their nicknames are part of the town's rich history.

A third huge procession down the self-same street came just before D-Day in 1944. At that time an invasion of continental Europe was impending and troop and equipment movements were huge throughout the land. For some days in that early summer, immense convoys of Army lorries, tanks, tracked Bren-gun carriers and field and anti-tank guns completely filled Sandyhill Road and several miles of the Huntly road. Some of the crews had been driving and training for days, so that when the convoy stopped, every householder would bring a supply of tea, fruit, bread and biscuits (so far as rationing would allow – and sometimes further) to refresh these young men, who would so soon be fighting for their – and our – lives in France or Italy. We boys normally played on rope swings hanging from the trees at the back of the big wall which separated the street from the woods of the Duff House grounds. On those days we climbed the dyke only to find rows of big field guns and limbers (the detachable foreparts of gun-carriages) full of shells lined up in their dozens in the grass and nettles, and soldiers throwing camouflage nets over everything. There was, perhaps, little need for that, as German air activity had all but stopped by then – but one never knew. After all, the Jerries had been here before!

BANFF LINKS
David Findlay Clark

Along the north-facing shore of the Moray Firth, between Banff and the village of Whitehills to the west, lies Banff links, a mile-long stretch of fine golden sand. Separated from the machair, or grassy links, by a shingle bank, this has been for generations a favourite walk for adults, children and dogs. During the first half of the twentieth century, its landward edge carried a single-track railway line to Tillynaught and points west and south. Passengers then might have surveyed gentleman golfers testing their skills, fishermen drying, mending and tarring

Pre-Boer War Banff Volunteers encamped at Banff links.
(© BODIE COLLECTION)

their herring nets, or heard the shrill and delighted screams of hundreds of children on Sunday-school and other organised picnics. The diversity of uses was not, however, entirely conducive to the equanimity of these users.

The golfers, who had built a rather neat little wooden golf clubhouse, considered it was their golf course and that they had priority usage. With a sheriff and several lawyers as members, they were inclined to 'pull rank' on the other users. They, in turn, recognised this as common land and were equally keen to preserve their rights, and the children were mostly inclined to head for the sand and the sea – even if the temperature of the latter was little over 10 or 12°C. Mostly, however, there was a strained co-existence until the golfers eventually moved to Duff House Royal GC on the flat parkland on the other side of the town in 1910. The picnickers tended to cluster round the purpose-built shelters (one now reactivated by surfers), and those among them who were not munching sandwiches or pursuing several footballs with more fervour than skill, would be heading for the old clubhouse which, post-1910, became a wee tearoom and ice-cream parlour.

The sight of, say, 5–10 acres of brown fishing nets laid out flat over the short grass, dotted about with blue-clad fishermen wielding their shuttles and fixing new corks, was always impressive. Small boys would approach to seek the odd cork for a fishing line float and old boys would chat up a fisher, and perhaps smooth the path of diplomacy by a cigar or some tobacco before asking for a bit of torn net to cover their strawberry patch or fruit bushes. Mostly, both were forthcoming.

For many years there were, just above the shingle line, two or three tall poles with triangular wooden steps bolted to the sides of them which were climbed by Coastguards on the look-out for a ship in distress or difficulty. The extra height gave them a further horizon. Others were supposed to be forbidden to climb these, but there were few young lads of any spirit who could resist the climb.

Then came the war in 1939 and all was transformed. Quite suddenly, hundreds of soldiers spread over the sand at low tide, dug deep holes and planted very tall, straight poles at 50 yard intervals in both directions over the whole of the sandy area. This was to prevent enemy gliders landing. Soon after, the whole of the links, from the mouth of the Deveron to the edge of Whitehills, was a barbed-wire-entanglement-protected minefield covering all the grassy area up to the present pathway on the landward side. Huge cubic concrete blocks were also placed at strategic positions along the shore to act as tank traps. The urgency of this transformation was driven by the concern of our military leaders that a German invasion from Norway was impending. The greatest dramas to be wrought at the links were no more than a few roaming dogs blown up by mines, one or two others (mines, that is, not dogs) exploded by boys deliberately throwing large boulders over the barbed wire in an attempt to 'make a big bang' and, later on, a pile of dead ducks on the sand just beyond the barbed wire where a small stream enters the sea near the former Banff Distillery. They had drunk themselves to death on whisky released by the attack on the distillery of a German fighter/bomber on Saturday, 16 August, 1941. The whisky floated on the stream surface in which the ducks swam, and they knew no temperance. Unfortunately, the carcases could not be retrieved because they were within the minefield. They would have made welcome ameliorations of wartime rations to many had events ended otherwise.

In 2008 the beach is again pristine. There is a fine caravan site at the western end of the links, a well-equipped children's playground adjacent and the rest, somewhat diminished by erosion, is once more a popular public open space and walking/picnicking area, often sunlit and swept clean by bracing breezes or gentle southern zephyrs in turn.

Scotstown, with gasworks and railway line.

extracted, fetched into Banff by boat and train at the harbour station. There was always a pungent smell of hot coke. Smoke and steam would seem to rise from quite unlikely places – like fumeroles on a volcano – as the managers, 'Gassy' Wilson or Mr Pitt (as I thought, appropriately named) stalked about in their own officious way. It was a private enterprise – no British Gas then. The whole process seemed to the layman to be potentially dangerous and chemically relatively unsophisticated – enough to make people peer in curiously but move on, perhaps a little thankfully. After all, it was a great improvement on lighting your house with paraffin lamps and cooking over a fire.

In the early years of the twentieth century, many houses and all the streets were lit by gas, and many homes had gas cookers. After the Second World War, the lights were replaced by electric lamps, but these never carried the romance of those lit by a man with a short ladder and a pole with a wax taper that never seemed to blow out.

THE GASWORKS
David Findlay Clark

Right up to the early years of the second half of the twentieth century, a great drum-like steel gas container moved up and down in its lattice frame as its contents waxed and waned in relation to consumption and supply. Probably something like 60ft in diameter, it might be anything from 10 to 40ft high. This dark red painted cylinder could be seen best from Macduff, as it sat on the flat spit of land behind Banff harbour – the only remaining relic of Banff Gas Works, still being used as a reservoir of 'town gas'.

The site is now mostly a car park, but during the previous half century, its furnace house, tall chimney and ancillary buildings were the scene of Vulcan-like fire-worshippers, black-faced, sweaty men who shovelled and raked coke from which the gas was

BLACKPOTS
David Findlay Clark

Hugh Miller, the Cromarty mason, natural historian, writer and geologist, wrote in *The Witness* newspaper in 1848 that he had visited the Banff area. He wrote:

The argillaceous deposit of Blackpots occupies, in the form of a green swelling bank, a promontory rather soft than bold in its contour, that projects far into the sea, and forms, when tipped thus with its column of smoke from the tile kiln, a pleasing feature in the landscape.

Blackpots had then, since 1766, been a busy and productive tile, pipe and brickworks, the products of which were to grace many a northern byre or house roof, to drain a large area of arable Banffshire and form the walls of many buildings. Now, in the early-twenty-first century, all that remains of this industry are a few shards of red tile and pipe all worn back near to the original clay they were made from as the waves of centuries wash over and over them.

Blackpots is described in the 1892 edition of the *Ordnance Gazetteer* as: '... a hamlet on the coast of Boyndie Parish, Banffshire, two and a quarter miles W by N of Banff. A manufacture of bricks and tiles, and a considerable salmon fishery are carried on.' There is, therefore, a small harbour with a narrow and rocky entrance from the north which, in the early days of the works, allowed boats not only to fish for the then abundant salmon but also to carry away the clay products to needy buyers in the south. The several long, low buildings where the tiles and pipes were dried, as well as a cottage for the foreman and the high-chimneyed kiln, were established by

a Dr Saunders, who owned the adjacent farm. A small team built the works, and over the years these were to employ between nine and 11 workers who lived locally.

In 1788 Alexander Saunders notified the Earl of Findlater of his intention to build 'a comfortable dwelling-house and two more sheds'. The works were prosperous and productive then. The house remains to this day, but everything else, though of immense historical and architectural importance, was bulldozed in 1977. The grassy prominence remarked on by Hugh Miller, Knock Head, is a raised beach carrying a broad seam of grey workable clay which was the raw material for the tileworks. It was dug out of the hillside above the works by two men who then wheeled it down 100 yards or so to the first shed on a four-wheeled bogie running on a narrow-gauge railway. It was shovelled into a near-vertical chute which carried it to a steam-driven compressing machine, from which it was extruded in the form of

Tile Works, Blackpots, near Whitehills.

(© Dr David Findlay Clark ARPS)

Blackpots Tile Works 1963. (© Dr David Findlay Clark ARPS)

The original small team who built Blackpots Tile Works, 1866.

(Courtesy of Mrs Stirton, Whitehills)

lengths of grey pipe, about 5ins in diameter and about 6ft long. These lengths were then chopped into four using a kind of wire cheese cutter before being picked up by a slim pole through them and stacked in the drying sheds. The drying sheds were long, single-storey clapboard buildings the walls of which could be hinged at the top and levered out at the bottom to let the wind through the pipes but keep the rain off them. Bricks were more simply made in moulds, as were the roof tiles. Later, after a period of fresh-air curing, all the products were stacked in the kiln and baked.

In 1900 the works were purchased by the Brodie family, solicitors in Banff, and only pipe and brick making was continued by them. Later still, in 1973, Brodie sold the works to a Mr Steele and only pipe making continued after that until the works closed down a few years later.

Mrs Stirton, a very senior citizen of Whitehills village, adjacent to the works, told the writer of how the place got its name. Apparently the first kiln built was inefficient and did not reach a temperature high enough to fire the clay sufficiently. The tiles and pipes should have turned from a grey/buff colour when they were put into the kiln to a warm, reddish-orange colour after firing. Unfortunately, the first products turned out black, not orange, and thus the place came to be named 'Blackpots'. Subsequently, a new kiln was built which did reach the requisite temperature and everything turned out fine! To this day it is likely that hundreds of miles of Blackpots drainage pipes lie under the surface of many a northern Scottish field. The site has now become a caravan site, the claypit a decorative pool in its midst, and only the tiny harbour offers itself as a watery play-area for children in summer.

BANFF HARBOUR
David Findlay Clark

The earliest references to a harbour at Banff are from Customs accounts of 1390 and from documents about the letting of salmon fisheries owned by the town to certain burgesses of the town. Then, however, there was no harbour as one might understand the word nowadays. Boats were simply drawn up above the high-tide mark onto a great shingle bar which stretched across Banff bay. Nevertheless, the fifteenth-century trade with London and the Low Countries was considerable. Woolfells, hides and, especially, salted salmon in barrels were the main products traded. To give some indication of the importance to the town of the salmon trade, it can be noted that the Customs duty paid at Banff for salmon exported during the second part of the reign of James III was £47. The total for the whole of Scotland at that time was £310.

It was only in the seventeenth century that moves were made by the town council to have a proper harbour built. In 1613, the council sought the (financial) assistance of the Convention of Royal Burghs to that end. As a result, in 1625 a contract was made to:

... cast, win and hew that pairt of the schoir, callit Guthries heaven lyand at the north pairt of the said burt of Banff... Beginnand at the wast at ane grene brea and craige in the chyngill discending thairfra down ane hollo goit lynallie to the North till it cum to ane low water- to ane heich craig at the eist pairt of the said heavin.

Guthrie's Haven, which became part of Banff harbour (note the dog).

(© BODIE COLLECTION)

127

The shingle bar, 1890. Looking towards Banff.

Boats in Banff harbour.

Banff harbour with 'Zulus' in the late-nineteenth century.

Boys sitting on Banff's harbour pier before the lighthouse was built.

Throughout the second half of the seventeenth century there were constant references in old town documents to both weather- and topography-determined difficulties of entering Guthrie's haven and to the need to raise money to pay for the new harbour. Personal donations; appropriation of fines, for example for fornication; circular letters to all the churches in Scotland (approved by an Act of the Scottish Parliament in 1697) requesting cash help – all were mobilised in the cause. Cash donations subsequently came in from all parts of Scotland for the development of the harbour. There was then a strong sense of the common weal in Scotland which was in part eroded by the Union a few years later. The following year, 1698, the town council pleaded for financial support because the town had lost 16 vessels, either shipwrecked or taken by the French 'during King William's wars'. The council argued that they were spending money on mending the ruinous steeple and Tolbooth and that their 'water mouth was inaccessible'. As a result the Convention of Royal Burghs contributed 500 merks. Cramond, in the *Annals of Banff*, records that a Banff merchant, Thomas Murray, made in his will a deed of gift so that all the rents from properties he owned would, for 20 years following his death, be applied 'for the

support, reparation, deepening and cleaning or otherways improving the new harbour of the burgh, commonly called Guthrie haven.'

Just as today, the planning and financing of developments such as making a new harbour took up nearly three-quarters of a century (plus ça change, plus c'est la même chose!). Mr Smeaton, the nationally known civil engineer responsible for, among other fine works, the Eddystone lighthouse, now on

A steamboat at Banff, c.1910.

Buildings along Banff harbour quays.

Banff harbour full of boats.

Plymouth Hoe, was engaged to oversee the work and, on 28 October 1775, Guthrie's Haven (now the inner harbour) was officially declared complete. In between times there had been various upsets and modifications required. There was constant pressure to extend the east pier to make the approach easier in poor weather, and at one stage some 60ft of it was washed away in a storm. Moreover, there was constant need for the town to mobilise workers of all ages and sexes to clear out sand and shingle from the harbour mouth, where it was constantly accumulating after gales and spates from the River Deveron. The silting up could become so severe that some larger ships ('of a hundred tons or more') carried in only a half cargo so as to lie less deeply in the water.

It is a sobering thought that all these civil engineering works were carried out by a limited number of toiling men and boys, using only such hand tools as picks and shovels, and horses and carts. Many were working, literally, for pennies, and some would have known that they would never see the end result of their labours. Nevertheless, some 20 years after the opening, and subject to later developments, the harbour was doing business with London and the Baltic. Mahood reports that:

About 1798, eight brigantines of about 100 to 210 tons each, 14 sloops, chiefly 60, 80 and 100 tons, belonged to Banff, some of which were in the London trade. Shipbuilding was carried on with success.

Gale damage at Banff harbour, 1983.

(© Dr David Findlay Clark ARPS)

For ten years from 1818, after designs by Thomas Telford, an engineer as talented and famous as Smeaton, a new pier and breakwater were built to form a new outer harbour. One of the reasons for the expansion was that, three years earlier, the herring fishing was started up in the district and the harbour was quietly changing from a trading harbour to one that would also accommodate a fishing fleet of smaller vessels, Fifies and Zulus. These were mainly wooden sail-driven boats, largely open decked and without engines. Often they were owned by merchants or landowners who rented the boats and small houses in the seatown of Banff to the fishing families.

It was a relatively hard life of, at times, almost indescribable toil and severity, not only for the men but for whole families. In general, larger boats of about ten tons then might cost about £24, and small four-tonners approximately half that amount. To a crew purchasing a boat the proprietors allowed a sum of about £11 and in return received an annual rent of £5.3s.3d. and a stated quantity of fish for a period of seven years, reckoned to be the reasonable life of a boat at that time. In addition to this, crews were often compelled to carry for the owners freight, often building materials, and other cargoes free of charge.

Sometimes fishermen who were unwilling to go to sea in bad conditions to meet these requirements were placed in 'joogs', or manacled with irons by the proprietors.

As late as the beginning of the nineteenth century such manacles could be seen attached to a large house on the east side of the Burn of Buckie. When I think how, having sailed a small boat out of Banff for a number of years, I and my cronies at the Sailing Club debated from time to time the advisability of going out when things were 'coorse' in the bay, the pressure on these ancient crews must have been almost unbearable. There was no stress counselling in those days. The reality of work or starve simply killed off, one way or another, those who could not cope.

Things were not quite so bad in Banff itself because at that time the town council had a direct interest in the fishing industry. Some boats were the property of the council and were rented to fishermen who were also advanced small sums for equipment and given small grants to build houses in the seatown of the burgh. In return, the fishermen were bound to serve in the white fishing industry for seven years and were liable to imprisonment if they deserted. A yearly rent for a boat under this scheme was in the region of £20, and the fishermen had to maintain the craft in good repair during their engagement. Town council records show that between the years 1775 and 1794 the price of a boat was £5.11s.1d!

The women had an especially tough time then. Often, before there was a harbour, they would have had to haul the boats up onto the shingle bank. They, with the children, would have collected bait from the rocks and pools in all weathers and then spent hours baiting the hooks on the long lines for white fishing. To cap it all, they would have had to carry their men out through the shallows to put them aboard their boats with dry feet. The construction of a harbour therefore alleviated the worst of these duties but did not eliminate all of them. However, the harbour was still essentially a trading harbour, accommodating the schooners and brigantines engaged in the runs to and from London, Leith, the Low Countries and the Baltic. The inner harbour might be packed with fishing boats after 1815, but the outer harbour was the province of these larger ships.

It was reported that in 1836 10–12 vessels of about 100 tons each made, on average, nine voyages each in a year and carried 11,000 tons of freight to London. Grain, barrels of herring and salmon, cured pork and some live cattle were taken there and to other ports. On the return voyages, coal and groceries were brought in, and the ships that went further afield brought in iron and timber from Sweden, hemp from Russia and flax from Holland. Even though the herring fishing burgeoned in the first half of the nineteenth century, and nearly 22,000 barrels of herring were exported, there remained a very substantial import/export trade through Banff.

Among the fishing boats, the Fifies and Scaffies were being rapidly replaced by the bigger and stronger Zulus. These took up more room in the harbour, and their presence and other influences quietly promoted the policy to develop new harbours at Macduff and Whitehills, both only a few miles distant. Then, in the early years of the twentieth century, came the age of steam, and both fishing and commercial boats were bigger and more independent of the weather. In 1916 35 steam drifters, ten sailing boats and one motor boat were registered at Banff. The harbour had an associated shipyard, a sawmill and a Morton Patent Slip, so steam drifters of 80–90ft in keel length were being built. Just before the First World War such boats cost about £3,000.

The war resulted in the loss of some ships and crews, but it has been noted that one of the main influences effecting the decline of Banff harbour as a trading port was the development of the railways. Ironically, although built originally to assist in the distribution of goods brought in by sea, and for the haulage to a harbour for export, the railway, because of its capacity and speed, soon took over the carriage of all goods, not only in Scotland but throughout the UK.

Moreover, the two world wars resulted in motor-powered and steam drifters being requisitioned for inshore coastal protection, mine-sweeping and other Admiralty duties. In the Second World War, the addition of a small platform with one or two Lewis guns, a couple of Carley floats and a coat of grey camouflage paint converted them, at a stroke, to weapons of war. Several of these small coastal patrol boats were relatively easy targets for stray raiders in the form of Heinkel 111s or Junkers 88s of the Luftwaffe. Several nights of the writer's boyhood and early adolescence were punctuated by the staccato exchange of machine-gun fire in the bay and the occasional crump of heavier weaponry and bombs as these exchanges took place.

For all that, it is probably true to say that, if the Second World War brought no substantial damage to Banff harbour itself, the second factor influencing its decline was the fact that the changing course of the River Deveron over the years had led to progressive silting up of the port. When the Earl Fife built a harbour at Macduff, across the bay, which had none of these problems, most of the boatmen who wanted to keep a commercial advantage moved to Macduff. However, a boatbuilding yard continued production at Banff harbour for several more years after the war ended, but even that had closed by the mid-1950s.

While there are records of a great north-easterly gale destroying the harbour in October 1819, just after work to develop it had commenced following Telford's plans in 1816, perhaps the event most likely to have had drastically adverse effects on the contemporary harbour at Banff occurred on 31 January and 1 February 1983. During that night and the whole of the following day, exceptionally fierce northerly or north-north-westerly gales did what none had succeeded in doing over the previous couple of centuries. On 1 February two huge waves, estimated at around 50–60ft high and 400–500m long, rolled in from the north and burst with a roar and a great flare of green water and spume across the length of the north (lighthouse) pier. When the water poured away it could be seen that much of the breakwater wall and pier decking had simply disappeared. The magnificent Kemnay granite stonework designed by Messrs Smeaton and Telford had been picked up bodily and flung about the bottom of the outer basin as if the great four-feet cubed blocks were no more than pebbles. A 50m length of the wall had been stripped down to the level of the pier decking. The sight of the whole north harbour wall being shattered in seconds was truly awesome. The Banff Sailing Club hut, all 50 by 18ft of it, was lifted bodily from its foundations by the wave, torn from its service pipes – fresh water and sewage as well as electric cables – and floated and buffeted 23ft from its original position, while the power lines sparked and fizzed in the water and the fresh water-main added its skyward jet to the general maelstrom. A concrete wall some 6ft high by the local gas-control building simply disappeared.

Happily, the then regional authority immediately set to work to reconstruct the wall and the pier decking. Skilled stonemasons reset the great granite capping blocks and whinstone masonry. Not only was this done because of the historical associations of the harbour but, more practically, because of the wall's importance as a coastal defence against erosion. Perhaps, too, the expectation that the harbour, in due course, might well recover at least some of its lost glories under sail played a part in the decision. Within a year the new wall had risen, Phoenix-like and stronger than ever before. The harbour has since emerged from destruction and decline and has continued to develop as an important amenity and recreational facility.

Then, in 2006, the Aberdeenshire Council made an important decision to develop Banff harbour into a modern marina, fully equipped with pontoon berths for over 80 yachts, motorboats and other craft. At the time of writing this marina is nearly full of motorboats and yachts, mostly recreational craft but a few lobster boats. Thus the harbour has come full cycle, from a haven for canvas-sailed fishing boats of two centuries ago, through a commercial phase, to once again reflecting the prosperous hinterland in a pontoon-equipped haven for sailing boats of an entirely different stamp.

FREEMASONRY
Hugh Miller

The many surviving eighteenth-century buildings seen today in Banff bear testimony to the abilities of countless skilled stonemasons. They would have been instrumental in the development of the community and were held in high regard. After labouring all day, the masons would have gathered into 'guilds' or 'lodges' in the evenings, mainly for social enjoyment, but also to share experience and improve their knowledge of their trade.

Not one, but two such lodges which appeared in Banff are today known as Lodge St Andrew No. 52 and Lodge St John Operative No. 92. They were consecrated in 1749 and 1764 respectively. Lodge St Andrew, which meets in the Town Hall on Castle

Bailie Davidson, who built much of modern Banff, in his Freemason's regalia.

Street, claims to have received an earlier charter from Lodge Kilwinning in Ayrshire. The first reference to a lodge in Banff is in 1703. It is thought that Lodge St John was formed by 'working' masons, and up until 1800 only admitted operative masons. The brethren of that lodge built their own lodge in 1798 on the Braeheads, overlooking Banff harbour. In 1999, Lord Burton, the Grand Master Mason of Scotland, honoured Lodge St Andrew No. 52 by his presence on the occasion of its 250th anniversary. The master of Lodge St Andrew at that time was the late brother Ewan MacGregor. Lodge St John will attain that milestone in 2014.

For the more efficient running of the craft, Grand Lodge in Edinburgh saw fit to decentralise its responsibilities and set up provincial grand lodges (32 in 2008). The Banffshire province, which follows the old county boundary, was erected in 1801 and today consists of 15 daughter lodges – from Macduff in the east to Portgordon in the west and Aberlour in the south. The provincial master is elected by the daughter lodges nowadays, but the office was originally held by four peers of the realm – George, the 9th Marquis of Huntly (1801); James, the 4th Earl Fife (1827); James, the 5th Earl Fife (1848) and Alexander, the 6th Earl Fife (1881). Duff House in Banff was the seat of the Earls Fife. Since then, two brethren from St John Operative No. 92, James Grant in 1906 and Charles M. Napier in 1959, and one brother from St Andrew No. 52, George MacGregor in 1964, have been elected to that important office.

In 1806, the Prince of Wales (later George IV) was installed as Grand Master Mason of Scotland. In his anticipated absences at royal duties, seven acting grand masters were elected. One of these was James (Duff), the 4th Earl Fife, who had the great honour of occupying the Chair of Grand Lodge in Edinburgh, between 1814 and 1816. This reflected great glory on the North East of Scotland and Banff in particular. Further south, however, it may have been wrongly assumed that he came from Fife. Even today, people make the same mistake. The 4th Earl had been Master of Lodge St Andrew No. 52 in 1813, again in 1818 and later in 1827, when, as mentioned earlier, he became Provincial Master of Banffshire, a position he held for over 20 years.

The Earls Fife supported both lodges and presented many treasured gifts. A beautiful silver punch bowl inscribed 'To his worthy brethren of Lodge St Andrew Banff from Lord Fife' is perhaps the most precious.

A less valuable, but equally cherished, inscribed gold-mounted horn snuff mill was given to Lodge St John Operative by James, the 4th Earl, past grand master, in 1836. A silver punch ladle with a large silver coin soldered inside is still used to serve traditional St John's punch on installation nights. The coin had been tossed into one of the two china punch bowls dated 1801, inscribed with old lodge No. 120, by the Earl Fife during a lodge harmony. Intriguingly a large painting of a lady seated in a tall chair hangs in the upstairs hall of Lodge St Andrew and that very chair is still used by the master to this day. Seemingly, the lady depicted, whose surname was Chalmers and who was related to the founder of the hospital of that name, was discovered amongst hay during an early meeting of that lodge held in a barn. Having witnessed some of the masonic meeting, she was made to swear on oath of secrecy as to what she had seen and heard. She wears an apron in the lodge colours and is referred to as the lady mason. A smaller painting also hangs in Chalmers Hospital. The large painting is signed John Mitchell Pinxit (Latin – 'he painted'), 1852.

In 1774 the brethren of Lodge St John helped build what is still the present bridge over the River Deveron to the design of John Smeaton, best remembered for the Eddystone lighthouse. James Robertson was engaged as foreman and, being master of St John, was well respected. The estimate for the seven-span Moray sandstone bridge was £4,548.14s.11d. At that time lead was priced at 2d./lb and the 10cwt required cost only £9.6s.8d! The final cost on completion in 1780 was £9,000. When it comes to builders' estimates, nothing has changed. The marks of the operative masons are clearly visible under the arch on the Macduff side. It is little coincidence that the first record in Scotland concerning masonic marks can be found in the lodge minutes of 1778.

In the minutes around 1790 we read of depute masters of St John being given commissions to visit certain towns and admit members to the operative lodge. Amongst others, the list includes Inverness, Gardenstown, St Fergus, Inverurie, Aboyne and Dunrobin. St John Operative, Banff, must have attained a most important status in those early days.

Masonry uses the customs and tools of the stone-mason as allegorical guides to shape man's moral and spiritual values. Belief in a Supreme Being is essential, and high moral standards, truthfulness and an observance of the laws of the land are demanded. The masonic handshake, often regarded with suspicion, is nothing more sinister than a form of recognition, and is based historically on the old stonemasons who could neither read nor write. It is certainly not a secret society, but a society with a few secrets, and as the success of the recent Doors Open Day demonstrated, has nothing whatever to hide.

One entrance to the Town and County Club.

(© TOMMY BOD)

THE TOWN AND COUNTY CLUB
Robert Carter

The Banff Town and County Club can lay claim to being one of the oldest institutions in the town. Nowadays only a handful of similar associations exist in the North East, and surely few can boast as their headquarters an architectural gem, one of the largest provincial town houses of eighteenth-century Scotland, described in the guidebooks as 'very precious'.

Mirroring in its own distinctive fashion the social and recreational mores of the town and district, stretching back over a long and chequered life to the Victorian era, the private club in Banff's Boyndie Street occupies a unique place in the community.

It was, in its early years, very much a 'male preserve', where town and gown met, a haunt of the business and professional men who had first promoted its foundation. Today much has changed, and although it continues to maintain a somewhat low profile, the aura of exclusivity that once marked its presence in the town has long since gone.

The members, men and women, meet in comfortable surroundings to enjoy the various amenities provided for them. Visiting guests, who are always welcome, immediately become aware of a special ambience, an atmosphere of calm and peace, as they come through the portals.

They can join their hosts relaxing in the main lounge, with its spiral stairway leading to a small gallery, or visit the reading and television room where an Adam-style fireplace dominates. Elsewhere in the building they find a library, a dining-room for small functions and two billiard–snooker rooms.

Outdoors, in spacious grounds, is a three-rink

The bar of the Town and County Club, Boyndie Street, Banff, with John Haefner, manager since the late 1980s.

(© TOMMY BOD)

bowling green, Banff's first, and alongside is the former tennis court, which in the 1930s was the scene of garden parties and which now is where regular barbecues are held.

Such, then, is the Banff Town and County Club of today, housed in the former residence of the distinguished Robinson family, who built it in 1772. Nevertheless, it is a little-known fact that it was not the original home of the club. That was a building in nearby South Castle Street.

The Club's founding in 1881 arose from a move in the town to resuscitate a defunct reading-room run by the local literary society. A 'Banff Town and County Club and Newsroom' was established, the main object being 'the provision and maintenance of a club and newsroom at Banff for the social intercourse, recreation and intellectual improvement of the members.'

Formerly owned by the Chalmers family of Cluny, wealthy merchants and shipowners, the new club's first premises were leased. Adapted to provide a reading-room where members and subscribers could browse through the daily, weekly and monthly press, the apartments also provided card and games rooms plus a smoke (!) room.

It was not long before the club was on the move. The South Castle Street property, the members agreed, was not really fit for purpose, and when the nearby imposing mansion in Boyndie Street came on the market in 1884 they moved speedily to acquire it. Following completion of limited interior alterations they moved in, and then embarked on laying out Banff's first proper bowling green, along with tennis courts. Ambitious plans for a community hall in the grounds were eventually abandoned. Incidentally, one of Banff's first telephones was installed in the building.

Over the years, and particularly during the early part of the twentieth century, a fluctuating membership roll and balancing the books exercised the club council, the body appointed annually by members to supervise the running of the club's affairs. After the First World War things took a decided turn for the better, and the then unprecedented decision in 1930 to seek a liquor licence under the Licensing Acts ushered in a new era.

During the Second World War military personnel stationed in the area were welcomed to the club and accorded the privilege of honorary membership. Subsequently, the pre-war pattern of club life was resumed, with bridge tournaments, ladies' nights and, more recently, Burns nights, musical entertainments, quiz night competitions and bowling matches becoming regular features. The 'at homes' and garden parties once popular in the 1930s did not survive into the post-war era.

Down through the years the maximum fixed membership has been raised from the original permitted 100 to 225, and the private nature of the club continues to be reflected in a voting procedure strictly enforced following an application from those applying to join. In a significant innovation during the 1960s a new category of 'lady associate' member was created, albeit ladies had always been welcomed as guests.

The club celebrated its centenary in 1981 with a memorable dinner and the publication of its history. The latter records the anniversary as coinciding with 'a period of expansion and quiet prosperity'. That situation persists today, along with a determination on the part of its council and members to endeavour to maintain the rich and historic character of an ancient townhouse of bygone days.

BANFFSHIRE FIELD CLUB, 1880–2008
Caroline Leggat

The Banffshire Field Club was founded in 1880 by a few interested local men, among whom was Thomas Edward, the naturalist. An enthusiastic membership soon gathered. That summer three excursions were held, led by John Horne, geologist, to Gamrie, Revd John Wilson to Fyvie, and William Cramond, historian, to Cullen.

The club was part of the Northern Association of Literary and Scientific Societies and hosted their third annual joint meeting, in Banff, with representation from Edinburgh, Aberdeen, Inverness, Ross-

Banffshire Field Club members on an outing, learning about wild mushrooms.

shire and Nairn. Following the reading of papers by various members and supper at the Fife Arms Hotel, by 8a.m. next day hundreds of spectators watched the procession of carriages, each drawn by a pair of horses, first stop at the Old Church of Boyndie, then at Boyne Castle, followed by the Old Kirk of Cullen and finally Cullen House. A business meeting was held on the lawn before the carriages took the guests back to Banff.

Following a paper by Mr Thomas Edward, the club decided to print his paper and distribute it to other societies, and also decided that all future papers would be printed by the *Banffshire Journal* and be free to members. This is the source of the transactions held by the club's transactions secretary today, available for a modest sum to anyone interested in a particular subject.

An early secretary was James Spence, who founded the Buchan Field Club, which in 2008 is still in existence. Another member, William G. Craib, botanist, compiled *The Flora of Banffshire*, published by the *Banffshire Journal* in 1912. He later became Professor of Botany at Aberdeen University and added three further supplementary lists.

During the First World War, the club continued to meet, but no excursions were held.

Postwar, 1923–37, contributions to meetings were from Mr Alistair Tayler and his sister Henrietta, among others. From 1925 Dr W. Douglas Simpson, librarian at King's College, Aberdeen University, contributed articles and led excursions to Boyne, Findlater, Spynie and Elgin Cathedral, Auchindoir, Rhynie, Essie and Rothiemay Castle. Many of his printed talks have detailed sketch maps and photographs, still available from the transactions.

From 1939 to 1958, the club was in abeyance, but after a public meeting in Cullen in 1958 it was reformed as 'The Banffshire Society', quickly gathering 203 members and four juniors. 'Society' prizes were given for studies in botany, natural history and biology, to encourage young people to join.

Sadly, the rebirth of interest was short lived, and in 1974, at a public meeting in Cullen Parish Church Hall, it was decided to reform the club as the Banffshire Field Club, its aims, agreeing with the 1880 constitution, are 'to explore the district... inquiring into the Geology, Botany, Natural History, Archaeology etc.' Members are drawn from a wide area – from the previous County of Banffshire and further afield.

On 10 September 2005, Banffshire Field Club celebrated the 125th anniversary of its founding with a lunch at the Banff Springs Hotel. The chairman was Mr James A.S. McPherson, CBE, FSA Scot, JP and there was an audio-visual presentation, 'Tribute to Thomas Edward', by Dr David Findlay Clark, OBE, DL.

In 2008 the club meets from October to April at 2.15p.m. on the second Saturday of the month in Keith Community Centre. Outdoor excursions are arranged in summer. Membership costs £5.00 per annum. Most transactions from 1880 to 1939 are available from the transactions secretary.

◆━━◆

MUSIC IN BANFF
Alistair Mason

The people of Banff have had a lot of pleasure from music over the years, but it has not really been a place of pilgrimage for lovers of music. Our local fiddle composer, Isaac Cooper, wrote some good strathspeys, but he was not on a par with William Marshall of Fochabers, say. Scott Skinner performed here, and dedicated tunes to Banff people. It is always pleasant to think that Robert Burns wrote the words 'O' a' the airts the wind can blaw' to fit the lovely tune 'Miss Admiral Gordon's Strathspey', and Miss Admiral Gordon lived in Carmelite House in Low Street, so it's probably a local tune. In the twentieth century, James Robertson, the school janitor at the academy, wrote a pipe march, 'Farewell to the Creeks', that lots of people recognise without knowing it came from Banff.

Banff Preservation & Heritage Society members giving a guided tour to Field Club members from beyond Banff, in 2006.

Singers of the Banff Operatic Society, in HMS Pinafore *in 1968.*

A nautical group from the Banff Operatic Society – HMS Pinafore in 1968.

Banff Highland games at Princess Royal Park, 1930.

(© Bodie Collection)

Mr Hossack, looking back on nineteenth-century Banff, said that the girls' boarding schools, for which Banff at one time was famous, meant that the towns-people developed a cultured taste in music.

In the twentieth century Banff had a great tradition of amateur musical performance. The Choral and Operatic Society, set up in 1925/56 – the two societies merged in 1955 – led by Mr and Mrs Harold George, played to packed houses. Over the years they produced every one of the Gilbert and Sullivan operas, which is a rare achievement for an amateur society. For more than ten years, from the 1990s, Gareth John ran very successful Deveron Festivals of classical music, bringing in top musicians – and Sandi Thom, a Macduffer, went to Banff Academy.

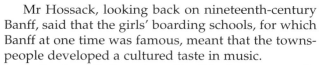

DEVERONVALE FOOTBALL CLUB
James McNaughton

For many years the local towns of Banff and Macduff had separate football teams, but they combined in the 1930s, and in 1938 they made the bold move of bidding for Highland League status. The name for the new club was to be Deveronvale FC, and in July 1938 they gained admittance to the league, going on to lose their first game 4–0 at Forres. The first season wasn't to be very successful as the new club tried to find its feet, and the outbreak of war was to hold up the club's progress.

After the war, Vale didn't have to wait long to gain their first honour, and lifted the Aberdeenshire Cup in 1947/48 by beating Peterhead 5–4 on aggregate in the final. The winning goal was scored by Jock Stephen, who was carried shoulder high to the dressing-rooms by his team mates. The trophy, presented to Vale president ex-provost J.C. Rankin, was put on display in Harry Watson's shop window.

This competition has proved to be the club's most successful to date, as they have gone on to win it in 1950/51 (beating Peterhead again over two legs),

1951/52 (beating Huntly over two legs), 1961/62 (beating Fraserburgh over two legs), 1965/66 (beating Buckie Thistle over two legs) 2000/01, when they ended a 35-year wait for cup success, beating Fraserburgh 2–1 in a nail-biting final at Peterhead, and most recently in 2006/07, beating Inverurie Locos 1–0 in the final at Keith, thanks to an Ian Murray penalty.

Vale appeared in the Scottish Cup for the first time in 1947/48, and in doing so became the first Highland League club to play a competitive match at Hampden Park, losing 8–2 to Queens Park. In 1960/61, Vale defeated Stirling Albion 1–0 in the first round at Banff, before losing 4–2 to Aberdeen at Pittodrie in the second round in front of 14,200 fans.

The season 2006/07 saw Vale embark on their greatest ever Scottish Cup run. Beating Montrose 3–2 in the first round, Fraserburgh 2–1 in the second round, Elgin City 5–4 in the third round, Vale progressed to the fourth round for the first time in the club's history, where they were to put up a brave fight before being narrowly beaten 1–0 by Partick Thistle.

The club's first Qualifying Cup success came in 1951/52, beating Clach 5–4 on aggregate. As the victorious side returned from Inverness with the trophy, Banff householders cheered from their door-ways as the bus passed through the town to the Plainstones, where large crowds were waiting to greet their heroes home. But it was to be a good 50 years before they would experience their next success in the competition, when they defeated Buckie Thistle in the final at Keith in 2001/02, with goals from Jamie Watt (2) Ian Murray (2) and Robbie Brown.

In 1977/78 Vale won the Bell's Scotch Cup, defeating Huntly in the final, with a young Jim Leighton in goal. After a 2–2 draw, Vale went on to win on penalties, with Les Mason scoring the all-important winner. They then had to wait till 1994/95 to secure their next trophy, beating Cove Rangers in the Aberdeenshire Shield final at Keith, courtesy of a Paul Bridgeford penalty. The Vale won the shield for a second time in 2002/03, beating Inverurie Locos in the final at Keith 3–2, with goals from Ian Murray (2) and Mike McKenzie.

But the club's greatest success came in season 2002/03, when they won the Highland League title for the first time. On 29 March 2003, a solitary strike from record goal-scorer Ian Murray was enough to give Vale a 1–0 victory at Keith, and clinch the league championship. The jubilant players and fans celebrated in the middle of Kynoch Park before heading back to Banff and Macduff to party long into the night. It was a proud moment for local lads Scott Anderson and Nigel Montgomery as they jointly lifted the league trophy after the last home game against Huntly, in front of their families, friends and hundreds of fans.

In season 2005/06 Vale were celebrating championship success for a second time. This time it was a much closer affair, in one of the most exciting title races for many years. It took a 1–1 draw at Cove in Vale's final game of the season to secure the vital point required to win the league, and as the final whistle blew, the large, vibrant travelling support joyfully spilled onto the pitch to cheer Mark Chisholm as he held the League Trophy aloft.

GOLF
James McNaughton

The Banff Golf Club was formed on 5 May 1871 at a meeting in the Court House Buildings, Banff, of several gentlemen favourable to the formation of a golf club. Rules and regulations were duly drawn up, and, on 3 August 1871, the council met at the links, which were deemed ready for play. The annual subscription was fixed at 5s., with an entrance fee of 20s. In the early days a large part of the course, that did not then go beyond the burn, including the greens, was covered by fishermen's nets, and if a ball landed on the nets, the fishermen promptly either threw the ball back or threw it onto the beach, where inevitably it was lost.

Of course there had been golf in Banff before. Francis Brown was up before the Burgh Court in 1637 for stealing golf balls, among other things. In 1828 Banff had an archery and golf club, honorary captain the Earl Fife, though the real captain was W. Bartlet, but 1871 was the start of golf as we know it.

At one time the ladies played a nine-hole course within the links course, a certain number of holes being common to both courses. This, however, was found to cause congestion, and, as the play of the ladies improved in time, the ladies' course was

The old clubhouse at Banff links, c.1890.

(© BODIE COLLECTION)

The original Duff House golf pavilion.   (© Bodie Collection)

The second Duff House and golf pavilion, c.1910.

(© Bodie Collection)

abandoned, leaving both sexes free to play the same course.

The Banff Golf Club was amalgamated with Duff House Royal on 1 January 1925, when it was agreed, among other things, that 'both courses be maintained in good condition'. Unhappily, the harsh realities of the economic situation caught up with the club and the office-bearers were compelled to abandon the links. Sadly, the site reverted to nature way back in 1929.

Duff House Royal Golf Club had been founded in 1910. On the invitation of the directors of Duff House Ltd, the members of the Duff House golf course met within the skating rink on Tuesday, 1 March 1910 for the purpose of discussing with the directors the future of the course and the formation of a club. (The golf course itself was in fact officially opened on Saturday, 17 July 1909 with a match between two of the giants of their day, J.H. Taylor and James Braid.) The motion was carried to form a club with a patron, president and two members of the committee, each appointed from the burghs of Banff and Macduff and Duff House Ltd. His Grace the Duke of Fife was elected patron in recognition of his having gifted the land to the communities of Banff and Macduff. The word 'Royal' was added to the Duff House title in December 1923 at the request of Her Royal Highness the Princess Royal.

The present course was reconstructed by the brilliant golf architect brothers Dr A. and Major C.A. Mackenzie, whose hallmark is to be found in the two-tier greens common to Britain and America. The original 'Barton' pavilion was erected at this time, and served to meet the needs of golfers until the first major reconstruction in 1962 following the purchase of 35 acres at the break-up of the Fife estates. The reconstructed 'Barton' pavilion was again extensively altered in 1971 to mark the centenary of organised golf in Banff, and there is now little of the original building. The first official exhibition game played at Duff House Royal, on 30 July 1924, was played by the British and American Open champion, Ted Ray, partnered by the club captain, W.W. Walker, against Sandy Herd and club professional Sam Dornan, who won 3 and 2.

In 1961 the club purchased the top part of the course, extending to 35 acres, for the sum of £3,000; in 1970 an area of ground and buildings around the Barnyards were purchased for £750; and finally in 1973 the remaining 65 acres, together with the stables and other buildings, were purchased for £10,000 with the assistance of a Scottish Sports Council Grant of £5,000 and a donation of £2,000 from Banff Town Council. In 1974 further major reconstruction to the clubhouse was authorised to make it more or less what it is at the present day.

In recent times the club has gone from strength to strength and attracts visitors from far and wide. The annual five-day tournament in August has long been regarded as one of the most popular in the North East of Scotland, attracting entries from all parts of the UK and further afield, and is a boon for local shopkeepers and hoteliers. In 2007 the club appointed its first full-time administrator and looks forward to its centenary in 2010 with confidence.

⊷ ⊷ ≍✦≍ ⊶ ⊶

THE BOWLING CLUB
James McNaughton

Banff Bowling Club was founded in 1903, although bowling had been played in Banff for many years before then, principally at the Town and County Club in Boyndie Street. By 1901 the game had proved so popular with the august and select members of the 'T and C' that the three rinks there were no longer adequate and, since there was insufficient ground there to form a fourth rink, it was decided to call a public meeting to discuss the formation of a bowling green for the town of Banff.

The meeting was called for 13 November 1901 in the council chamber. The meeting was well attended and was advised that five possible sites for a bowling green had been identified, the most suitable being one above the Ramsay School on land belonging to Seafield Estates in Seafield Street. A deputation had already had a preliminary discussion with the then factor of Seafield Estates, a Mr Campbell, by whom they were very favourable received. A 21-year lease was offered, but clearly a club would be required to be formed with a proper constitution. The meeting agreed to proceed with the formation of a properly constituted club, with local solicitor James Forbes as its first president. A 21-year lease was negotiated and contractors employed to lay out the rinks and construct a pavilion. The formal opening took place on Wednesday, 27 May 1903, with a game played by representatives from neighbouring clubs and home players, and on 3 and 4 July a bazaar was held with a view to liquidating the debts the club had incurred in constructing the green and pavilion. The notice in the *Banffshire Journal* of 2 June 1903 advertising the bazaar lists the distinguished patrons and patronesses – most of the titled landowners in the area – and it was to be opened by Alexander Asher,

Esq., LLD, KC, MP, Dean of the Faculty of Advocates.

The club has continuously occupied its Seafield site since 1903 and has for many years been the owner of the feu. In 1921 it joined the Highland Bowling Association. In 1981 a new clubhouse with a frontage of 120ft and six indoor carpet bowling facility was built with Sports Council and local government grant and loan aid at the cost of over £90,000. In 1986 the lounge was extended, giving the club its present first-class bowling and social facility.

BANFF SAILING CLUB
David Findlay Clark

In the late 1960s Banff harbour was largely silted up and only an amendment proposed by this writer, then a town councillor of Banff, prevented it being totally filled in to become a car park. The legacy of Smeaton and Telford would have been desecrated had that proposal gone ahead. The writer then also built a small Mirror dinghy and became a lone sailor from the harbour. Very soon, however, one or two others – James McPherson, Tom Hendry and the late Sheriff Croan – all brought boats to sail out of the harbour. One or two small work-boats and the occasional water-skier joined up to form Banff Watersports Club, but as the 1970s progressed it became apparent that there were too many conflicting interests, and the Banff Sailing Club was formed.

The town council was persuaded to dredge the middle basin using a bulldozer and lorries, and the Sailing Club gradually moved from a broken-down shed in the harbour compound to a bigger and better wooden HQ which, in the great gales of 1983, was itself torn 23ft from its foundations and seriously damaged. Later, the club acquired a small building on the quayside which is still used.

Through the 1980s and '90s, there was regular sailing and racing, and such was the growth of the club, then about 18 yachts and dinghies, that it joined up with the Royal Findhorn Sailing Club to found the

Banff bowling club, c.1920. (© BODIE COLLECTION)

The winners of a bowling competition.

The Banff–Stavanger boat race, 1996.

(© DR DAVID FINDLAY CLARK ARPS)

139

Some members of Banff sailing club in the early 1980s.   (© Dr David Findlay Clark ARPS)

Banff–Stavanger Race – a serious ocean race of about 285 nautical miles which, at its peak, attracted an entry of over 50 yachts and crews. This race continues, from Banff to Stavanger one year and in the opposite direction the other.

Very recently, Aberdeenshire Council decided, in the face of increasing demand for sailing berths locally, to embark on a major project to create an 86-berth marina at the harbour. That was completed in 2007 and now makes a stirring sight – even if, proportionately, fewer of the boats in it actually sail very much as compared with the few intrepids of the earlier days of the club, who would venture out in tougher conditions and one or two of whom sailed smallish yachts to the Azores and French canals (Peter Inglis), to the west coast or, on various voyages, round the UK (Andy Kennedy).

What is clear is that Banff provides wonderful opportunities for the casual and the intrepid sailor alike. The Sailing Club is small but welcoming, but sailors who need not be members of the club will still enjoy the freedom of the open sea and the whistle of the wind in their halyards.

YOUTH ORGANISATIONS
David Findlay Clark

In the 1930s, and even a decade later, and in spite of the war, there were lots of opportunities for boys and girls to join the various youth organisations, such as the Life Boys and Boys' Brigade, the Cubs and Boy Scouts, the Girls' Guildry and so on. These tended to meet in various halls and schools on Friday or other evenings after children had been fed with their evening meal.

There was locally something of a rivalry between Boys' Brigade and Scout groups – though it was probably less than the rivalry then between the two towns of Banff and Macduff. Mostly it was kept in check by the officers of these organisations, who gave up a lot of their own free time to support and instruct the many children who attended the meetings and won various badges for skills such as camping, first-aid, sport, signalling, natural history and so on.

The highlight of the year for the Scouts, Guides and BBs (as the Boys' Brigade was abbreviated) was the annual camp, when a bus or lorry would transport the company to a field or other site out in the country at varying distances from home. The writer can remember a very curtailed camp in a field less than a mile from the town when the few bell tents had to be painted with camouflage paint and the police had to be informed about who was in the camp and how long they would be there. That was during the Second World War, and no lights could be shown after dark because of the blackout, and food was scarce and rationed. The local farmers were always very good about supplying free potatoes and vegetables and an occasional rabbit for the campfire pot. By the end of the war, camps again became more far flung, to such places as Dufftown or Anstruther, and became, in a variety of ways that our parents might not have liked, more 'adventurous'.

Care was taken by those in charge of camps to keep boys and girls well separated (preferably by many miles). There was, however, in this writer's memory, a wonderful occasion when our BB tents were quickly pitched in a field (near Dufftown as I

Other Sports in Banff

Banff rugby club game at Duff House, 1990.

(© Dr David Findlay Clark ARPS)

Above: *An Edwardian tennis party.*

(© Bodie Collection)

Right: *Banff cricket club in action at Duff house grounds.*

(© Dr David Findlay Clark ARPS)

Banff cricket team in the 1970s.

remember) which, we were unaware at the time, was immediately adjacent to a Girl Guide camp from a different town in the next field. The unrestrained glee of the older boys when this was discovered, and a certain amount of encouragement from the older girls over the dyke, set the 'bosses' to a hasty conference – with the result that next day the girls had, by early morning, all gone to a new site which we never discovered. What a disappointment!

Armistice Day, 11 November, was also a key date in the youth organisations' calendar. Flag bearers, bugle bands and carefully inspected uniforms were the order of the day. The BBs especially were strong on 'drill' and were expected to set the standard of smartness and decorum. All paraded to the Parish Church after the usual ceremony of wreaths at the war memorial. I was a bugler and can remember several such wintry days when I feared I'd never hit the high notes because my lips were frozen stiff. The drummers had an easier time, we believed.

Nevertheless, many boys and girls learned life skills and gained knowledge of a kind different from what was supplied at school and which served us well in later life. We did not then appreciate the contributions of the adults who sustained these organisations and gave up huge amounts of their precious free time to lead us. There are still those who carry on those traditions now. They should be honoured and appreciated.

BANFF HOTELS
David Findlay Clark

The role of hotels in enhancing tourism in North Scotland is little more than two centuries old. Prior to that there were, of course, a variety of small inns and other hostelries, some of which developed into coaching inns such as the Black Bull in Low Street, where Samuel Johnson and his scribe and companion, Boswell, spent a night. In the late-nineteenth and early-twentieth centuries, however, public houses, the vast majority without any accommodation for travellers, proliferated. In Banff, in the 1920s and '30s, there were as many pubs as there were places of public worship. The pious would prefer, perhaps, to put that the other way round.

Many townspeople will have special memories of establishments mentioned here and perhaps of others not remarked on. These memories of theirs may delight or horrify in their own way. What is told here is bound to be selective and episodic rather than representative. The writer's own memories have been enhanced by those of Mrs Anne Meldrum, now in her 90s but as sharp as a tack.

By far the most important hotel of the twentieth century, apart from Duff House, which had a short life as a hotel, was the *Fife Arms*, a Trust House. It

The Royal Oak Hotel, Bridge Street, Banff, known as Barclays Hotel in 2008. (© BODIE COLLECTION)

The Temperance Hotel, or Rose's Hotel, at the bottom of the Strait Path. (© BODIE COLLECTION)

was the hotel favoured by the gentry of the time – relatively moneyed people who came to shoot and fish in season and who preferred a slightly cluttered Victorian elegance, good service, food and privacy when sought. The hotel had access to several salmon pools on the River Deveron and areas for rough shooting as well. The hotel was managed by Miss Connon, later to become Mrs Simpson on marriage. Most stories derive from her reputation as a total martinet – toward guests and staff alike. She was quite regal in the deference she expected from all and sundry, and presided over every event or occasion in the hotel in queenly style. During the Second World War, several important guests, such as the exiled King Haakon VII of Norway and his son, Crown Prince Olaf, Group Captain Sir Max Aitken, CO of the Banff Strike Wing, and others, were all reported as being somewhat in awe of her. She herself always changed into evening dress of black velvet chenille after midday and ensured that her staff were impeccable in dresses, cuffs and sparkling white aprons (the female staff anyway) which were so stiffly starched as to put anyone brushing against them at hazard of being cut. Mrs Simpson was a stickler for

The bus for Banff ready to leave from Macduff Harbour – pity the poor horses with all the passengers they had to carry!

Horne's bus to Macduff outside the former Crown Hotel, 1930s.

(© Bodie Collection)

The bar of the Ship Inn on Deveronside, Banff, which was used in the film Local Hero. (© TOMMY BOD)

The Railway Inn, c.1900. (© BODIE COLLECTION)

close observance of the licensing laws and would allow not the tiniest relaxation, no matter who her guests, clamouring for more drink, might be.

Anne Meldrum tells one rather charming story of how one of Mrs Simpson's bootboys or porters at last turned the tables on his virago of a boss. The lad had erred in bringing afternoon tea to Mrs Simpson's private room on an ordinary tray. Berating him, she told him that nothing was ever brought to her by staff except on a silver salver. Some weeks later, the same lad was called to bring more coals for her fire. He hastened to do so – bringing them on a silver salver! Her response was not recorded.

In the 1930s the door was guarded by a porter in full dark-maroon uniform with brass buttons and peaked cap. He would open the car doors of the guests, see to their luggage, guns and fishing tackle, and later was responsible for laying out, against the names of the fishermen, the day's catch, with the weights and flies or lures used, on a great enamel tray on a table just inside the main door. This was a relatively common practice in the better hotels of the day. The successful guests might specify which of the fish might be taken to the kitchens for cooking.

One stage-coach inn, with a date stone of 1732, which in due course became a good hotel, was the

Seafield Hotel at the town end of Sandyhill Road. Even into the 1930s it had an arched and cobbled entrance to the left of the main door leading to a cobbled area where the coach could be drawn in and the ostler might see to the horses. The domestic premises of the hotel stretched well back from the road and were mainly on the first floor. On the ground floor the public rooms led off from the entrance hall. This writer remembers the frequent sight of Mr Willie Wilson, son of the proprietors and latterly proprietor himself, waiting at the front door either to welcome his guests back from their sport, or to encourage others into the bar. The Seafield Hotel was never seen to be quite as 'high-class' as the Fife Arms, but it had its aspirations. As at the latter, the day's trophies were also laid out in the hall for all to see. Sometimes the odd cynic amongst us would wonder whether Willie had bought some of the fish at the High Street fishmonger's. Willie had the knack, however, of suggesting that the sportsmen had been successful largely because they were customers at his hotel.

Willie was a bespectacled, lean man of medium height with a fast-talking style, slightly bird-like in his mannerisms, and a heavy smoker – as many were in those days. He favoured very wide check 'plus fours', rather fancy diamond-patterned socks to just below the knee and sturdy brogues which made his feet look rather larger than they really were. He was a very respectable golfer and his time away from his hotel was usually spent at Duff House Royal GC.

The Second World War put paid to much of that, however. Mr Wilson retired and died, and at various times after the war the hotel was run by a Mr Webster and by Mr and Mrs Stevenson. They were all very skilled in the culinary arts, although the link with fishing and shooting was broken by changes in ownership of the river pools and moors. For a time excellent food was to be had there in salubrious premises (updated and refurbished by the latter owners), but subsequent to the death of Mr Stevenson, the hotel gradually changed its character. The arched courtyard was built up as a bland white harled wall, save for its just-discern-ble date-stone, and now it is a nightclub for the young.

The *Royal Oak Hotel* in Bridge Street and the now destroyed *Crown Hotel*, adjacent to Old Market Place, were both residential and supported public functions. Mr Smith, part-time farmer, at the Royal Oak, and Mr and Mrs Millar at the Crown were the proprietors in the mid-twentieth century. There was also *Swordanes Links Hotel* down by the beach between Banff and Whitehills. For a time it was run by a demobbed RAF pilot, Dick Webster, and his wife, Vi. Dick was the son of a well-known grocer in the High Street, but his later interest in cuisine compelled him into the hotel. The food was unquestionably nothing short of excellent, but Dick was almost as much a martinet about his guests sitting down exactly when called to the table as Mrs Simpson at the Fife Arms had been generally. He felt strongly that the food was spoiled if it was not eaten immediately it was served from the kitchen. Vi did her best to make him sound less fierce than a RAF station warrant officer!

The *Railway Inn* above the harbour was less residential than its contemporaries, but all were much favoured by service men and women during the Second World War. After one notable air victory by aircraft from the Banff Strike Wing over a German squadron, the air and ground crews celebrated their safe return with several drinking parties at all these establishments and, being somewhat overenthusiastic, ended up in 'jankers' (see page 98).

Two hotels in the town were originally private houses of some grandeur. The *County Hotel* in High Street was originally the elegantly fronted Moray House, which first housed Provost Robinson, one of Banff's best-known provosts. Later occupants included Dr Hugh Smith, local GP and surgeon, and architect Jack Meldrum, one of the moving spirits of Banff Preservation & Heritage Society, and his wife Anne. *Carmelite House* hotel in Low Street was originally the home of Admiral Gordon, and subsequent owners have sustained its reputation both as a home and as a hotel.

The *Market Inn* on High Shore, however, is unquestionably the oldest Banff hotel, boasting origins in 1585. It still carries a reputation as a genial hostelry with a wide client range, but is more pub than inn now. By contrast, *Banff Springs Hotel*, on the west side of town, is the most recently built hotel, though it has undergone several changes of ownership in the past few decades. Originally built and owned by a consortium of local businessmen, it got its name because of that group's wish to celebrate Banff's link with the famous hotel of the same name in Banff, Alberta, Canada. Representatives from there were present at its opening. A slick, well-appointed modern hotel, its reputation has tended to vary depending on the ownership (and chefs) of the time. But then, it never had its Mrs Simpson, its Willie Wilson, its Dick Webster or its Bob Millar.

For all its colourful characters, the hotel trade in Banff has always been reputed for warmth of hospitality, the range of activities it can make available and the food and beverages it offers. From Dr Samuel Johnston and Boswell, to rich and not so rich, kings and commoners alike, all are still welcome.

⊶ ⊨✦⊨ ⊷

BANFF IN CANADA
Norman Allan

I remember many years ago George Sandison, who used to have a chemist's shop on the High Street, telling me that it was his uncle Harry Sandison who was responsible for giving Banff, Canada, its name.

Some time later this was confirmed when local historian Monica Anton showed me a cutting from a 1939 edition of the *Banffshire Journal* in which an ageing Harry Sandison had been interviewed. Harry Sandison had emigrated from Banff to Winnipeg in Canada, and there he had a good friend, another Scot called MacTavish. One day, while they were having a chat, MacTavish, who was an official in the Canadian Pacific Railway, mentioned that shortly he was travelling to Montreal to attend an executive meeting of that company. The CPR had decided to create a holiday resort in the Rockies and had chosen a site beside a popular hot spring near one of its sidings. On the agenda for the meeting was a choice of name for the new project. Harry suggested the name of his home town, Banff, and MacTavish agreed to the suggestion. At the subsequent board meeting MacTavish submitted his proposal of Banff. One of the board members, George Stephen, jumped up immediately and went over to confer with the board chairman, George Smith. Stephen and Smith then proposed Banff as the name, and the resolution went through unopposed. I may say that George Stephen (later Lord Mount Stephen) was a Dufftown chiel and George Smith (later Lord Strathcona) came from Forres. Subsequently Harry Sandison was officially thanked for his suggestion.

A Banff bobbie meets a Mountie in High Street, Banff, in 1996. (© Dr David Findlay Clark ARPS)

FOND MEMORIES OF SHOPPIES
Jim Mortimer

The Banff that I wi'd ca' tae mind,
Jist is a laddie aye lang, lang syne,
I walked the streets the other day
Trying to rouse my memory.
I stopped outside a wee shop door,
Wonderin' fa' had the shop before,
Some hidna changed it was good to see.
Although a generation on maybe.
I stood outside the auld Toon Hall
And thocht o' shops I could recall.

Ham and eggs fae Charlie Brodie
Photographs fae Albert Bodie
A pair o' boots fae John A Dunn,
Tae fae Grigors, half a pun.
McConnachie and Ironside,
Cloth fae Tarty, twa yards wide.
Hector Innes for Chiver's jelly.
Strippet balls fae Candy Nellie.
Aye, that was Banff afore the Forties.
Playing billiards doon at Tortie's.
Jimmy Williamson's fish and chips,
Ellis for salve for chappit lips.
Some bilin' beef fae Johnny Wood,
Or maybe jist a mealie pud.
Jackie Field to cut yer hair,
Seeds and things fae Willie Kerr.
Odds and ends fae Annie Pirie,
Auld Mrs Findlay's shop was eerie.
Graham's for things like coriander,
Pills fae Willie Alexander.
A Christmas card fae Margaret Conn.
Some sugar from Henry Littlejohn.
Maybe a rabbit fae Lachie Mark.
Or Ley's in High Street for a sark.
Willie Massey for bicycle brakes,
Stevenson's for grand oatcakes.
Willie Clark for good white baps,
Dickie Webster for ginger snaps.
Simpson's for a' oor music books,
For indoor plants we'll go to Cook's.
Wallpaper at Alex Watt's
Archie Hutcheson for ties and hats.
Isy Mack for lucky tatties,
Shoes for mendin' went to Wattie's.
Greig Kynoch for a bit o' lamb,
John Greenlaw for a jar o' jam,
Auld George Milne for fine ground coffee.
Mrs Fyffe for my Saturday toffee.
Jimmy Law for wedding cake.
Peter Lyon for spads or rakes.

There's more, of course, but I did nae bad.
The nostalgia made me feel quite sad.
I was lucky, I had kent them all.
So I walked away from the auld Town Hall.

John A. Dunn, Low Street, Banff. (© BODIE COLLECTION)

Grocer's shop, Low Street, Banff, Pyramids in 2008.

(© BODIE COLLECTION)

Webster's grocer's shop, now an estate agents's, High Street, Banff, c.1900. (© BODIE COLLECTION)

Strait Path shops, c.1910. (© BODIE COLLECTION)

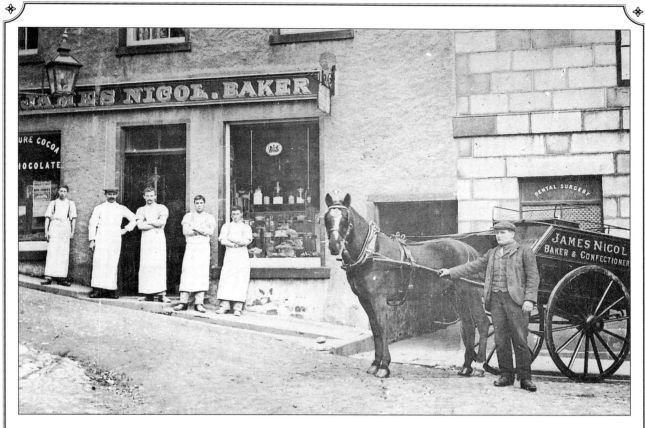

Baker's shop at the foot of Strait Path, Banff, c.1910.   (© Bodie Collection)

The Longmore & Fraser shop, Banff High Street, in the nineteenth century. At the time of writing this is the site of the Royal Bank of Scotland.   (© Bodie Collection)

Haberdashery shop, North Castle Street.

(© BODIE COLLECTION)

The corner of Boyndie Street and North Castle Street in 1930. There is a newsagent's still on the corner in 2008, but the road is a lot wider. (© BODIE COLLECTION)

BANFF BUSINESSES 50 YEARS AGO
Alistair Mason

Egg Grading and Packing

Banffshire Egg Packers Ltd came into being in 1941, organised by a Mr Ritchie on Bridge Street. After the war the egg packers moved to Battery Green under Mr Duffus, who had 17 staff, six of them qualified testers.

The original Post Office, Castle Street, c.1890.

(© BODIE COLLECTION)

Motor Garages

Horne's garage evolved from a coaching business. Mr Horne owned the Crown Hotel and had stables beside it. They first had horse-drawn and later motor buses running between Banff and Macduff. From 1912 Horne's were dealers for Ford motorcars, and from 1915 Fordson tractors.

Another garage was Massie & Beveridge, which closed in 1944 – the site became the Post Office garage. Ex-provost J.R. Gordon started a garage in 1920. After a fire they moved in 1949 to Elmbank, complete with four floors and hydraulic lifts.

In 1923 the Davidson brothers began a Banff–Macduff bus service, and a twice-weekly bus to Aberdeen. In a few years they had a fleet of buses and an hourly service to Aberdeen. SMT took over the bus service, but the Davidsons continued with garage work, Vauxhall and Bedford agencies, tractor repairs, etc. They had a taxi-hire business too.

High Street shops, c.1950. (© BODIE COLLECTION)

Another firm was Watson's, behind Banff prison. Mr Fyda from Poland was the force behind Agra Motor & Agricultural Engineers.

Bakery Trade

The oldest baker's in Banff was Melvin's on Bridge Street, belonging to Bailie Law, founded in 1865.

The Post Office and Graham's store on Carmelite Street, c.1910. (© BODIE COLLECTION)

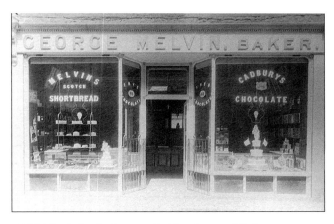

1930 The baker's shop on Bridge Street, 1930.

(© BODIE COLLECTION)

From the 1880s came William Clark's on Seafield Street. There was also Chalmers on Strait Path and Stevenson's on Castle Street.

Grocery Trade
Probably the oldest grocer's was Grahams, founded by a Mr Duncan. The names of those running it kept changing – Anderson & Walker, Ritchie (in the 1940s) and then Malinowski, one of our Second World War Polish links.

The five licensed grocers in Banff were Collie's, Graham's, Grigor's, Milne's, and Webster's. Webster's could claim to have been there for 120 years, the proprietor's father having taken over in

1895. They also had a café at the Plainstones. The Grigors had owned their shop since 1911, and before that it had been a general store.

There were lots of grocers: Scott on the High Street, Brodie's, Whyte's, McGregor's, Falconer's, Thomson's, McLeay's, Robertson's, Nissen's and Andrew's. Somehow they fought off the chain stores: Lipton's had closed down. There was a Co-op.

Butchers and Fishmongers
Gordon's of Low Street had taken over from Dickson's in 1920. Wood Bros was as old, and Innes's (though it had changed hands – Mr Pirie, then Mr Kynoch). Donald's and Alexander's had been there for years.

Gone were the days when you could stroll to the harbour and get fish for the asking. There were two fishmongers, Copland's, who still smoked at the harbour with oak chips, and Mair. Copland's fish came from Macduff, Mair's from Whitehills.

The Clothing Trade
For tailors, there was Bowden's on Bridge Street, Ley's on High Street, and Stuart's on Strait Path. Bowden's was a good gentleman's tailor, hit by the demise of Duff House, and had well-dressed shop windows.

There were four big draper's shops, Milne's, Lobban & Crichton, Rankine's and Garden's, all dating from the 1880s. The names would carry on though new proprietors were running the shop. Thus Lobban & Crichton was owned by Bailie

Raffan, and then by the Watsons of Gerriesfield. Major Bodie, who ran Garden's, was a grandson of the founder.

For children's clothes you went to Mrs Bottomley of Bridge Street. Burnett & McCulloch (husband and wife) specialised in Scottish knitwear. Mr Hutcheson of Carmelite Street was in the same shop for 50-odd years. Everyone knew Miss Jean Pirie of Strait Path, and for babywear there was Miss Donald of Bridge Street.

Hairdressers

There was an Edinburgh firm called Fenton's who had a branch on High Street and trained local hairdressers. Fentons was divided into two salons, first class and third class. There was a shelf for the numbered shaving mugs of the individual customers in the first-class salon. The manager from 1884 was Robert Urquhart, who set up his own business on Bridge Street. Mr R.B. Field took over Fenton's, where he had trained, after 1918, and his son succeeded him in 1945. There was also Mr Sheriffs, in the old dentist's on Strait Path. The ladies' hairdresser was Munro's on Carmelite Street. Mr Munro introduced the machineless perm and specialised in tinting.

Bookshops

Mr Henderson had a lending library on Strait Path, as well as selling books and other things. There were books on sale in Mr Duthie's shops on Low Street, and in Miss Conn's and Mrs Watson's. On High Street there was Mr Joss's, who took over the business from the late Provost Gordon.

We hope that these names, and the pictures of old shops, will refresh memories of Banff 50 and more years ago. I should admit gratefully that Roy Milligan found the articles this material comes from in the back numbers of the Banffie.

DISTILLERY MAN OF BANFF
Roy Alexander and Christina Ord

Roy Alexander, now 65 years of age, was born at No. 2 Sandyhill Road, Banff, and left school at the age of 15 to start his working career as a malt man in Banff distillery at Inverboyndie. While there he also worked at the tun room as a masher and in the still house, although after only three years he left to join the RAF. He says it was the best job he ever had.

Roy explains some of his daily chores as an employee at the distillery:

The malt man's job is to wait for the dressed barley to be dropped from the steps to the malt barn floor, where the men spread it in varying thickness according to the weather conditions, and it is continuously turned in a circular spreading motion using a wooden shovel known as a malt shiel. The floor temperature is all-important in the production of the malt and the turning aerates the barley, which aids germination and keeps down carbonic acid gas. Malting is the process whereby the starch content of the barley is converted to sugar. The barley is then left to malt until it almost sprouts. At this point it is elevated to the kiln fire, which uses peat. Many distilleries have their own peat

Workers gather for a presentation outside Banff distillery (late 1950s).

Great Occasions

The ceremonial arch built for the Prince of Wales's visit in 1883. (© BODIE COLLECTION)

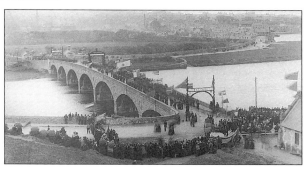

The visit to Banff of the Princess Royal, the Duchess of Fife, in 1920. (© BODIE COLLECTION)

A parade along Low Street, c.1905. (© BODIE COLLECTION)

Armistice Day parade through Low Street. (© BODIE COLLECTION)

Townsfolk gather at the Market Cross for the proclamation of King George V, 1910.

(© BODIE COLLECTION)

Lifeboat at Banff Bridge. (© BODIE COLLECTION)

Right: On her visit to Banff on 14 August 1961 the Queen is presented with a bouquet by the Primary School Dux.

mosses sourced locally; this peat is cut and stocked at the end of the distilling season. The peat firing of the kiln impregnates the malt with characteristic flavourings; each distillery has its own traditions about the usage and quantities of the peat, which gives the final bouquet of the product.

The dried malt is then stored in bins and is dressed and crushed to the consistency of fine meal. Grist mashing consists of mixing the grist with hot spring water in the mash tuns, which are huge metal vessels. The mixture resembles the consistency of porridge, and the full tun is for all the world like an outsize brown mash mixture. After mixing the liquid, the pure malt extract is drained off. This liquid, known as seet wort, is pumped up the fermenting vessels or wash backs in the tun room, which are usually made from oregon pine or larch. In the wash backs the wort is mixed with yeast in the proportion of 100 gallons of wort to one gallon of yeast. This yeast attacks the sugar content in the wort and the resulting fermentation is completed again. At this point knowledge and experience are essential, as a proportion of alcohol is formed and this resulting liquid has a distinct flavouring of beer, which is referred to as the wash.

Distilling is the final process, which consists of the production of spirits by the concentration of the alcohol in the wash. Usually two pot stills are arranged side by side resembling immense copper orbs with long bulbous necks, and each of these is heated by an individual furnace. The first still is known as the wash still and is considerably larger than the spirit still. The first distillation yields what are known as low wines. In the second distillation, alcohol, having a lower boiling point than water, can be separated, and the vaporised alcohol passes along pipes known as worms, which are immersed in water, and condenses back into liquid and can be collected as desired.

A careful note is kept of temperatures and specific gravities. Spirits are tested for impurities by adding water, which is collected in a spirit receiver. When the gravity drops below a certain point the remaining distillate is returned to the low wines receiver for re-distilling. When a suitable proof level for the whisky is reached this is then transferred to casks to mature in the bonded warehouses.

Thistle Whisky in Glasgow did the bottling for the Inverboyndie distillery when Roy worked there.

The closed season for the distillery was from July to September, when all the cleaning was done. Peats were cut and brought and stockpiled, and the cleaning of the water system, which was called ditching, had to be done. Any overgrowth of weeds or rubbish that might be lying in the ditches was cleared by hand. The water from Fiskaidly came down to the dam at Inverboyndie through a lead which was a concrete trough where the water entered the distillery. This was pumping day and night. Barley and coal were brought by rail in the siding at

Banff distillery, and the railway lorries were driven by Bob Annand and George Grant, who ferried the barley to the lofts and the coal to the still house.

The original owner of the distillery was Mr Simpson, a local man who lived at Colleonard. He also owned coach stables on what we now know as Golden Knowes Road. Sadly, Mr Simpson had a terrible accident when out with one of his horse-drawn gigs, which couped in heavy snow, resulting in Mr Simpson being smothered by the snow.

When the distillery was bombed during the war, it spewed out its whisky into the nearby burn, where many cows, sheep and ducks consumed the liquid and were rather intoxicated.

Also, a member of the fire brigade, who was helping to extinguish the fire, drank from the burn, using his hat to scoop up the liquid. Sadly he was fined for this act – well, it would have been a shame to let just the animals have a good time!

MACDUFF
James A.S. McPherson

Overlooked by the Hill of Doune, the twin towns of Banff and Macduff lie a mile apart on the curving shore of Banff Bay, with the estuary of the River Deveron between and linked by Smeaton's attractive seven-arch bridge.

Although similar in size and population and now having much in common, the towns are in other respects very different. Royal and Ancient Banff can boast a proud history of more than 1,000 years and is one of the oldest royal burghs in Scotland, having obtained its charter from Robert II in 1372. Macduff, by contrast, is a town of much more recent origin, becoming a Burgh of Barony in 1783.

Previously the settlement called Doune, or Down,

A pilot tug with Macduff in the background, c.1900.

(© BODIE COLLECTION)

The making of the road from Banff to Macduff (Palmer Cove). The men are using stone forks. (© BODIE COLLECTION)

comprised a cluster of cottages huddled between the beach and the braes. It lay within the Barony of Glendowachie, which for many years formed part of

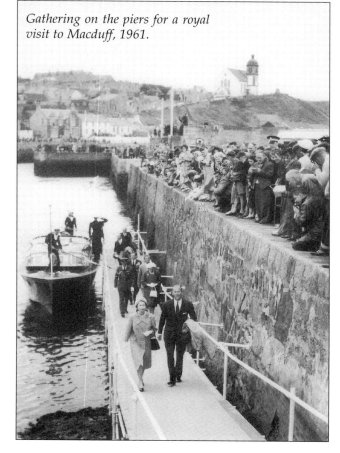

Gathering on the piers for a royal visit to Macduff, 1961.

the extensive lands of the Earls of Buchan until, in 1733, it was acquired by William Duff, Lord Braco, who became the 1st Earl Fife. Here, we can say begins, the history of Macduff.

The life of a Scottish fishing community in the eighteenth century was hard and hazardous, and it was fortunate for the people of Doune that Lord Fife became feudal superior at that time. During the second half of the eighteenth century Scottish landowners were beginning to show a new interest in the development of their estates, and the 2nd Lord Fife was no exception. Not only did he encourage

Platform party at the 600th anniversary of the Banff Charter 1972, Banff Castle grounds. Sitting beside Provost Gordon is Neil Paterson, whose 'Home Town' is reprinted at the beginning of this book.

153

land reclamation and new methods of farming, but he also appreciated the opportunities of exploiting the resources of the sea. That he proceeded to do with great vigour and enthusiasm, as the rapid development of Macduff and its harbour during his lifetime demonstrated. Old records disclose that in 1759 Doune had a population of under 400, yet by 1791 the population of the settlement, now the Burgh of Macduff, had increased to over 1,000. By 1891 the population had increased to 3,722 and the figure at the time of writing is 3,850.

The achievement of burgh status was a protracted and at times frustrating business for both Lord Fife and his factor, but eventually the charter declaring Macduff a Burgh of Barony passed through the requisite departments of state and was signed by King George III at the Palace of St James on 31 January 1783. Later that year Macduff Cross was erected on the hill overlooking the harbour. The cross bears the arms of the Earls of Fife and this inscription:

Macduff Cross rebuilt at Macduff by the Earl of Fife in 1783 when the place was constituted a Royal Burgh by George III. May it flourish, increase in opulence while its inhabitants gain the blessings of life by industry, diligence and temperance.

On 3 September 1783 the first town council was elected, and William Rose, Lord Fife's factor, became the first provost. A feature of the new town was the harmonious working relationship between successive Earls Fife as the feudal superior and the town council. Land and sea activities were combined and promoted in a very practical way. Lord Fife made lands on the outskirts of the burgh available for let to the feuars. These 'lotted lands' remained available for let to feuars until as recently as 1961, when the Duff House estate was sold.

The Victorian era saw the introduction of a piped water supply, first from wells within the burgh, later from Hungryhills, Silverford and Fortrie, and finally, in the 1960s, combining with neighbouring Banff from gravel beds near the Deveron. Street lighting, first by oil lamps, then by gas, came in 1837, with electricity 100 years later.

To attend church 250 years ago the inhabitants of Doune, being in the parish of Gamrie, had to walk seven miles to St John's Church on the headland overlooking Gamrie Bay, which was the Parish Church. In 1768 a building in School Hill was converted to a chapel of ease, and in 1805 Doune Church, now Macduff Parish Church, was built, the gift of the 4th Earl Fife. It continued as a chapel of ease until 1865, when the *quoad sacra* parish of Macduff was created. It was only then that Macduff had a permanent minister competent to preside at baptisms, marriages and funerals without a special dispensation from the parish minister at Gamrie. At that time the church was enlarged and the original

spire replaced by a three-storey tower with domed roof and cupola.

In 1844 the year following the Disruption, the seceders from Doune Church congregation built their own place of worship in Institution Street, where services were held until 1899, when a new Free Church at the junction of Duff Street and Clergy Street was built. After the Reunion in 1929 it was named Gardner Church in memory in Revd Joseph Gardner, who had been minister to the congregation for 43 years. In 1989 Gardner Church united with Doune Church to form Macduff Parish Church, and the Gardner Church building, now surplus to requirements, was sold to the local council and has since been used as an Arts Centre.

The first school mentioned in the records of Macduff was in School Hill, opened shortly after the establishment of the chapel of ease in 1768. In addition there was a Free Church school, several dame-schools and Murray's Institution, now the Knowes Hotel, known locally as 'The Ragged School', which was erected by public subscription in 1849 with the assistance of an endowment of £4,000 from John Murray, a London merchant who was a generous benefactor of the town. A new public school in Shand Street was built in 1872 to implement the provisions of the Education Act of that year when local school boards were established and schooling became compulsory.

The infant school was built in Fife Street in 1930, and in 1964 a new building to house the secondary department of Macduff High School was opened. The primary department remained at Shand Street until 1969 when, following a decision by Banffshire Education Committee to reduce the number of secondary schools in the county from 12 to four, Macduff High School was axed and all secondary pupils transferred to the new Banff Academy. Some years later the primary and infant departments moved to the Berrymuir building and the Shand Street building and site were sold for housing. After remaining vacant for a number of years, the infant school building was converted for use as an outreach centre for Buchan College.

Long before holidays became part of the normal pattern of our working lives, Macduff was attracting its visitors. The Mecca was the Well of Tarlair, a chalybeate spring discovered in the mid-eighteenth century. Lord Fife provided a well house in 1770 and hither flocked visitors from far and wide, eager to imbibe the health-restoring waters of Tarlair. Tarlair was just the beginning, and to cater for locals and visitors alike the bowling green was opened in 1905, Royal Tarlair Golf Course in 1926 and Tarlair swimming pool in 1931. Since the end of the Second World War facilities for sport and recreation have been increased and enhanced by a new bowling pavilion, providing ample space for social activities and indoor carpet bowling.

Facilities for squash have been provided and the old golf club house replaced by a modern custom-built pavilion, and in 1976 an extensive playing-field and pavilion were opened at Myrus. Macduff Old Folks' Association have a fine hall, opened in 1957, and a community centre, forming part of the Berrymuir school complex, was opened in 1974, catering for indoor activities for all age groups and for local clubs and youth organisations.

A memorable day in the history of the burgh was 14 August 1961 when, at the start of their tour of Banffshire coastal burghs, HM The Queen and the Duke of Edinburgh arrived at the harbour in the royal barge from the royal yacht *Britannia* anchored in Banff Bay to be welcomed by the Lord Lieutenant and Provost Robert Henry, who became Macduff's longest serving civic head.

It was 35 years later that their daughter, Princess Anne, the Princess Royal, visited Macduff to officially open Macduff Marine Aquarium, which has since become a major visitor attraction.

When Macduff celebrated its bicentenary in 1983 it had a housing stock of 1,566, 917 owned by the council and the remaining 649 in private ownership. Since then many council tenants have acquired their houses, and major private housing developments at Barnhill and to the south-east of the burgh have been completed, and of the increased housing stock the majority are now privately owned.

The life of Macduff, like other fishing communities along the Moray Firth, has always centred on its harbour. Several extensions and improvements were undertaken and financed by successive Earls Fife assisted by government grants and loans, particularly the 1878 extension, which involved the construction of a new north basin. In 1888 a number of the principal traders of the burgh, headed by Mr P.H. McPherson, timber merchant, and grandfather of the last provost, petitioned the town council to acquire the harbour. The council, recognising the importance of the question, was successful in negotiating the purchase of the harbour on extremely generous terms from the 6th Earl who became the 1st Duke of Fife. The Macduff Harbour Order, empowering the town council to purchase the harbour and to construct new improvement works and to maintain and regulate the harbour, became law on 24 December 1898. Further improvements were undertaken in 1903, and a major extension of the harbour, commenced in 1914 shortly before the outbreak of the First World War, was not completed until 1920. A commodious new basin which almost doubled the capacity of the harbour was officially opened by the Duke of Fife's widow, HRH the Princess Royal, on 25 May 1921. A modern slipway was constructed on reclaimed ground to the east of the harbour. Further improvements were carried out in 1955, and in 1965 a major scheme involving the deepening of the harbour, the construction of a new spur jetty and the

provision of a new fish market was completed. At the present time further improvements are being undertaken, including the upgrading of the slipway to accommodate larger steel boats.

Macduff has had a healthy history of fiercely maintained independence over its 225 years of life. It looks to the future with cautious optimism, drawing strength from the links forged between the town and its harbour which gave the town life and has sustained it through the years.

WHITEHILLS AND BOYNDIE
Ronald Lees

In the Parish Church at Whitehills are to be found the 'town bell' with a date on it of 1727 and a rather primitive chair, possibly of oak, carrying the date 1733 – thus indicating that the church in this area has been around a long time. But the first kirk, at Inverboyndie, may well have been set up over 1,000 years ago – at the site of and maybe as a result of the successful outcome of a battle there between Scots and Vikings. In these early days Inverboyndie and Banff were a single parish, being separated only in the early-seventeenth century.

Much later, in 1773, the auld kirk became unsatisfactory. A larger improved kirk was built inland at Boyndie, complete with a fishermen's gallery, and that remained in use till 1966, with services now centred in the Whitehills Church in the village. Sadly, the Boyndie Church was destroyed by fire and is now, like the older Inverboyndie Church, a ruin – possibly to be 'developed' in the future.

Much earlier signs of human activity in the parish are the 'kitchen midden' near the mouth of the Boyndie burn, the indications of Bronze-Age round-houses on the Hills of Boyndie, and it is said a Roman marching camp was detected near the crossroads above the village, while in the same area were the ruins of Buchragie House. The Brangan Stones at Tillynaught are probably named after St Brandon, while at the extreme west end of the parish are the remains of Boyne Castle – still in the ownership of the Seafield family and famously visited by Mary, Queen of Scots. In 1746 the Duke of Cumberland's men marched through the parish en route to Culloden. The First World War saw Whitehills men and boats off to war, with several medals won in an action in the Adriatic, while the Second World War saw the construction of an airfield for the RAF at Boyndie in response to the German invasion of Norway.

Whitehills, for most of its history, has been a fishing village populated by pretty independent-minded and self-reliant folk. We read of two girls being admonished for leaving a service in Cullen Parish Church to go back to Whitehills in 1644. In 1675 Geo. Watson got onto the burgess roll in Banff –

Whitehills.

but clearly fell out with his new fellows ('did express a bad expression, not to be repeated, and vilified the Magistrates and Council') and not surprisingly was fined and ordered to 'lay down his Burgess act'. In 1752 Whitehills fishermen were transporting stone to Banff, probably for the harbour improvements, and by 1809 they were supplying whitefish to Banff and Macduff – 'there being no proper fishermen here'. The village in 1792 had seen two persons 'sent on board a man of war' because of agitation concerning reform, and in 1832 'The Great Reform Meeting' in Banff welcomed with applause almost the whole population of Whitehills parading to the town – leaving only two aged and infirm men at home in the village.

Farming and fishing were, and are, the main occupations in the area, the two ways of life coinciding with several smallholdings, farms and dairies situated within the village. In the *Statistical Account* of 1790 the local minister praised the Seafield family for leading the agricultural improvement locally, but also noted that several of the local farmers had also been very forward thinking. Fishermen here, too, were not afraid to adopt new methods promptly,

enthusiastically engaging in the herring fisheries, then adopting the seine net methods when the herring trade declined after the First World War. They very early on started to use motor vans to sell their fish further inland, and, when fishing with small boats became less profitable, they invested in larger, more modern boats operating out of larger harbours in the North East. Their local harbour (run and owned by elected commissioners representing the community) was then adapted to become a successful marina.

Other sources of employment have been the Blackpots tileworks, producing mainly field drains and some roof tiles, and Ladysbridge Asylum – later Hospital – which provided over the years for hundreds of patients with mental problems or learning difficulties until closed down in the '90s as facilities in the community became available to those who needed them.

Within the parish an active community council, a lively church and a successful school have combined to make a progressive and friendly community, well deserving of the title of Scottish Community of the Year in 2001.

Appendices

The Provosts of Banff

1541, 1543, 1548	Sir Walter Ogilvie of Dunlugas	1776–79	Alexander Dirom
1549	Sir Walter Ogilvie of Boyne	1779–82	John Innes
1550–52	Sir Walter Ogilvie of Dunlugas	1782–84	James Shand
1567	George Ogilvie	1784–87	George Robinson
1600	George Ogilvie	1787–90	John Innes
1620	Walter Ogilvie	1790–93	George Robinson
1624	George Ogilvie of Carnowsie	1793–96	George McKilligin
1625	Walter Ogilvie of Dunlugas	1796–99	George Robinson
1626	Rt Hon. Walter Ogilvie of Banff	1799–1802	George Garden Robinson
1627	Sir George Ogilvie of Banff	1802–05	George Robinson
1628–38	George Baird of Auchmedden	1805–08	George Garden Robinson
1639–45	Alexander Douglas	1808–11	George Robinson
1646–47	Sir James Baird of Auchmedden	1811–14	George Garden Robinson
1648	Walter Mair of Pitgair (elected September)	1814–17	George Robinson
		1817-20	George Garden Robinson
1648 and 1649–50	Alexander Douglas MD (elected October 1648)	1820–23	George Robinson
		1823–26	George Garden Robinson
1652	John Urquhart	1826–28	George Robinson
1653	Alexander Douglas	1828–31	George Garden Robinson
1654 and 1656–59	John Urquhart	1831–33	James McKilligin
1661–66	Sir James Baird of Auchmedden	1833–38	Peter Cameron
1667–69	John Gordon of Balmad	1838–40	George Alexander
1670–78	Thomas Ogilvie	1840–44	T.H. Richardson
1679–87 and 1689	Walter Stewart	1844–50	William Scott
1690–91	Alexander Leslie of Kininvie	1850–51	[Judicial Managers]
1692 and 1694	Walter Stewart	1851–53	William Scott
1695–99	Alexander Leslie	1853–59	Robert Duncan
1700–01	Robert Sanders	1859–60	Thomas Adam
1701–04	Alexander Leslie	1860–63	Robert Duncan
1705	Robert Sanders	1863–67	Thomas Adam
1706	John Mark	1867–75	James Wood
1707 and 1708	Robert Sanders	1876–81	William Coutts
1708–12	John Mark	1882–88	James Williamson
1714	George Gairden	1888–94	James Smith
1714 (October)	John Mark	1894–96	Alexander Ramsay
1715-16 and 1718	Robert Stewart	1896–1902	Henry Munro
1718–20	William Scott	1902–05	Peter Lyon
1721–24	Robert Stewart	1905–08	William Alexander
1724 and 1726	William Scott	1908–11	James Christie
1727–28	George Gairden	1911–17	Joseph A. Rankine
1729–32	James Shand	1917–20	Adam Walker
1732–35	William Duff	1920–23	Andrew B. Murray
1735–38	Alexander Innes	1923–29	John R. Gordon
1738–41	Patrick Forbes	1929–32	John Stephen
1741–44	Alexander Innes	1932–35	James Christie
1744–48	James Innes	1935–38	James C. Rankine
1748–50	Alexander Innes	1938–50	John C.H. Addison
1750–53	James Innes	1950–56	James J.M. Thomson
1753–56	Alexander Innes	1956–59	James B.S. Law
1756–59	James Bartlet	1959–62	George O. Robertson
1759–61	Alexander Innes	1962–67	William C. Smith
1761–64	James Shand	1967–71	Allan Anderson
1764-67	Patrick Duff	1971–75	Alexander W. Gordon
1767–70	Alexander Dirom		
1770–73	James Shand		
1773–76	Patrick Duff		

Rectors of Banff Academy

We begin the list when the school was first called an Academy rather than a Grammar School. Earlier names are given in the *Annals of Banff*.

1786–92	Dr George Chapman
1792–1830	John Cruickshank
1830–43	James Smith
1843–47	William McDowell
1847–50	John Leask
1850–55	George Weir
1855–57	David H Paton
1857–73	James Hunter
1873–75	James Moir
1875–1900	Dr John Wilson
1900–02	James Mair
1902–24	Dr Charles M. McPherson
1924–30	Arthur F. Murray
1930–37	David McKenzie
1937–59	Alexander S. McHardy
1959–65	Baillie T. Ruthven
1965–91	Robert I. Scott
1991–93	Keith McCorkindale
1993–2005	George Sinclair
2005-	David Dunn

Ministers of Banff Parish Church since the Reformation

Pre 1574–c.1589	William Lawtie
1590 – after 1615	John Guthrie
Pre 1629–60	Alexander Setone
1661–79	Alexander Setone II
1679–99	Patrick Innes
1699–1716	William Hunter (deposed – see Episcopal Church)
1716–53	James Innes
1753–61	Dr Robert Traill
1762–92	Andrew Skene
1793–1821	Abercromby Gordon
1821–43	Francis Grant
1845–72	Dr Robert Bremner
1873–1925	Dr William Straton Bruce
1925–62	Dr David Findlay Clark
1962–67	James Wilkie
1967–85	Alex S. Geddes
1986–90	Austin U. Erskine
1990–97	Stuart D. Jeffrey
1998-	Alan Macgregor

Clergy of St Andrew's, Banff

William Hunter was deposed as parish minister of Banff in 1716. His followers worshipped in private houses until 1723.

1723–1752	Alexander Murray
1752–55	John Barclay
1755–68	Nathaniel Morgan
1768–69	Michael O'Clare
1769–94	Charles Cordiner

The church was 'Qualified' from 1746 to 1792. From 1778 to 1792 there were two Episcopal chapels, the ministers of the Scottish one being:

1778–84	William Smith
1786–91	Jonathan Watson
1791–97	John Skinner (1792-94 jointly with Charles Cordiner)
1798–1815	James Milne
1815–62	Alexander Bruce
1862–93	James Davidson
1893–1913	Alexander Boyd
1914–19	John E. Fyffe
1920–26	James C. Wilson
1926–37	Frederick G. Barrett-Ayres
1937–38	Kenneth Dodds
1939–44	James A. Craig
1945–51	George M. Chaplin
1951–53	Stephen S. Horsley
1953–57	Harry Fairburn
1958–61	Douglas W.M. Grant
1961–65	E. Miles Copley
1966–67	William Paterson
1967–70	Ferdinand R.J. St John

From then on the church has been served from Turriff and then (1998) Buckie

Ministers of the Free, United Free and Trinity and Alvah Church

1843–57	Francis Grant
1857–64	Archibald Smellie
1864–1905	James Watson Geddie
1905–21	Patrick L.K. Mudie
1921–24	John Rankine
1925–29	James Rae
!929–36	James Mackie
!937–41	William W. Peden
1942–49	W. Reid Findlay
1949–61	George B. Urquhart
1961–71	John L. Blair
1971–94	Harold A.M. Steven

Books on Banff

William Cramond (1891–93) *Annals of Banff* (2 vols), New Spalding Club

H. Hamilton (1961) *Banffshire* (Third Statistical Account of Scotland)

James Imlach (1898) *History of Banff and Familiar Account of its Inhabitants and Belongings*

A.E Mahood (1919) *Banff and District*

Charles McKean (1990) *Banff and Buchan: An Architectural Guide*

E.I. Spriggs (ed.) (1919) *Banff and District*

Nigel Tranter (1974) *The North East* (the Queen's Scotland)

The various pamphlets of the Banff Preservation & Heritage Society, including *Royal and Ancient Banff* and the offprints of the Transactions of the Banffshire Field Club

Subscribers

Christian R. Allan, Banff
Dr Norman Allan, Banff, Scotland
Alec and Isobel Angus, Banff, Scotland
Naomi Appleby, Itlaw, Alvah
Shan K. Austin Frost, Eden
Audrey Badcock, Ashburton, Devon
Richard Bagshaw, Cowhythe
Margaret Barclay, Mount Cotton, Queensland, Australia
Dr David M. Bertie, Peterhead, Aberdeenshire
Nancy Booth, Banff
William C. Brown, Speuss, Germany
Alan S. Bruce, West Hartford, Connecticut, USA
Margaret Bruce, Fraserburgh, Scotland
Stanley Bruce, Banff, Scotland
Charles J. Burnett Esq, Ross Herald
John and Fiona Calder, Banff
Iona M. Cameron, Edinburgh
Duncan F. Cameron, Turriff
Duncan G. Cameron, Turriff, Scotland
Lester Ferguson Cameron, Aberdeen, Scotland
C. M. Campbell, Clunie Street, Banff
William Campbell, Inverarnie, Inverness
Robert T. Carter, Banff, Scotland
Mrs J. Cartwright, Gardenstown, Banff
David J.W. Chalmers, Banff
Alexander H. Chalmers, Banff
Alexander G. Chalmers, Banff
Mary Cheyne, Banff, Scotland
Stewart Cheyne, Banff, Scotland
Sylvia Clark, California, USA
Duncan C. Clark, Banff, Scotland
Alexander G. Clark, Westray, Huntly
Helen Clark, Banff, Scotland
Isabella J. Clark, Banff, Scotland
Dr David Findlay Clark, O.B.E. D.L, Banff
Gordon West Cook, Son of Bob Cook
Alexandra Cooper, Macduff, Scotland
Louise I. Cooper, Keilhill, Banff
Mr and Mrs C.B. Cotton, Sheffield
Leslie W. Craib, Banff, Scotland
Shona Craig, Lagrasse
Isabelle Cruickshank, Banff
Mrs C. Cunyngham-Brown, Shetland
W. Davidson, Whitehills, Banffshire
Ian Tennant Dawson, Banff, Scotland
David Dawson, Banff, Scotland
Betty and Doug Dennistoun, Hillpark, Banff
Lexie Devlin, Banff, Scotland
Lorna K. Dickson, Whitehills, Scotland
Lexy Docherty, St Andrews, Fife
Nicholas Dolphin, Banff, Scotland
Symon and Lesley Donald, Banff
Helen Dow, Aberdeen
Elizabeth Duguid, Banff, Scotland
Dr Stuart H.W. Duncan
Thelma A. Duncan, Banff
Kevin Duncan, Banff, Scotland
Marcia and Ian Edwards, Banff, Scotland
Joan Ellis, Macduff
William Espie, Banff
Mr and Mrs S. Esslemont, Colleonard, Banff
Lesley J. Ewen, Banff, Scotland
Robert Ferguson, Banff
Patricia M. Findlater, Edinburgh

Geraldine Finnie, MacDuff, Scotland
Madeline V. Flory, Banff
Leona C. M. Foote, Banff, Scotland
Michael J. Foote, Banff, Scotland
Hilda French, Banff
David Fusco and Iona Sim, Banff
Elizabeth Gabriel, Granddaughter of Provost Paterson, Macduff
Trish and Nick Gale, Thornlea, Banff
Mrs Sara A. Gaston, Edinburgh
Mrs Helen Gibson, Clunie Street, Banff
George Gordon, Kirkside
Mr and Mrs Frank Annand Grier, Midlothian, Virginia, U.S.A
Jack Hadden, Kilkeel, County Down
M. Hall, Banff
Jean Hamilton, Crovie
Beatrice A. Hay, Banff, Scotland
Irene Henderson, Portsoy
John and Anne Henderson, Banff
Margaret W. Hendry, Macduff
Nicholas Hide, London
Christopher J. Holt-Miller, Kingston-upon-Hull, East Yorkshire
Rebecca Howland, re. 3 High Shore, Banff
Dr J. Douglas Hunter, Newcastle Upon Tyne
Doreen Hutcheson, Banff
L. Inglis, Banff
Mrs P.S. Johnston, Scotstown, Banff
Peter W. Johnston, Scotstown, Banff
Alexander G. A. Johnston, Macduff
Kate Jones, re. 3 High Shore, Banff
Oonah Jones, née Law, ex. 3 High Shore, Banff
Katherine Kennedy (née Baron), Pontefract
Nicol James Kindness, Macduff
Yvonne A. Knowlson, Turriff, Scotland
Jamie Laing and Natalie Laing, Banff
Helen J. Lamb, Banff, Scotland
Brian J. Lamb, Banff, Scotland
Elizabeth A. Law, Macduff
Grace Law, Banff, Scotland
Nellie Law, née Crichton, ex. 3 High Shore, Banff
Tom and Mary Leel, Banff
A. and R. Lees, Whitehills, Banff
Stewart T. Lippe, Banff, Scotland
Diane Lizana (née Wilson), Chile
Dane Love, Lochnoran House, Auchinleck, Scotland
Carol Lovie, Cuminestown
Mr and Mrs Ronald A. Lyall, Macduff
James P. Lyall, Wolverhampton, England
Kay Mackay (Murdoch family, Banff), Surrey
Angus Mackenzie, Dunfermline
Alistair Mackenzie, Dunfermline
Dr and Mrs A. S. Mackenzie, Dunfermline
Stephen L. Mackie, Macduff
Mr John J. Mackie
Pamela Maclennan-Brown, Banff, Scotland
James Donald MacLeod, Robina's Quay, Australia
Rob and Brenda MacPherson, Macduff
L. Mair, Banff
Ms Wendy Mann, Gardenstown, Scotland
Harry and Meg Mantell
Michael Marsden, Macduff, Scotland

Dr Alistair Mason, Banff

Alan F. Masson, Banff, Scotland

Mr and Mrs Forbes Masson, Banff, Scotland

Angus D. A. McAllister (Jnr), Banff

Angus C. McAllister (Snr) (Piper), Banff

McAllister's, Banff, Scotland

Pat and Andy McAngus, Macduff

I. McBain, Aberdeen

N. McBain, London

Dr A.P. McBain, Banff

Stuart A. McCallum, Edinburgh (formerly of Banff), Scotland

Ian Lippe and Moira McClennan, Banff

M.J.D. McConnachie, Boyndie

Ian McConnachie, Deerson, Kent

Moira McGregor, Ruthin, North Wales

Ian, Isobel, Stuart and Andrew McGregor, Thurso, Scotland

Neil McHardy, Memsie, Fraserburgh

Andrew George McIntosh, Inverboyndie, Banff

Christine McIntosh, Macduff, Scotland

Isabel McIntyre, Peterculter, Aberdeenshire

Jean McIntyre, Banff, Banffshire

Frances M. McKay, Banff

Colleen A. McKay, Sydney, Australia

McKenzie Family, Banff, Scotland

David W.W. McLean, Cheshire

Ronald McLeay, Blairgowrie

Jim and Pauline McNaughton, Banff

Mrs Helen M. McPherson, Macduff, Scotland

J.A.S. McPherson, CBE, Macduff, Scotland

D and S. McRae, Banff

Margaret McRobert, Stonehaven, Scotland

Anne Meldrum, Banff, Scotland

Tom and Kate Miller, Banff

Fiona H. Miller, Caceres, Spain

Jean and Douglas Miller, Banff, Scotland

Iain D. Miller, Boston U.S.A

Dr Robert W. Milligan, Lumphanan, Kincardineshire

Roy A. Milligan, Banff, Banffshire

Master Sandy R.G. Milne, Banff

R.W. Milne, Macduff, Banffshire

Mr W. J. Milne, Hornchurch, Essex

Mr Joseph Milne, N.S.W., Australia

A.M. Moir, Romford, Essex

M.N. and D.S. Moloney, Moulton, Lincs

Mrs Margaret Morgan (née Robertson), Dunfermline

Lady Morison, Banff, Scotland

Evelyn M. Morrison, Banff, Scotland

William John Murray, Banff, Scotland

Charles Murray, Banff, Scotland

Roy S. Murray, Banff, Scotland

Stuart P. Murray, Clovenfords, Galashiels

Alan and Brenda Neish, Banff

Jean W.P. Nutall (née Donald), Banff

Dagmar C. O'Donovan, Nr Windsor, Berks

Helen J. Ogg, Westhill, Aberdeenshire

Kaitlyn E. Oliver, Banff

Sara L. Oliver, Banff

Barry J. Ollason, Eshaness

J. Margaret S. Ollason, Banff

Mr Stephen Ord, Banff

Mr John Ord, Banff, Scotland

Jockey Ord, Whinhill Terrace, Banff

The Revd Canon Jeremy Paisey, Buckie, Scotland

Isabel Perks, Banff, Banffshire

John D.G. Perks, Morningside, Edinburgh

Christine Pert, Nr Sandend

Jesper Funck Petersen, Inverichnie, By Banff

Mr and Mrs E. Phillips Grier, Jnr, Virginia Beach, Virginia, U.S.A.

Colonel and Mrs E. Phillips Grier, Snr, Longmanhill Top Croft, Banff

G.D. Raymond, Banff, Aberdeenshire

M. Reilly, Aberdeen

Gordon P. Rennie, North Wales

Mrs Terry Richardson, a granddaughter of many residents of Banff

C. A. Ritchie, Banff, Scotland

John Malcolm Robb, London

F.M. Ross, Clunie Street, Banff

John Ross, Kirkcaldy

John Roy, Banff 7/1/72

Mr Ewan S. Roy, Banff, Scotland

Mr Michael J. Roy, Banff, Scotland

Mr John M. Roy, Macduff, Scotland

Mr and Mrs Tristan Russell, Forglen, Banffshire

Mr John Russell

Ms Caroline Russell

William G. Rust, Banff, Scotland

John and Sandra Scrudis, Durn House, Portsoy

Patricia Seligman, Banffshire, Scotland

John F. Sellar, Macduff, Scotland

Mrs M. Seymour-Griffin, Surrey

Charles Shepherd, Banff, Scotland

Andrew and Louise Simpson, Banff

Alison Smith, Macduff

John L.A. Smith LCGI, Longmanhill, Banff

Erika Speirs, Farnham, Surrey

Stevens Family, Hammersmith, London

Ian Strachan, Macduff

Elma Strachan, Banff, Scotland

Helen Summers, Macduff, Scotland

Arnold and Janet Swinglehurst, Warrington

Mrs Beryl Tacon, Banff

Beryl Tacon, Banff, Scotland

Mrs Mary Taylor, Stonehaven

Nikki L. Taylor, Banff, Scotland

Andrew and Elizabeth Taylor, Banff

Ian Thain, Banff, Scotland

The Jenkins Family, Whitehills

The Robertson Family, Banff, Scotland

John Thomson, Banff

Robert A. Thomson

Norman Tonner, Banff

Monica Townsend, re. 3 High Shore, Banff

Drs James and Shona Vance, Banff

Marie B. Walker, Turriff

W. Mark Watson, Little Haywood, Staffordshire

Cynthia A. Watson, Exeter

Nellie Watt, Banff

John D. Watt, Banff

Chris Weir, Bristol

George M. Weir, Banff

Mrs E. West, Castle Lane, Banff

Ian and Pat Williams, Macduff

George P. Wilson, 'Mon Abri', Banff

Mr Charles Wilson, Banff

Alicia and Sara Wood, Banff, Scotland

Mr Robert J. and Mrs Edna Wood, Whitehill, Banff, Scotland

Peggy Wright, Auds Boyndie

Mr and Mrs Tony Wright, Alvah, Banff